W9-BMZ-573

# SUMMER LINK

## MATH plus READING

Thinking Kids®
An imprint of Carson-Dellosa Publishing LLC
Greensboro, North Carolina

Thinking Kids®
An imprint of Carson-Dellosa Publishing LLC
P.O. Box 35665
Greensboro, NC 27425 USA

ISBN  978-1-4838-0468-2

06-105197784

# Table of Contents
## by Section

Summer Link Math . . . . . . . . . . . . . . . . . . . . . . . . . . . . . . . . . . . . . . . . . . . . . . . .7

Summer Link Reading . . . . . . . . . . . . . . . . . . . . . . . . . . . . . . . . . . . . . . . . . . . .99

Summer Link Test Practice . . . . . . . . . . . . . . . . . . . . . . . . . . . . . . . . . . . . . .192

# Summer Link Math
# Table of Contents

Place Value . . . . . . . . . . . . . . . . . . . . . . . . . . . . . . . . . . . . . . . . . . . . . . 8–10

Rounding and Estimating . . . . . . . . . . . . . . . . . . . . . . . . . . . . . . . . . . . 11–14

Mean, Median, and Mode . . . . . . . . . . . . . . . . . . . . . . . . . . . . . . . . . . 15–17

Counting and Comparing . . . . . . . . . . . . . . . . . . . . . . . . . . . . . . . . . . . 18–20

Addition . . . . . . . . . . . . . . . . . . . . . . . . . . . . . . . . . . . . . . . . . . . . . . . . 21–24

Subtraction . . . . . . . . . . . . . . . . . . . . . . . . . . . . . . . . . . . . . . . . . . . . . 25–27

Multiplication . . . . . . . . . . . . . . . . . . . . . . . . . . . . . . . . . . . . . . . . . . . . 28–34

Division . . . . . . . . . . . . . . . . . . . . . . . . . . . . . . . . . . . . . . . . . . . . . . . . 35–39

Order of Operations . . . . . . . . . . . . . . . . . . . . . . . . . . . . . . . . . . . . . . . . 40

Decimals, Fractions, and Percents . . . . . . . . . . . . . . . . . . . . . . . . . . . . . 41–48

Adding, Subtracting, Multiplying, and Dividing With Money . . . . . . . . . . 49–54

Time . . . . . . . . . . . . . . . . . . . . . . . . . . . . . . . . . . . . . . . . . . . . . . . . . . 55–56

Customary and Metric Systems . . . . . . . . . . . . . . . . . . . . . . . . . . . . . . . 57–64

Geometry . . . . . . . . . . . . . . . . . . . . . . . . . . . . . . . . . . . . . . . . . . . . . . 65–79

Patterns . . . . . . . . . . . . . . . . . . . . . . . . . . . . . . . . . . . . . . . . . . . . . . . . . 80

Venn Diagrams . . . . . . . . . . . . . . . . . . . . . . . . . . . . . . . . . . . . . . . . . . . . 81

Graphs . . . . . . . . . . . . . . . . . . . . . . . . . . . . . . . . . . . . . . . . . . . . . . . . 82–84

Ratio . . . . . . . . . . . . . . . . . . . . . . . . . . . . . . . . . . . . . . . . . . . . . . . . . . . . 85

Probability . . . . . . . . . . . . . . . . . . . . . . . . . . . . . . . . . . . . . . . . . . . . . . 86–87

Glossary . . . . . . . . . . . . . . . . . . . . . . . . . . . . . . . . . . . . . . . . . . . . . . . . . 88

Answer Key . . . . . . . . . . . . . . . . . . . . . . . . . . . . . . . . . . . . . . . . . . . . . 89–97

Developmental Skills for Fifth Grade Math Success . . . . . . . . . . . . . . . . . . . 98

# Summer Link Reading
# Table of Contents

Summer Before Grade 5 Recommended Reading . . . . . . . . . . . . . . . . . . . 100

Parts of Speech and Word Usage . . . . . . . . . . . . . . . . . . . . . . . . . . . 101–114

Editing . . . . . . . . . . . . . . . . . . . . . . . . . . . . . . . . . . . . . . . . . . . . . . 115–116

Research . . . . . . . . . . . . . . . . . . . . . . . . . . . . . . . . . . . . . . . . . . . . . 117–121

Reading Comprehension . . . . . . . . . . . . . . . . . . . . . . . . . . . . . . . . 122–167

Summarizing . . . . . . . . . . . . . . . . . . . . . . . . . . . . . . . . . . . . . . . . . . 168–172

Types of Writing . . . . . . . . . . . . . . . . . . . . . . . . . . . . . . . . . . . . . . . 173–176

Sentences . . . . . . . . . . . . . . . . . . . . . . . . . . . . . . . . . . . . . . . . . . . . 177–180

Glossary . . . . . . . . . . . . . . . . . . . . . . . . . . . . . . . . . . . . . . . . . . . . . . . . 181

Answer Key . . . . . . . . . . . . . . . . . . . . . . . . . . . . . . . . . . . . . . . . . . . 182–190

Developmental Skills for Fifth Grade Reading Success . . . . . . . . . . . . . . . 191

This page intentionally left blank.

# SUMMER LINK MATH

# Place Value

**Place value** is the value of a digit, or numeral, shown by where it is in the number. See the number 1,234,567.

**Directions:** Write each numeral in its correct place.

1. The number 8,672,019 has:

    __2__ thousands          __1__ ten              __6__ hundred thousands
    __8__ millions           __9__ ones             __7__ ten thousands
    __0__ hundreds

2. What number has:

    6 ones                  3 millions              9 tens
    7 hundreds              4 ten thousands          8 thousands
    5 hundred thousands

    The number is __3,548,796__ .

3. The number 6,792,510 has:

    __9__ ten thousands       __6__ millions          __5__ hundreds
    __0__ ones               __2__ thousands          __1__ ten
    __7__ hundred thousands

4. What number has:

    5 millions              3 tens                  6 thousands
    1 hundred               8 ten thousands          4 ones
    0 hundred thousands

    The number is __5,086,134__ .

Name _____

# More Place Value

**Directions:** Draw a line to connect each number to its correct written form.

1. 791,000                  Three hundred fifty thousand

2. 350,000                  Seventeen million, five hundred thousand

3. 17,500,000           Seven hundred ninety-one thousand

4. 3,500,000            Seventy thousand, nine hundred ten

5. 70,910                   Three million, five hundred thousand

6. 35,500,000          Seventeen billion, five hundred thousand

7. 17,000,500,000      Thirty-five million, five hundred thousand

**Directions:** Look carefully at this number: 2,071,463,548. Write the numeral for each of the following places.

8. ___6___ ten thousands

9. ___1___ millions

10. ___5___ hundreds

11. ___2___ billions

12. ___4___ hundred thousands

13. ___7___ ten millions

14. ___3___ one thousands

15. ___0___ hundred millions

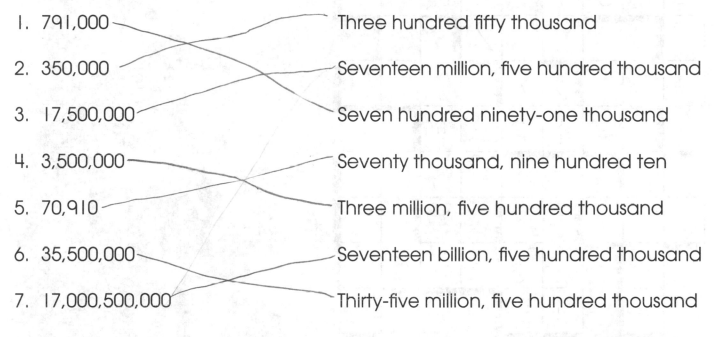

# Place Value Puzzles

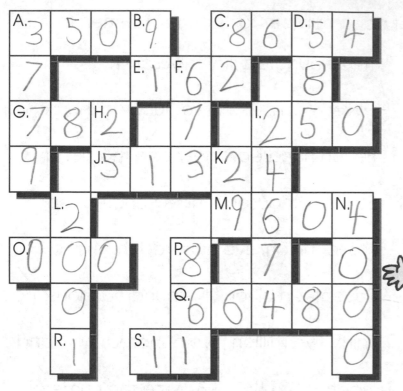

The crossword puzzle grid (with handwritten answers):

Row 1: A. 3 5 0  B. 9  C. 8 6  D. 5 4
Row 2: 7  E. 1  F. 6 2  8
Row 3: G. 7 8  H. 2  7  I. 2 5 0
Row 4: 9  J. 5 1 3  K. 2 4
Row 5: L. 2  M. 9 6 0  N. 4
Row 6: O. 0 0 0  P. 8  7  0
Row 7: 0  Q. 6 6 4 8 0
Row 8: R. 1  S. 1 1  0

**Directions:** Complete the puzzle.

## ACROSS

A. 3 thousand 5 hundred 9
C. 100 less than 8,754
E. one hundred sixty-two
G. seven hundred eighty-two
I. 100, 150, 200, ___
J. 1, 2, 3, 4, 5 mixed up
L. two
M. 100 less than 9,704
O. three zeros
P. eight
Q. 10,000 more than 56,480
R. one
S. 1 ten, 1 one

## DOWN

A. 10 more than 3,769
B. ninety-one
C. 28 backwards
D. 5 hundreds, 8 tens, 5 ones
F. 100 less than 773
H. 5, 10, 15, 20, ___
I. ten less than 24,684
K. 2 tens, 9 ones
L. two thousand one
N. 1000, 2000, 3000, ____
R. eight hundreds, 6 tens, 1 one

# Rounding

**Rounding** a number means to express it to the nearest ten, hundred, thousand, and so on. When rounding a number to the nearest ten, if the number has five or more ones, round up. Round down if the number has four or fewer ones.

**Examples:**

Round to the nearest ten:        84 ⟶ <u>80</u>        86 ⟶ <u>90</u>

Round to the nearest hundred: 187 ⟶ <u>200</u>    120 ⟶ <u>100</u>

Round to the nearest thousand: 981 ⟶ <u>1,000</u>    5,480 ⟶ <u>5,000</u>

**Directions:** Round these numbers to the nearest ten.

87 ⟶ <u>90</u>    53 ⟶ <u>50</u>    48 ⟶ <u>50</u>    32 ⟶ <u>30</u>    76 ⟶ <u>80</u>

**Directions:** Round these numbers to the nearest hundred.

168 ⟶ <u>200</u>    243 ⟶ <u>200</u>    591 ⟶ <u>600</u>    743 ⟶ <u>700</u>    493 ⟶ <u>500</u>

**Directions:** Round these numbers to the nearest thousand.

895 ⟶ <u>1,000</u>  3,492 ⟶ <u>3,000</u>  7,521 ⟶ <u>8,000</u>  14,904 ⟶ <u>15,000</u>  62,387 ⟶ <u>62,000</u>

| City Populations | |
|---|---|
| City | Population |
| Cleveland | 492,801 |
| Seattle | 520,947 |
| Omaha | 345,033 |
| Kansas City | 443,878 |
| Atlanta | 396,052 |
| Austin | 514,018 |

**Directions:** Use the city population chart to answer the questions.

Which cities have a population of about 500,000?
<u>Cleveland, Seattle, Kansas, Austin, Austin</u>

Which city has a population of about 350,000?
<u>Omaha</u>

How many cities have a population of about 400,000? <u>2</u>

Which ones? <u>Atlanta and Kansas City</u>

# Rounding Off With Roundball

| TEAM | BUILDING | SEATING CAPACITY |
|------|----------|------------------|
| Atlanta Hawks | The Georgia Dome | 34,821 |
| Dallas Mavericks | Reunion Arena | 18,042 |
| Utah Jazz | Delta Center | 19,911 |
| Orlando Magic | Orlando Arena | 17,248 |
| Charlotte Hornets | Charlotte Coliseum | 24,042 |
| Milwaukee Bucks | Bradley Center | 18,717 |
| Houston Rockets | The Summit | 16,285 |
| Portland Trail Blazers | Rose Garden Arena | 21,401 |

**Directions:** Round off the seating capacity of each team's home arena to complete the chart.

| Team | Seating capacity to the nearest . . . | | |
|------|----------------|-----------------|---------------------|
| | hundred seats | thousand seats | ten thousand seats |
| Hawks | 34,800 | 35,000 | 30,000 |
| Mavericks | 18,000 | 18,000 | 20,000 |
| Jazz | 19,900 | 20,000 | 20,000 |
| Magic | 17,200 | 17,000 | 20,000 |
| Hornets | 24,000 | 24,000 | 20,000 |
| Bucks | 18,700 | 19,000 | 20,000 |
| Rockets | 16,300 | 16,000 | 20,000 |
| Trail Blazers | 21,400 | 21,000 | 20,000 |

# Estimating

*w. Calc. for 2 questions*

To **estimate** means to give an approximate rather than an exact answer. Rounding each number first makes it easy to estimate an answer.

**Example:**

$$\begin{array}{r} 93 \\ + 48 \\ \hline \end{array} \rightarrow \begin{array}{r} 90 \\ + 50 \\ \hline 140 \end{array} \qquad \begin{array}{r} 321 \\ + 597 \\ \hline \end{array} \rightarrow \begin{array}{r} 300 \\ + 600 \\ \hline 900 \end{array} \qquad \begin{array}{r} 1,859 \\ - 997 \\ \hline \end{array} \rightarrow \begin{array}{r} 2,000 \\ - 1,000 \\ \hline 1,000 \end{array}$$

**Directions:** Estimate the sums and differences by rounding the numbers first.

| | | |
|---|---|---|
| $\begin{array}{r} 68 \\ + 34 \\ \hline 102 \end{array} \rightarrow \begin{array}{r} 70 \\ + 30 \\ \hline 100 \end{array}$ | $\begin{array}{r} 12 \\ + 98 \\ \hline 110 \end{array} \rightarrow \begin{array}{r} 10 \\ + 100 \\ \hline 110 \end{array}$ | $\begin{array}{r} 89 \\ + 23 \\ \hline 112 \end{array} \rightarrow \begin{array}{r} 90 \\ + 20 \\ \hline 110 \end{array}$ |
| $\begin{array}{r} 638 \\ - 395 \\ \hline 243 \end{array} \rightarrow \begin{array}{r} 600 \\ - 400 \\ \hline 200 \end{array}$ | $\begin{array}{r} 281 \\ - 69 \\ \hline 212 \end{array} \rightarrow \begin{array}{r} 300 \\ - 70 \\ \hline 230 \end{array}$ | $\begin{array}{r} 271 \\ - 126 \\ \hline 145 \end{array} \rightarrow \begin{array}{r} 300 \\ - 100 \\ \hline 200 \end{array}$ |
| $\begin{array}{r} 1,532 \\ - 998 \\ \hline 534 \end{array} \rightarrow \begin{array}{r} 2,000 \\ - 1,000 \\ \hline 1,000 \end{array}$ | $\begin{array}{r} 8,312 \\ - 4,789 \\ \hline 3,523 \end{array} \rightarrow \begin{array}{r} 8,000 \\ - 5,000 \\ \hline 3,000 \end{array}$ | $\begin{array}{r} 6,341 \\ + 9,286 \\ \hline 15,627 \end{array} \rightarrow \begin{array}{r} 6,000 \\ + 9,000 \\ \hline 15,000 \end{array}$ |

Bonnie has $50 to purchase tennis shoes, a tennis racquet, and tennis balls. Does she have enough money?

Yes

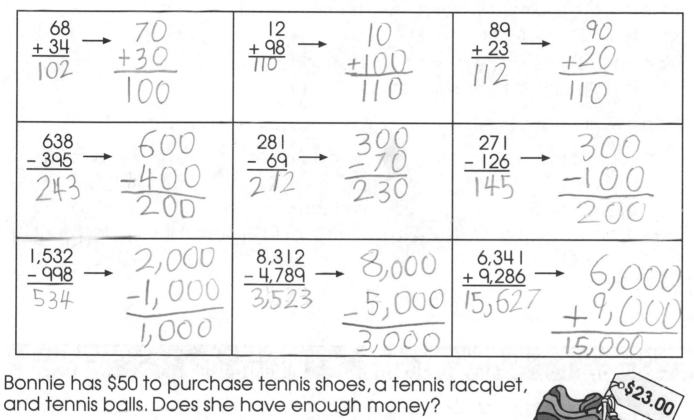

$23.00

$16.00

$3.00

# Estimate by Rounding Numbers

Estimate by rounding numbers to different place values. Use these rules.

**Example:** Round 283 to the nearest hundred.

- Find the digit in the place to be rounded.   ②83
- Now, look at the digit to its right.   ②83
- If the digit to the right is less than 5, the digit being rounded remains the same.
- If the digit to the right is 5 or more, the digit being rounded is increased by 1.   ②83   Rounds to 300
- Digits to the right of the place to be rounded become 0's. Digits to the left remain the same.

**Examples:** Round 4,385 . . .

| to the nearest thousand | to the nearest hundred | to the nearest ten |
|---|---|---|
| 4,385 | 4,385 | 4,385 |
| 3 is less than 5. | 8 is more than 5. | 5 = 5. |
| The 4 stays the same. | The 3 is rounded up to 4. | The 8 is rounded up to 9. |
| 4,000 | 4,400 | 4,390 |

**Directions:** Complete the table.

| NUMBERS TO BE ROUNDED | ROUND TO THE NEAREST THOUSAND | NEAREST HUNDRED | NEAREST TEN |
|---|---|---|---|
| 2,725 | 3,000 | 2,700 | 2,730 |
| 10,942 | 11,000 | 10,900 | 10,940 |
| 6,816 | 7,000 | 6,800 | 6,820 |
| 2,309 | 2,000 | 2,300 | 2,310 |
| 7,237 | 7,000 | 7,200 | 7,240 |
| 959 | 1,000 | 1,000 | 960 |

# What Is the Mode?

**Directions:** There are three kinds of averages: the **mode**, the **median**, and the **mean**. The **mode** is the number that occurs most often. Find the mode.

3, 6, 9, 5, 12, 5, 7, 8 ___5___     11, 7, 9, 11, 3, 8, 9, 10, 11 ___11___

8, 5, 6, 4, 7, 11, 10, 9 ___NONE___     5, 7, –2, 4, –5 , –2, 0, 2, 1 ___–2___

4, 7, 5, 6, 7, 4, 3, 4, 8, 4, 7, 7 ___7 & 4___     3, 4, 3, 2, 0, 0, 1, 2, 0, 1 ___0___

3, 3, 3, 3, 3, 3, 3, 3, 3, 3 ___3___     1, 2, 3, 4, 5, 6, 7, 8, 9 ___NONE___

1, 2, 3, 1, 2, 3, 1, 2, 3, 1, 2, 3 ___1,2 & 3___ 13, 12, 10, 15, 12, 14, 12, 11 ___12___

**Directions:** Solve.

1. All of Jill's throws landed 24 feet away. What is the mode? ___24___

2. Look at Rob's data for his first ten throws in the first box below. How far would he have to throw the javelin on the the 11th throw so that the data would have two modes? ___22___

3. Write a list of 6 numbers that have no mode. ___13, 97, 42, 1, 2,000, 500___

4. Which javelin thrower had a higher mode, Kate or Adam? ___Kate___

| ROB | | | | KATE | ADAM |
|---|---|---|---|---|---|
| **Throw** | **Distance** | **Throw** | **Distance** | 22 feet | 21 feet |
| 1 | 23 feet | 6 | 20 feet | 23 feet | 20 feet |
| 2 | 26 feet | 7 | 24 feet | 24 feet | 23 feet |
| 3 | 21 feet | 8 | 23 feet | 24 feet | 24 feet |
| 4 | 23 feet | 9 | 22 feet | 21 feet | 21 feet |
| 5 | 25 feet | 10 | 22 feet | 22 feet | 22 feet |
| | | | | 22 feet | 25 feet |

Name _____

# Jumping the Median

The **median** is another kind of average.
When ordering a list of numbers from least to greatest, the median is the number that falls in the middle. Look at Anna's maximum high jumps for the last week.

| Day | Height |
|-----|--------|
| Monday | 62 inches |
| Tuesday | 64 inches |
| Wednesday | 62 inches |
| Thursday | 64 inches |
| Friday | 60 inches |
| Saturday | 61 inches |
| Sunday | 64 inches |

Order the numbers: 60, 61, 62, **62,** 64, 64, 64. The number 62 falls in the middle. It is the median.

The mode is 64 inches. In some cases, the median and mode are the same number.

If there is an even number of heights, there will be two numbers in the middle. To find the median, add the two middle numbers and divide the sum by 2.

**Example:** 2, 2, 3, 4, 6, 6, 7, 9

The numbers 4 and 6 are both in the middle.
4 + 6 = 10; 10 ÷ 2 = 5. The median is 5. The median does not have to be a number in the list.

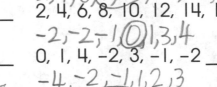

**MEDIAN**

The middle number in an ordered list of numbers

**Directions:** Find the median.

355 68 9 12
3, 6, 9, 5, 12, 5, 8 _____ 7

4 5 6 7 9 10 11 11
11, 6, 4, 7, 5, 9, 11, 10 _____ 8

4, 5, 6, 7, 9, 10, 11
7, 5, 6, 4, 7, 11, 10, 9 _____ 8

Don't even need to organize
3, 3, 3, 3, 3, 3, 3, 3, 3, 3 _____ 3

18, 34, 39, 46, 47, 55, 55, 61, 67
55, 34, 67, 39, 47, 18, 46, 55, 61 _____ 47

3, 7, 8, 9, 9, 10, 11, 11
11, 7, 9, 11, 3, 8, 9, 10 _____ 9

-4, -3, -2, -1, -1, 1, 2
-4, 2, -3, -1, 1, -1, -2 _____ -1

2, 4, 6, 8, 10, 12, 14, 16
2, 4, 6, 8, 10, 12, 14, 16 _____ 9

-2, -2, -1, 0, 1, 3, 4
0, 1, 4, -2, 3, -1, -2 _____ 0

-4, -2, -1, 1, 2, 3
2, -2, 1, -1, 3, -4 _____ 0

# What Do You Mean?

Probably the most common average is the **mean**. To find the mean, add all the numbers in the list, then divide the sum by the total number of addends.

Suppose a hurdler completes his trials in the following times. Find the mean.

| Trial | Time in Seconds |
|-------|-----------------|
| 1 | 35 |
| 2 | 29 |
| 3 | 34 |
| 4 | 30 |
| 5 | 31 |
| 6 | 33 |

**MEAN**

The sum of all the numbers divided by the number of addends

Add the numbers: $35 + 29 + 34 + 30 + 31 + 33 = 192$
Divide 192 by 6 because there are 6 numbers in the list: $192 \div 6 = 32$.
The mean is 32 seconds.

The mean may or may not be a number in the list. The mean may also be different from the median and/or the mode.

**Directions:** Find the mean.

3, 6, 9, 5, 12 _____ 7

11, 5, 9, 11, 3, 7, 9, 9 _____ 8

3, 1, 0, 2, 0, 0 _____ 1

4, 6, −1, −1 _____ 2

−3, −2, −3, −1, −1 _____ −2

2, −1, 1, −2 _____ 0

3, 3, 3, 3, 3, 3, 3, 3, 3, 3 _____ 3

5, 9, 6, 2, 7, 9, 12, 4, 8, 8 _____ 7

9, 4, 5, 2, 6, 0, 3, 4, 3 _____ 4

6, 7, 3, 6, 4, 2, 7, 5 _____ 5

# Weighing In

**Example:**

A **number line** can be used to compare **integers**.
The farther to the right a number is, the greater it is.

3 is greater than –1.
2 is greater than –5.

```
◄─┼──┼──┼──┼──┼──┼──┼──┼──┼──┼──┼──┼──┼──┼──┼──┼──┼──┼──┼──┼──►
 -10 -9 -8 -7 -6 -5 -4 -3 -2 -1  0  1  2  3  4  5  6  7  8  9  10
```

**Directions:** Circle the greater number in each pair.

# Counting Puppies

Ty Half-awake has trouble sleeping. His mother suggested that he try counting puppies. So night after night, he lay awake counting puppies.

**Directions:** Each set of three numbers below contains the actual number of puppies Ty counted on a given night and two other numbers. The number he counted will always be the greatest number of the three. Circle the number of puppies in each row that is the greatest number. Then, circle the letter above the greatest number in each group, and use it to spell out the cause of Ty's sleeplessness.

| s | l | p |
|---|---|---|
| 110,001 | 110,010 | 110,100 |

| l | u | a |
|---|---|---|
| 221,112 | 222,111 | 212,211 |

| g | p | t |
|---|---|---|
| 523,567 | 523,746 | 523,476 |

| p | r | e |
|---|---|---|
| 991,991 | 919,911 | 991,191 |

| g | t | y |
|---|---|---|
| 432,342 | 423,432 | 432,423 |

| m | l | n |
|---|---|---|
| 955,449 | 959,454 | 959,445 |

| e | a | o |
|---|---|---|
| 723,327 | 772,332 | 773,223 |

| s | v | t |
|---|---|---|
| 401,101 | 410,410 | 410,401 |

| e | l | r |
|---|---|---|
| 883,833 | 838,388 | 838,833 |

The cause of Ty's sleeplessness was ___PUPPY LOVE___.

# The Old Ball Park

The fans, hot dogs, the "Wave," and the crack of the bat—these are just a few of the sights, sounds, and smells at the old ball park. American League teams have new parks and old parks, big parks and small parks.

**Directions:** Use the information from the chart to compare the sizes of these parks.

### American League Ball Parks

| Team | Park | Year Built | Seating |
|---|---|---|---|
| Anaheim Angels | Edison Intnl. Field | 1966 | 45,050 |
| Baltimore Orioles | Camden Yards | 1992 | 48,262 |
| Boston Red Sox | Fenway Park | 1912 | 33,871 |
| Chicago White Sox | Comiskey Park | 1991 | 44,321 |
| Cleveland Indians | Jacobs Field | 1994 | 43,368 |
| Detroit Tigers | Tiger Stadium | 1912 | 46,945 |
| Kansas City Royals | Kauffman Stadium | 1973 | 40,625 |
| Minnesota Twins | Metrodome | 1982 | 48,678 |
| New York Yankees | Yankee Stadium | 1923 | 57,545 |
| Oakland A's | Oakland Coliseum | 1968 | 43,662 |
| Seattle Mariners | Safeco Field | 1999 | 47,000 |
| Tampa Bay Devil Rays | Tropicana Field | 1990 | 44,207 |
| Texas Rangers | The Ballpark | 1994 | 49,166 |
| Toronto Blue Jays | SkyDome | 1989 | 50,516 |

1. What are the two teams that play in stadiums with seating between 50,000 and 60,000? _The New York Yankees and Toronto Blue Jays._

2. There are eleven teams that play in stadiums with seating between 40,000 and 50,000. List them in order from largest to smallest.
   1. _Texas Rangers_
   2. _Baltimore Orioles_ ✓
   3. _Seattle Mariners_
   4. _Detroit Tigers_
   5. _Anaheim Angels_
   6. _Chicago White Sox_
   7. _Tampa Bay Devil Rays_
   8. _Oakland A's_
   9. _Cleveland Indians_
   10. _Kansas City Royals_
   11. _Boston Red Sox_

3. Which team plays in the smallest park? _Boston Red Sox_

# Addition

**Addition** is "putting together" two or more numbers to find the sum.

**Directions:** Add. Fill the backpacks with the right answers.

*Good Work*

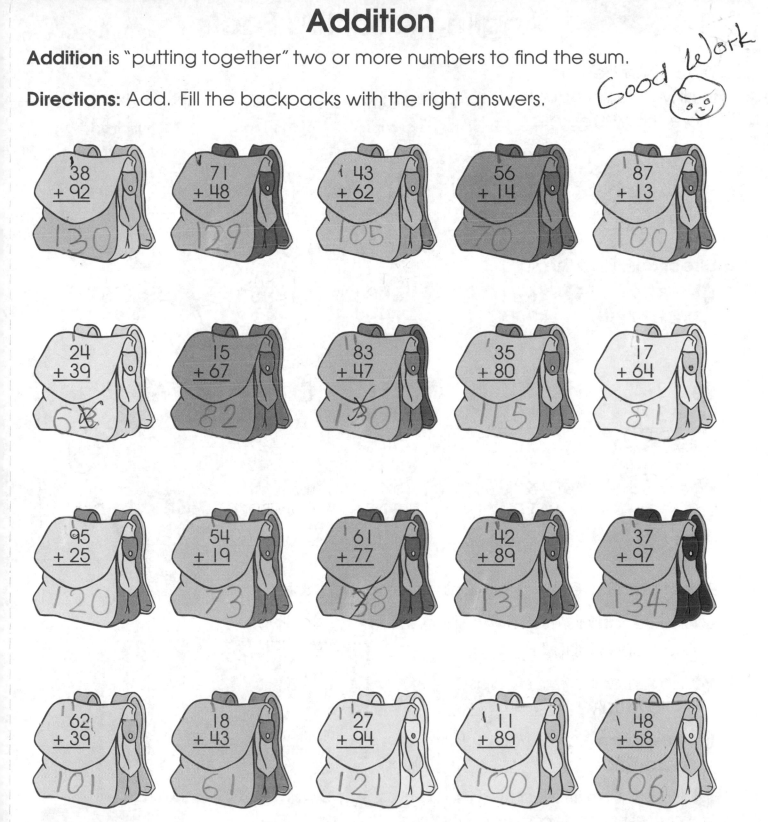

| | | | | |
|---|---|---|---|---|
| 38<br>+ 92<br>130 | 71<br>+ 48<br>129 | 43<br>+ 62<br>105 | 56<br>+ 14<br>70 | 87<br>+ 13<br>100 |
| 24<br>+ 39<br>63 | 15<br>+ 67<br>82 | 83<br>+ 47<br>130 | 35<br>+ 80<br>115 | 17<br>+ 64<br>81 |
| 95<br>+ 25<br>120 | 54<br>+ 19<br>73 | 61<br>+ 77<br>138 | 42<br>+ 89<br>131 | 37<br>+ 97<br>134 |
| 62<br>+ 39<br>101 | 18<br>+ 43<br>61 | 27<br>+ 94<br>121 | 11<br>+ 89<br>100 | 48<br>+ 58<br>106 |

# Angling Addition Facts

When numbers added in any column equal more than 9, regroup.

**Example:**

| Add the ones. Regroup. | Add the tens. | Add the hundreds. |
|---|---|---|
| 1 | 1 | 1 |
| 486 | 486 | 486 |
| +109 | + 109 | + 109 |
| 5 | 95 | 595 |

**Directions:** Find the sums.

1.  852
    +137
    **989**

2.  661
    +307
    **968**

3.  649
    +144
    **793**

4.  953
    + 28
    **981**

5.  537
    +253
    **790**

6.  267
    +325
    **592**

7.  807
    + 92
    **899**

8.  366
    +324
    **690**

9.  478
    +206
    **684**

10. 655
    +239
    **894**

11. 763
    +229
    **992**

12. 833
    +156
    **989**

13. 581
    +309
    **890**

14. 99
    +100
    **199**

**Directions:** Solve the problems by using the table.

15. How many lures did the shop sell in July and August? _____ **353**

16. How much live bait was sold in July? _____ **279**

17. How many lures were sold in September? _____ **354**

18. How much live bait was sold in August and September? _____ **1,044**

Dakota Tackle Box

| Month | Live bait | Lures |
|---|---|---|
| July | 279 | 138 |
| August | 479 | 215 |
| September | 565 | 354 |

1.  138
    +215
    353

2.  479
    +565
    1,044

# One-Digit Multiplication

Here's how to do 1-digit multiplication without regrouping.

**Multiply the ones.**

```
  2,043
x     2
      6
```

**Multiply the tens.**

```
  2,043
x     2
     86
```

**Multiply the hundreds and thousands.**

```
  2,043
x     2
  4,086
```

**Directions:** Multiply.

```
   41        33       103       122       101     1,214
 x  2      x  3      x  2      x  4      x  8     x    2
```

```
  230     3,422       689     3,321     9,738     1,011
 x  3     x    2      x  0     x    3     x    1     x    6
```

```
   32     1,022     5,903     4,413       204        24
 x  3     x    4      x    1     x    2     x  2      x  2
```

**Directions:** Write a numeral in each box to make the multiplication problem true.

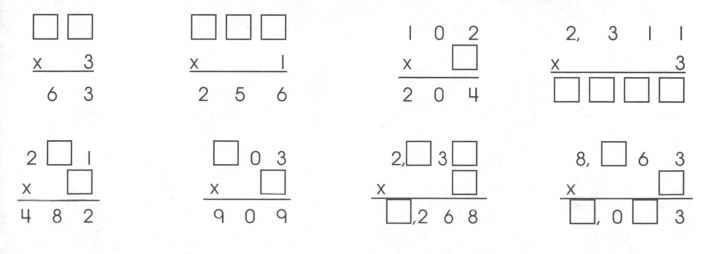

Name _____

# Sailing Through Multiplication

**Directions:** For each multiplication problem, color in the matching answer in the picture below.

**Example:**

```
  33
x  5
-----
 165
```

```
  24        97        82        76        54        62        42        23
x  6      x  2      x  7      x  2      x  7      x  8      x  6      x  7
-----     -----     -----     -----     -----     -----     -----     -----


  37        86        24        46        58        22        52        21
x  3      x  2      x  5      x  2      x  4      x  8      x  4      x  8
-----     -----     -----     -----     -----     -----     -----     -----
```

# Multiplying With Molly

**Directions:** Write the problem and the answer for each question.

**1** Molly is the toughest football player in her school. She ran for 23 yards on one play and went 3 times as far on the next play. How far did she run the second time?

**2** Molly keeps a rock collection. She has 31 rocks in one sack. She has 7 times as many under her bed. How many rocks are under her bed?

**3** Molly had 42 marbles when she came to school. She went home with 4 times as many. How many did she go home with?

**4** Molly stuffed 21 sticks of gum in her mouth in the morning. In the afternoon, she crammed 9 times as many sticks into her mouth. How many sticks did she have in the afternoon?

**5** Molly did 51 multiplication problems in math last week. This week, she did 8 times as many. How many did she do this week?

**6** Molly did 21 science experiments last year. This year, she did 7 times as many. How many experiments did she do this year?

# Multiplication (Two-Digit Multiplier)

**Example A**
**(no regrouping)**

```
      21
x     44
      84
+    840
     924
```

**Step 1** Multiply by ones.
4 x 1 = 4
4 x 2 = 8
**Step 2** Multiply by tens.
Add zero in the ones column.
4 x 1 = 4
4 x 2 = 8
**Step 3** Add.
84 + 840 = 924

**Example B**
**(regrouping)**

```
      67
x     58
     536
+  3,350
   3,886
```

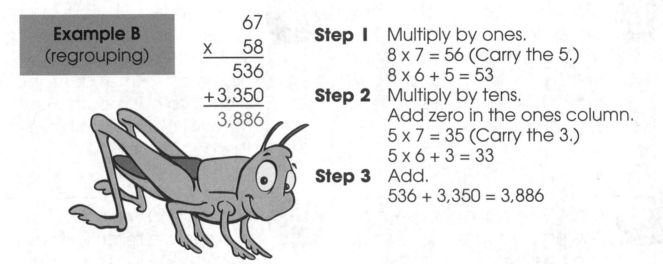

**Step 1** Multiply by ones.
8 x 7 = 56 (Carry the 5.)
8 x 6 + 5 = 53
**Step 2** Multiply by tens.
Add zero in the ones column.
5 x 7 = 35 (Carry the 3.)
5 x 6 + 3 = 33
**Step 3** Add.
536 + 3,350 = 3,886

**Directions:** Multiply.

| | | | |
|---|---|---|---|
| 1. | 43 x 33 | 2. | 55 x 46 | 3. | 78 x 68 |

1.  43
    x  33

2.  55
    x  46

3.  78
    x  68

4.  39
    x  27

5.  21
    x  87

6.  77
    x  24

7.  44
    x  16

8.  80
    x  71

9.  65
    x  49

# Two-Digit Multiplication With Regrouping

**Example:**

**Steps:**

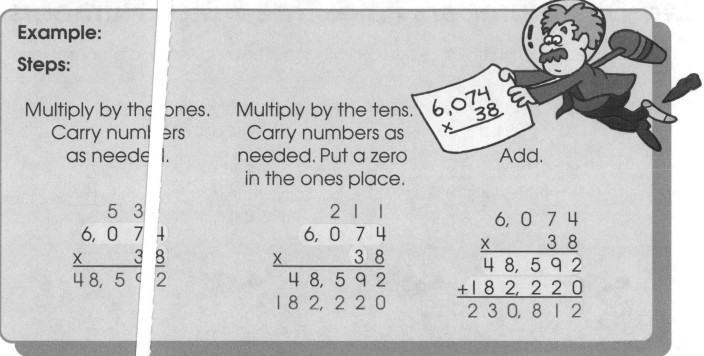

Multiply by the ones. Carry numbers as needed.

Multiply by the tens. Carry numbers as needed. Put a zero in the ones place.

Add.

```
    5 3
  6, 0 7 4
  x     3 8
  4 8, 5 9 2
```

```
    2 1 1
  6, 0 7 4
  x     3 8
  4 8, 5 9 2
  1 8 2, 2 2 0
```

```
  6, 0 7 4
  x     3 8
  4 8, 5 9 2
  +1 8 2, 2 2 0
  2 3 0, 8 1 2
```

**Directions:** Multiply along each diagonal of the square. Write the answer in the oval.

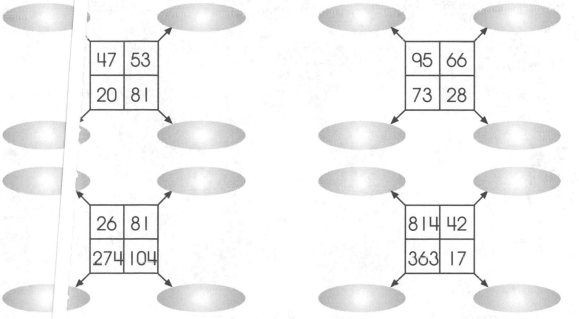

What is the pattern of the answers on opposite corners? Why is that so?

_____

# Multiplication:
# Two-Digit Numbers Times Three-Digit Numbers

Follow the steps for multiplying a two-digit number by a three-digit number using regrouping.

**Example: Step :** Multiply the ones. Regroup.

**Step 2:** Multiply the tens. Regroup. Add.

```
                    2 2
  287             2 8 7
x  43           x   4 3
_____          _____
                  8 6 1
```

```
  287             287
x  43           x  43
_____          _____
                  861
1 1,4 8 0      +11,480
               _____
                12,341
```

**Directions:** Multiply.

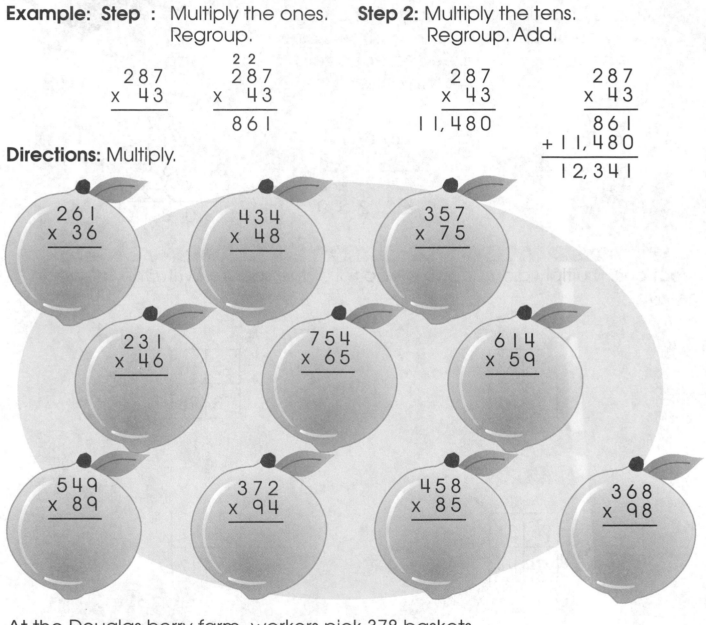

```
  261           434           357
x  36         x  48         x  75
```

```
  231           754           614
x  46         x  65         x  59
```

```
  549           372           458           368
x  89         x  94         x  85         x  98
```

At the Douglas berry farm, workers pick 378 baskets of peaches each day. Each basket holds 65 peaches. How many peaches are picked each day? _____

# Backward Multiplication

Division problems are like multiplication problems—just turned around.
As you solve 8 ÷ 4, think, "how many groups of 4 make 8?" or "what number 'times' 4 is eight?"

**2** x 4 = 8, so 8 ÷ 4 = **2**.

**Directions:** Use the pictures to help you solve these division problems.

9 ÷ 3 =

6 ÷ 2 =

16 ÷ 4 =

10 ÷ 5 =

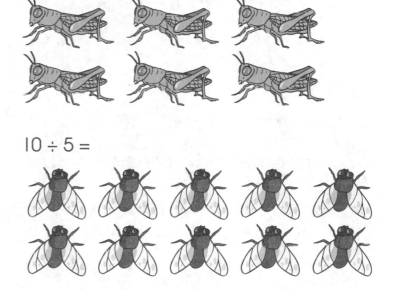

20 ÷ 1 =

18 ÷ 3 =

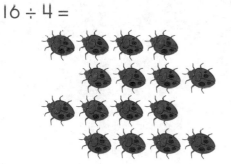

Name _____

# Divide by One-Digit Numbers

Here's how to divide by a one-digit number.

**Without a remainder**

dividend⟶ 81 ÷ 3 = _____
                    ↓
                 divisor

1.  Rewrite the problem.

    3⟌81

2.  Divide into the tens.
3.  Multiply the partial product.
4.  Subtract.

    $$\begin{array}{r} 2\phantom{1} \\ 3\overline{)81} \\ -6\phantom{1} \\ \hline 2\phantom{1} \end{array}$$

5.  Carry down the 1 in the ones place.
6.  Divide.
7.  Multiply the partial product.
8.  Subtract.

    $$\begin{array}{r} 27 \\ 3\overline{)81} \\ -6\downarrow \\ \hline 21 \\ -21 \\ \hline 0 \end{array}$$

81 ÷ 3 = 27 ⟵ quotient

**With a remainder**

dividend⟶ 52 ÷ 6 = _____
                    ↓
                 divisor

1.  Rewrite the problem.

    6⟌52

2.  Divide into the tens. If the divisor is larger than the tens, divide into the first two digits.
3.  Multiply the partial product.
4.  Subtract.

    $$\begin{array}{r} 8\phantom{1} \\ 6\overline{)52} \\ -48 \\ \hline 4 \end{array}$$

5.  Write the remainder.

    $$\begin{array}{r} 8R4 \\ 6\overline{)52} \\ -48 \\ \hline 4 \end{array}$$

52 ÷ 48 = 8R4 ⟵ quotient

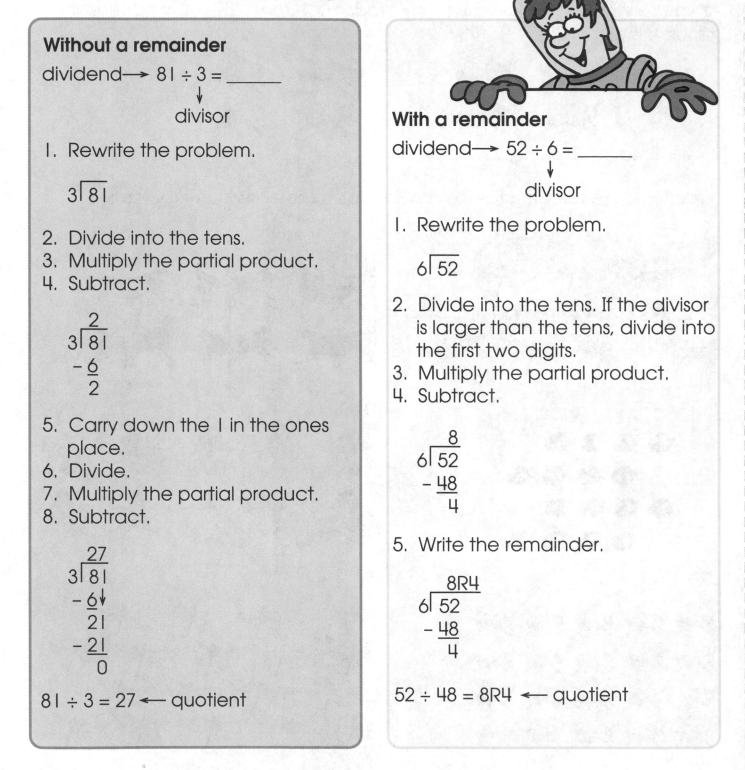

# Zeros in the Quotient

Some problems will have a zero in the quotient.

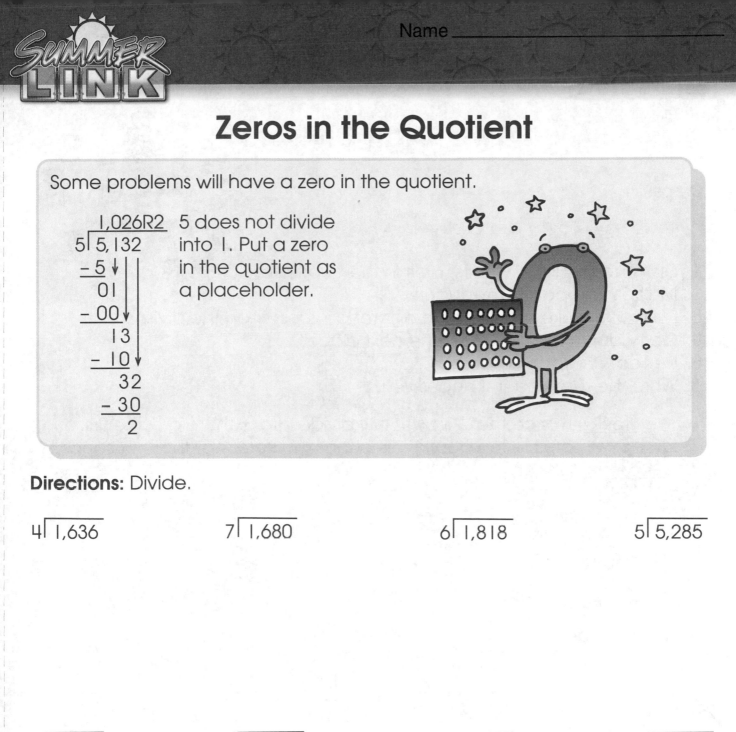

$$
\begin{array}{r}
1,026\,R2 \\
5\overline{)5,132} \\
-5\phantom{,132}\downarrow \\
\hline
01\phantom{00} \\
-00\phantom{0}\downarrow \\
\hline
13\phantom{0} \\
-10\phantom{}\downarrow \\
\hline
32 \\
-30 \\
\hline
2
\end{array}
$$

5 does not divide into 1. Put a zero in the quotient as a placeholder.

**Directions:** Divide.

$4\overline{)1,636}$        $7\overline{)1,680}$        $6\overline{)1,818}$        $5\overline{)5,285}$

$5\overline{)5,025}$        $9\overline{)21,654}$        $8\overline{)8,320}$        $6\overline{)24,300}$

# Two-Digit Divisors

**Steps:**

$$3{,}549 \div 23 \longrightarrow 23\overline{)3{,}549}$$

1. Estimate to place the first digit in the quotient.
2. Multiply the partial product.
3. Subtract. Make sure that the difference is less than the divisor.
4. Carry down the digit from the next place.
5. Repeat for each place.
6. Write the remainder, if necessary.

```
        154R7
  23) 3,549
     - 23↓
        124
      - 115↓
          99
        - 92
           7
```

Notice that 23 does not divide into 3. Therefore, the first digit in the quotient is in the hundreds, not the thousands, place.

**Directions:** Divide.

$$29\overline{)4{,}092} \qquad 33\overline{)7{,}524} \qquad 11\overline{)3{,}925} \qquad 58\overline{)9{,}979}$$

# Wisconsin's Nickname

**Directions:** What is Wisconsin known as? To find out, solve the division problems below. Then, find the answers at the bottom of the page and write the corresponding letter on the line above the answer.

T. $14\overline{)1218}$          E. $23\overline{)1633}$          S. $53\overline{)2756}$

A. $38\overline{)1596}$          A. $61\overline{)5185}$          E. $18\overline{)1764}$

T. $22\overline{)1628}$          R. $40\overline{)2520}$          D. $55\overline{)4400}$

G. $31\overline{)1364}$          B. $12\overline{)780}$

___  ___  ___  ___  ___  ___     ___  ___  ___  ___  ___
65   85   80   44   71   63      52   74   42   87   98

# My Dear Aunt Sally

**Example:**

To solve a problem with several operations, follow the rules of My Dear Aunt Sally.

**My D**ear =    **M**ultiplication/**D**ivision

**A**unt **S**ally =   **A**ddition/**S**ubtraction

Do all multiplication and division steps first, in order from left to right.

Then do all addition and subtraction steps, in order from left to right.

These rules are called the Order of Operations.

$$4 \times 8 + 36 \div 6 - 7$$
$$32 \quad + \quad 6 \; - \; 7$$
$$38 \; - \; 7$$
$$31$$

**Directions:** Follow the Order of Operations to solve.

$4 + 5 \times 3 - 6 =$ _____

$8 \div 4 + 3 \times 2 + 2 =$ _____

$2 + 3 \times 2 - 4 + 2 \times 2 =$ _____

$4 \times 5 - 8 \div 2 + 5 \times 2 =$ _____

$3 \times 3 + 3 - 3 \times 3 - 3 =$ _____

$4 - 3 + 6 \div 2 + 4 \times 2 =$ _____

$5 \times 2 - 3 + 5 - 6 \div 3 =$ _____

$6 - 2 + 3 - 2 \times 4 + 3 =$ _____

$9 \div 3 + 5 - 4 \div 2 + 6 =$ _____

$8 - 4 \div 4 + 2 \times 3 - 2 =$ _____

# Dare to Compare

**Directions:** Compare the fractions below. Write =, <, or > in each box.

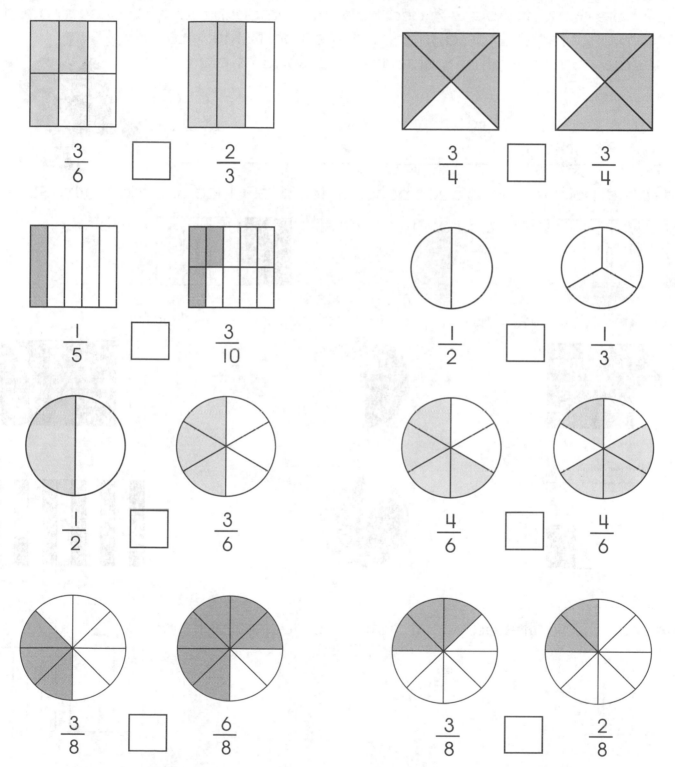

$\dfrac{3}{6}$ ☐ $\dfrac{2}{3}$          $\dfrac{3}{4}$ ☐ $\dfrac{3}{4}$

$\dfrac{1}{5}$ ☐ $\dfrac{3}{10}$          $\dfrac{1}{2}$ ☐ $\dfrac{1}{3}$

$\dfrac{1}{2}$ ☐ $\dfrac{3}{6}$          $\dfrac{4}{6}$ ☐ $\dfrac{4}{6}$

$\dfrac{3}{8}$ ☐ $\dfrac{6}{8}$          $\dfrac{3}{8}$ ☐ $\dfrac{2}{8}$

# Doing Decimals

Just as a fraction stands for part of a whole number, a decimal also shows part of a whole number. And with decimals, the number is always broken into ten or a power of ten (hundred, thousand, etc.) parts. These place values are named tenths, hundredths, thousandths, etc.

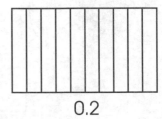

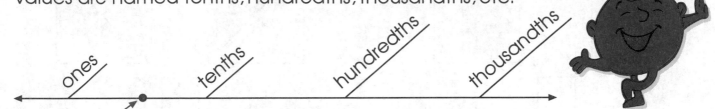

A **decimal point** is a dot placed between the ones place and the tenths place.

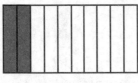 0.2 is read as "two tenths." 0.4 is four tenths

**Directions:** Write the answer as a decimal for the shaded parts.

_____        _____        _____

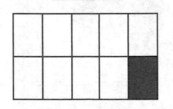  

_____        _____        _____

**Directions:** Color the parts that match the decimal numbers.

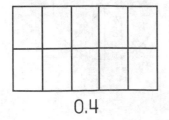 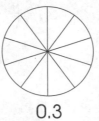 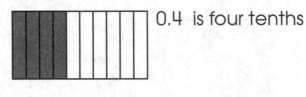

0.4              0.3              0.2

# Decimals

A **decimal** is a number with one or more places to the right of a decimal point.

**Examples:** 6.5 and 2.25

Fractions with denominators of 10 or 100 can be written as decimals.

**Examples:**

$\frac{7}{10} = 0.7$

$$\frac{0}{\text{ones}} \cdot \frac{7}{\text{tenths}} \frac{0}{\text{hundredths}}$$

$1\frac{52}{100} = 1.52$

$$\frac{1}{\text{ones}} \cdot \frac{5}{\text{tenths}} \frac{2}{\text{hundredths}}$$

**Directions:** Write the fractions as decimals.

$\frac{1}{2} = \overline{10} = 0.\underline{\hspace{1cm}}$

$\frac{2}{5} = \overline{10} = 0.\underline{\hspace{1cm}}$

$\frac{1}{5} = \overline{10} = 0.\underline{\hspace{1cm}}$

$\frac{3}{5} = \overline{10} = 0.\underline{\hspace{1cm}}$

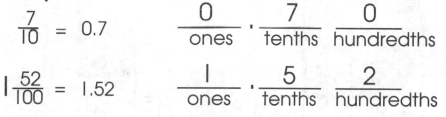

| $\frac{63}{100} =$ | $2\frac{8}{10} =$ | $38\frac{4}{100} =$ | $6\frac{13}{100} =$ |
|---|---|---|---|
| $\frac{1}{4} =$ | $\frac{2}{5} =$ | $\frac{1}{50} =$ | $\frac{100}{200} =$ |
| $5\frac{2}{100} =$ | $\frac{4}{25} =$ | $15\frac{3}{5} =$ | $\frac{3}{100} =$ |

# More Puzzling Problems

## Across

3. 7.333 = seven and three hundred thirty-three _____

5. 67.02 = sixty-seven and _____ hundredths

6. 490.1 = four hundred _____ and one tenth

7. 0.512 = five _____ twelve thousandths

9. 8.06 = eight and _____ hundredths

10. 0.007 = _____ thousandths

12. 11.3 = _____ and three tenths

13. 300.12 = _____ hundred and twelve hundredths

15. 62.08 = sixty-two and _____ hundredths

18. 70.009 = _____ and nine thousandths

19. 9.3 = _____ and three tenths

20. 10.51 = _____ and fifty-one hundredths

21. 1,000.02 = one thousand and two _____

## Down

1. 6.5 = six and five _____

2. 0.428 = four hundred _____ thousandths

3. 8,100.1 = eight _____ one hundred and one tenth

4. 3.02 = three and two _____

8. 0.685 = six hundred _____ thousandths

11. 50.19 = fifty and _____ hundredths

14. 0.015 = _____ thousandths

16. 430.7 = four hundred thirty and seven _____

17. 73.4 = seventy-three and four _____

# Adding Money

**Example:**

**Steps:**

1. Align the decimal points.
2. Add.

$4.32
+ $2.19
$6.51

$10.43
$ 4.25
+ $12.04
$26.72

**Directions:** Rewrite the problems and align the decimal points. Then, add.

$1.15 + $2.25 =                    $2.09 + $1.46 =

$1.11 + $5.35 =                    $3.87 + $2.95 =

$10.42 + $2.54 =                   $8.12 + $3.29 =

$11.13 + $10.26 =                  $4.03 + $2.99 =

$42.80 + $103.25 + $32.54 =        $3.64 + $49.39 + $1.00 =

# Subtracting Money

**Example:**

**Steps:**

1. Align the decimal points.
2. Subtract.

$$
\begin{array}{r}
\$14.32 \\
- \ \$ \ 5.43 \\
\hline
\$ \ 8.89
\end{array}
$$

**Directions:** Rewrite the problems and align the decimal points. Then, subtract.

$4.15 - $2.25 =                    $2.09 - $1.46 =

$3.93 - $0.44 =                    $6.06 - $3.85 =

$7.83 - $2.17 =                    $26.32 - $12.88 =

$11.13 - $10.26 =                  $4.03 - $2.99 =

$43.76 - $0.94 =                   $104.65 - $4.87 =

# Minute Men

**Directions:** Draw the hour and minute hands on these clocks.

**Example:**

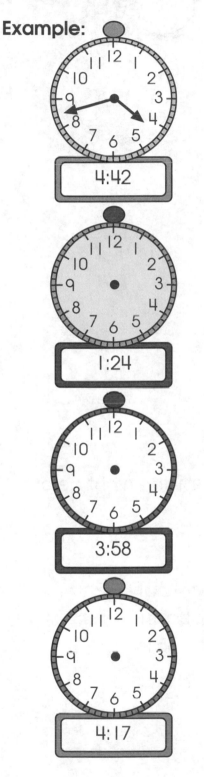

| | | |
|---|---|---|
| 4:42 | 9:03 | 6:51 |
| 1:24 | 7:33 | 10:11 |
| 3:58 | 12:01 | 2:49 |
| 4:17 | 5:36 | 8:23 |

# Time to Play Ball

**Directions:** Write the number of the matching clock in front of each sentence.

_____ Mary's coach says she should be in bed by 9:30 P.M. the night before a game.

_____ Tom's baseball team practices at 6:15 P.M.

_____ It was 6:08 P.M. when Mike arrived at practice.

_____ Coach told the team their next game was tomorrow at 4:45 P.M.

_____ The National Anthem was played over the loudspeaker at 4:35 P.M.

_____ Steve and Paul pitch to each other every day at 3:35 P.M.

_____ Emily went to see her friend Sue's game at 10:21 A.M.

_____ Coach had us practice running the bases at 2:37 P.M.

_____ Our game was rained out at 5:51 P.M.

_____ Sue's game was finished at 12:09 P.M.

# Length

Inches, feet, yards, and miles are used to measure length in the United States.

    12 inches = 1 foot (ft.)

    3 feet   = 1 yard (yd.)

    36 inches = 1 yard

    1,760 yards = 1 mile (mi.)

**Directions:** Circle the best unit to measure each object. The first one has been done for you.

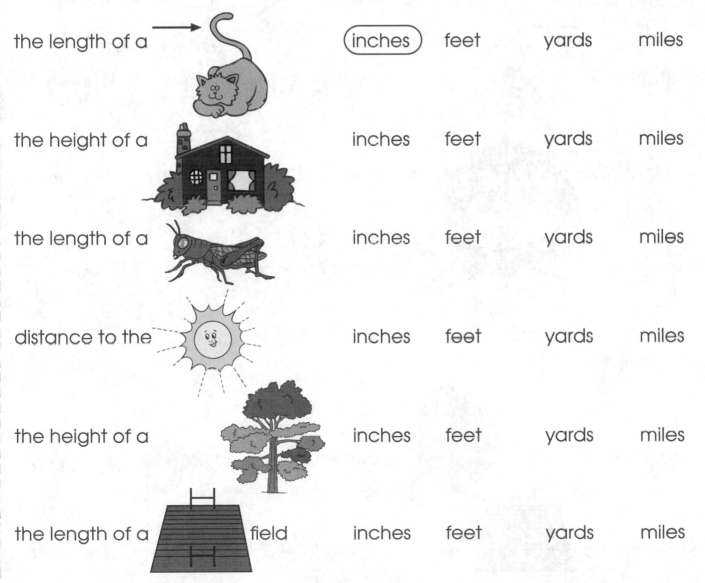

the length of a ➝      (inches)    feet    yards    miles

the height of a      inches    feet    yards    miles

the length of a      inches    feet    yards    miles

distance to the      inches    feet    yards    miles

the height of a      inches    feet    yards    miles

the length of a    field    inches    feet    yards    miles

# Length: Metric

**Millimeters, centimeters, meters,** and **kilometers** are used to measure length in the metric system.

> **1 meter = 39.37 inches**
> **1 kilometer = about $\frac{5}{8}$ mile**
> **10 millimeters = 1 centimeter (cm)**
> **100 centimeters = 1 meter (m)**
> **1,000 meters = 1 kilometer (km)**

**Directions:** Circle the best unit to measure each object. The first one has been done for you.

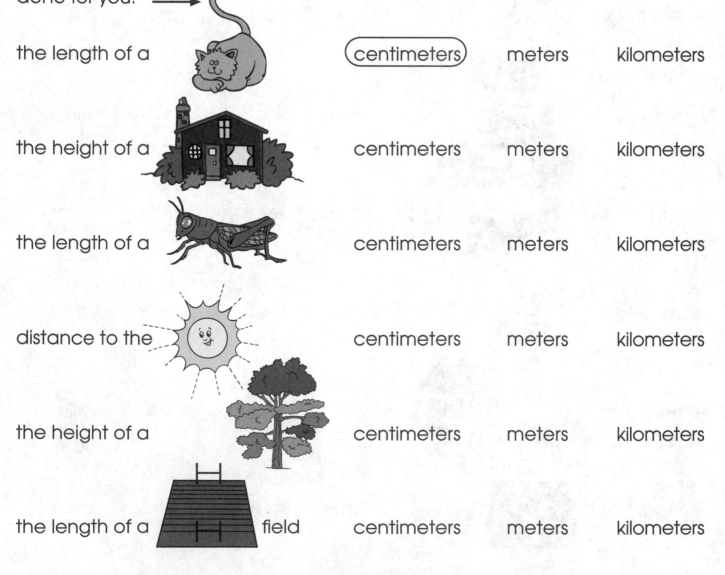

the length of a     (centimeters)     meters     kilometers

the height of a     centimeters     meters     kilometers

the length of a     centimeters     meters     kilometers

distance to the     centimeters     meters     kilometers

the height of a     centimeters     meters     kilometers

the length of a     field     centimeters     meters     kilometers

# Weight

**Ounces, pounds,** and **tons** are used to measure weight in the United States.

**16 ounces = 1 pound (lb.)**
**2,000 pounds = 1 ton (tn.)**

**Directions:** Circle the most reasonable estimate for the weight of each object. The first one has been done for you.

| | | | |
|---|---|---|---|
| 10 ounces | (10 pounds) | 10 tons |
| 6 ounces | 6 pounds | 6 tons |
| 2 ounces | 2 pounds | 2 tons |
| 3 ounces | 3 pounds | 3 tons |
| 1,800 ounces | 1,800 pounds | 1,800 tons |
| 20 ounces | 20 pounds | 20 tons |
| 1 ounce | 1 pound | 1 ton |

# Weight: Metric

**Grams** and **kilograms** are units of weight in the metric system. A paper clip weighs about 1 gram. A kitten weighs about 1 kilogram.

**1 kilogram (kg) = about 2.2 pounds**

**1,000 grams (g) = 1 kilogram**

**Directions:** Circle the best unit to weigh each object.

# Capacity

The **fluid ounce, cup, pint, quart,** and **gallon** are used to measure capacity in the United States.

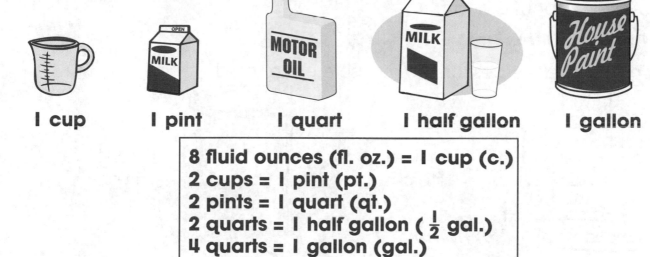

| I cup | I pint | I quart | I half gallon | I gallon |

**8 fluid ounces (fl. oz.) = I cup (c.)**
**2 cups = I pint (pt.)**
**2 pints = I quart (qt.)**
**2 quarts = I half gallon ( $\frac{1}{2}$ gal.)**
**4 quarts = I gallon (gal.)**

**Directions:** Convert the units of capacity.

13 gal. = _____ qt.          10 pt. = _____ c.          12 c. = _____ pt.

4 gal. = _____ qt.          16 qt. = _____ gal.          5 c. = _____ pt.

36 pt. = _____ gal.          12 qt. = _____ pt.          6 gal. = _____ pt.

16 c. = _____ qt.          32 oz. = _____ c.          16 oz. = _____ pt.

# Capacity: Metric

**Milliliters** and **liters** are units of capacity in the metric system. A can of soda contains about 350 milliliters of liquid. A large plastic bottle contains 1 liter of liquid. A liter is about a quart.

### 1,000 milliliters (mL) = 1 liter (L)

**Directions:** Circle the best unit to measure each liquid.

milliliters
liters

milliliters
liters

milliliters
liters

milliliters
liters

milliliters
liters

milliliters
liters

milliliters
liters

milliliters
liters

milliliters
liters

milliliters
liters

# Temperature: Fahrenheit

Degrees **Fahrenheit** (°F) is a unit for measuring temperature.

**Directions:** Write the temperature in degrees Fahrenheit (°F).

**Example:**

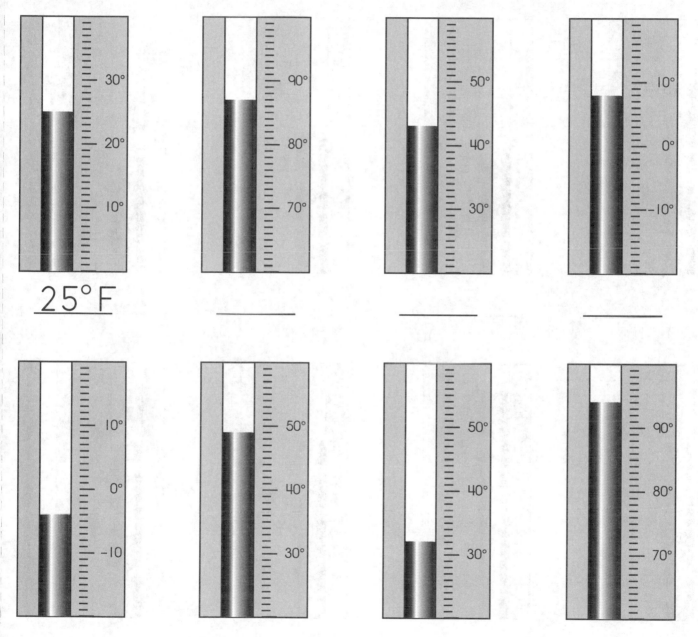

25°F

_____  _____  _____

_____  _____  _____  _____

# Temperature: Celsius

Degrees **Celsius** (°C) is a unit for measuring temperature in the metric system.

**Directions:** Write the temperature in degrees Celsius (°C).

**Example:**

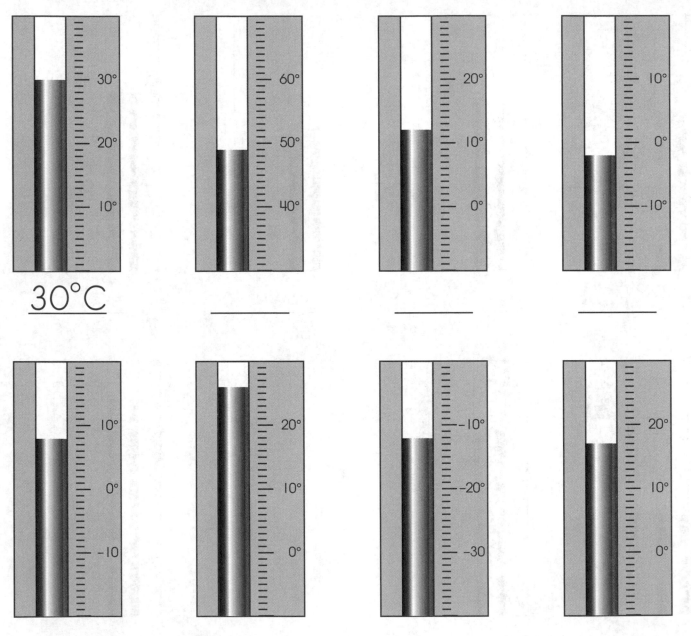

# Geometry

**Geometry** is the branch of mathematics that has to do with points, lines, and shapes.

**Directions:** Write the word from the box that is described below.

| | | | |
|---|---|---|---|
| triangle | square | cube | angle |
| line | ray | segment | rectangle |

a collection of points on a straight path
that goes on and on in opposite directions _____

a figure with three sides and three corners _____

a figure with four equal sides
and four corners _____

part of a line that has one end point
and goes on and on in one direction _____

part of a line having two end points _____

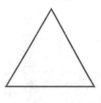

a space figure with six square faces _____

two rays with a common end point _____

a figure with four corners and four sides _____

# Similar, Congruent, and Symmetrical Figures

**Similar** figures have the same shape but have varying sizes.

Figures that are **congruent** have identical shapes but different orientations. That means they face in different directions.

**Symmetrical** figures can be divided equally into two identical parts.

**Directions:** Cross out the shape that does not belong in each group. Label the two remaining shapes as similiar, congruent, or symmetrical.

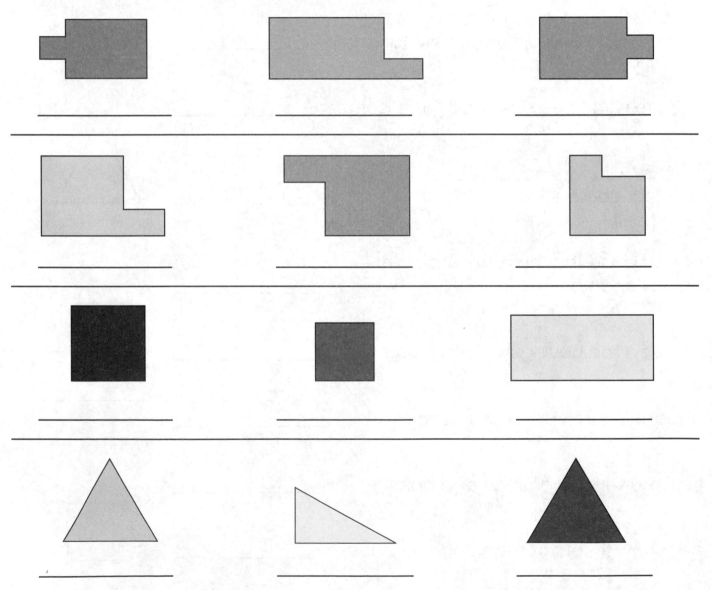

# Perimeter and Area

The **perimeter (P)** of a figure is the distance around it. To find the perimeter, add the lengths of the sides.

The **area (A)** of a figure is the number of units in a figure. Find the area by multiplying the length of a figure by its width.

**Example:**

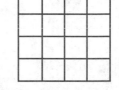

**P** = 16 units
**A** = 16 units

**Directions:** Find the perimeter and area of each figure.

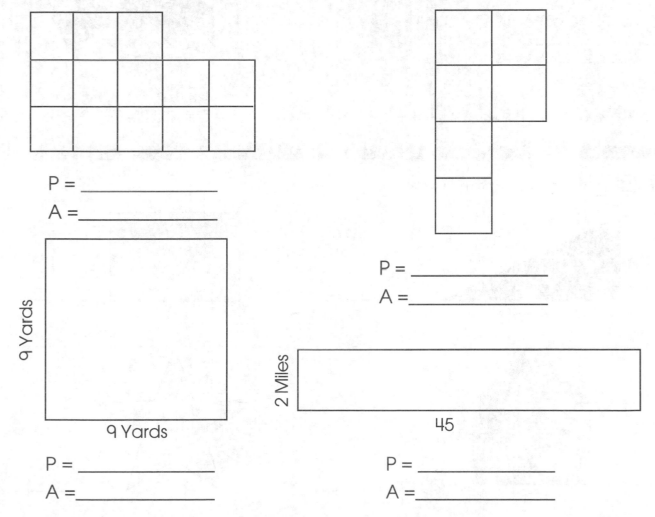

P = _____

A = _____

9 Yards

9 Yards

P = _____

A = _____

P = _____

A = _____

2 Miles

45

P = _____

A = _____

Name _____

# Perimeter

The **perimeter** is the distance around a shape.

**Example:**

Find the perimeter of a polygon by adding the lengths of each side.

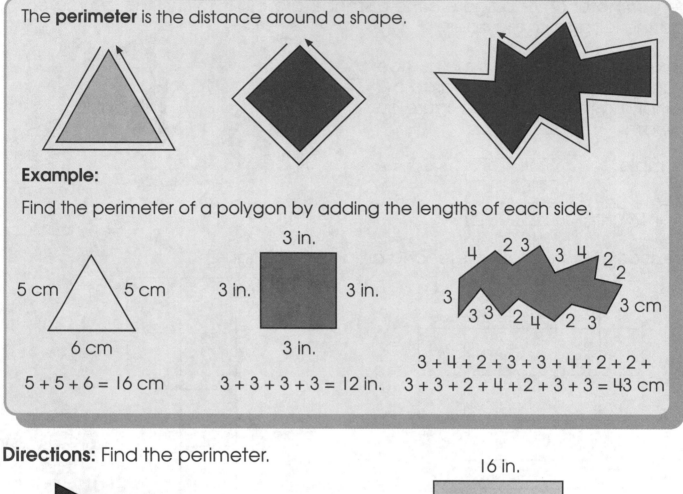

5 + 5 + 6 = 16 cm    3 + 3 + 3 + 3 = 12 in.

3 + 4 + 2 + 3 + 3 + 4 + 2 + 2 +
3 + 3 + 2 + 4 + 2 + 3 + 3 = 43 cm

**Directions:** Find the perimeter.

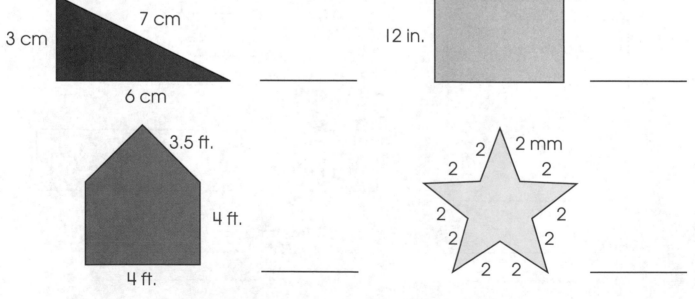

# Figuring Distance

**Directions:** Find the perimeter of each figure.

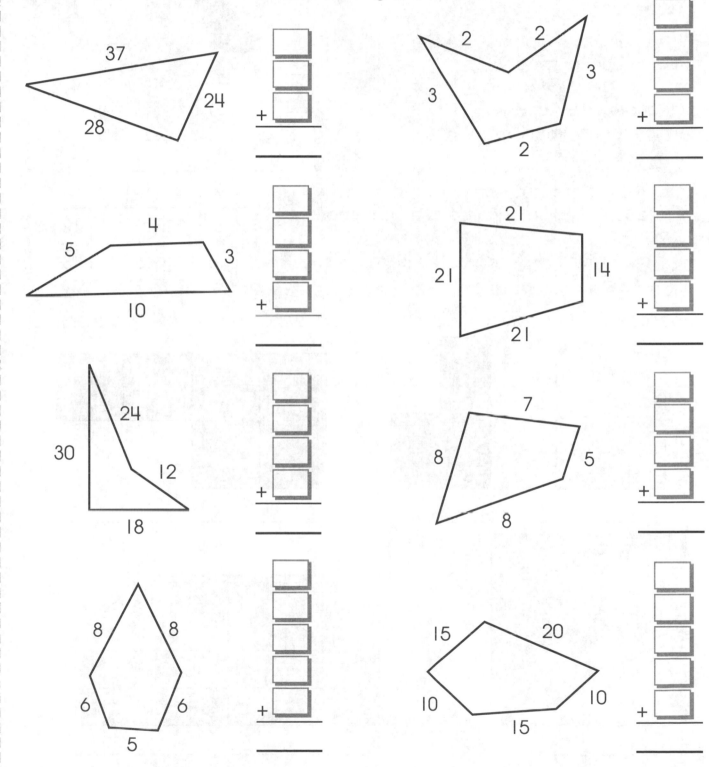

Name _____

# Area

**Example:**

The **area** of a shape is the amount of space it covers. Area is measured in square units, such as square centimeters (cm²) or square inches (in²).

One way to measure the area of a shape is to count the number of square units it covers.

The area of this rectangle is 18 square units.

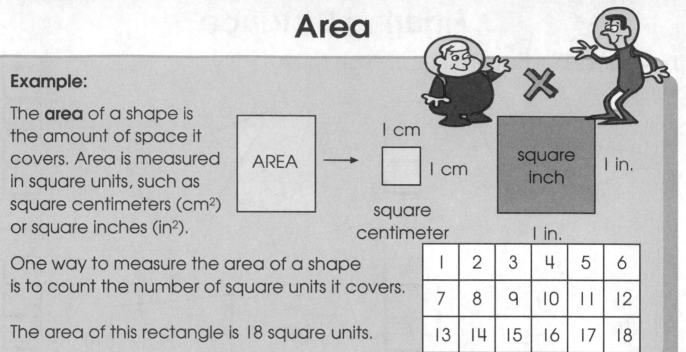

**Directions:** Find the area of each shape. Write the number of square units.

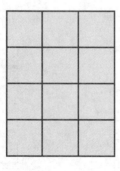

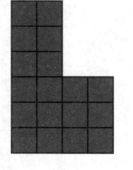

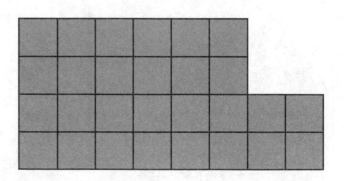

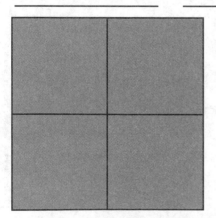

# Pump Up the Volume!

The **volume** of a 3-D shape is the amount of space it occupies. Volume is measured in cubic units, such as cubic centimeters (cm³) or cubic inches (in.³).

Imagine a box filled with unit cubes. The number of cubes is the volume of the box.

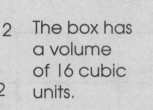

2
2
4

The box has a volume of 16 cubic units.

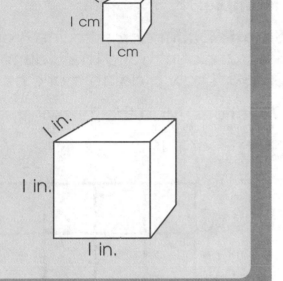

1 cm
1 cm
1 cm

1 in.
1 in.
1 in.

**Directions:** Find the volume of each shape in cubic units.

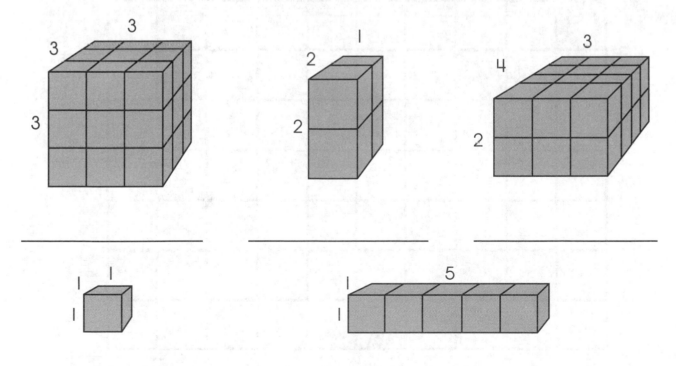

_____     _____     _____

_____          _____

# Ordered Pairs

An **ordered pair** is a pair of numbers used to locate a point.

**Example:** (8, 3)

**Step 1:** Count across to line 8 on the graph.
**Step 2:** Count up to line 3 on the graph.
**Step 3:** Draw a dot to mark the spot.

**Directions:** Map the following spots on the grid using ordered pairs.

(4, 7)      (9, 10)      (2, 1)      (5, 6)      (2, 2)      (1, 5)      (7, 4)      (3, 8)

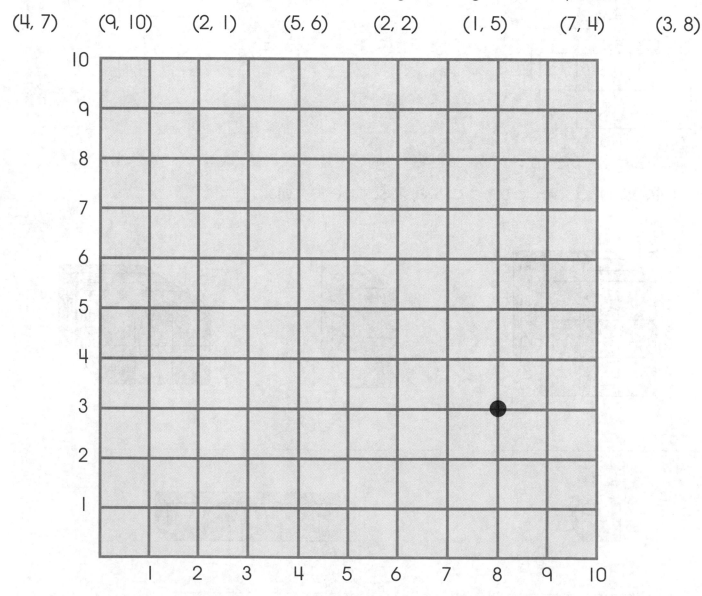

# Polygons

The word **polygon** means "many angles" and describes a shape that:

a) starts and stops at the same place (making it "closed").
b) can be traced without lifting the pencil or crossing or retracing any part.
c) is made of at least three line segments.

A **regular polygon** has sides that are all the same length.

      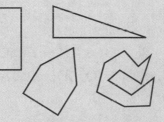      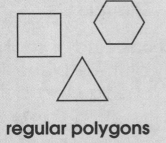

**shapes**                **polygons**            **regular polygons**

**Directions:** Circle any shape that is a polygon. Color any shape that is a regular polygon. If the shape is not a polygon, explain why.

# Plainly a Plane

A **plane figure** is a shape on a flat surface. The most common plane figures are shown below:

**Triangle**   **Circle**   **Square**   **Rectangle**

**Directions:** Find and label any shapes in the pictures below which remind you of any of these plane figures. Some of the pictures might suggest more than one plane figure. Label them all.

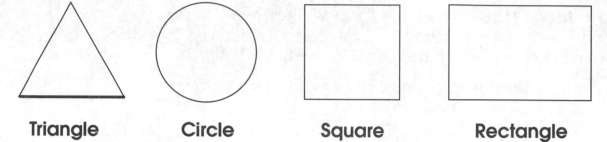

1.                          2.

3.                          4.

5.          6.          7.

**Directions:** Now, find a picture in a magazine or newspaper that suggests each of these plane figures. Either cut out and glue them or draw them on another sheet of paper. Label the plane figures.

# Circumference

**Circumference** is the distance around a circle. The **diameter** is a line segment that passes through the center of a circle and has both end points on the circle.

To find the circumference of any circle, multiply 3.14 times the diameter. The number 3.14 represents **pi** (pronounced pie) and is often written by this Greek symbol, $\pi$.

The formula for circumference is $C = \pi \times d$

    C = circumference

    d = diameter

    $\pi = 3.14$

**Example:**

    Circle A

    d = 2 in.

    $C = 3.14 \times 2$ in.

    C = 6.28 in.

**Directions:** Find the circumference of each circle.

4 in.

C = _____

6 in.

C = _____

| d = 10 in. | d = 14 in. | d = 3 yd. |
|---|---|---|
| C = _____ | C = _____ | C = _____ |

| d = 4 ft. | d = 8 ft. | d = 12 ft. |
|---|---|---|
| C = _____ | C = _____ | C = _____ |

Name _____

# Triangle Angles

A **triangle** is a figure with three corners and three sides. Every triangle contains three angles. The sum of the angles is always 180°, regardless of the size or shape of the triangle.

If you know two of the angles, you can add them together, then subtract the total from 180 to find the number of degrees in the third angle.

**Directions:** Find the number of degrees in the third angle of each triangle.

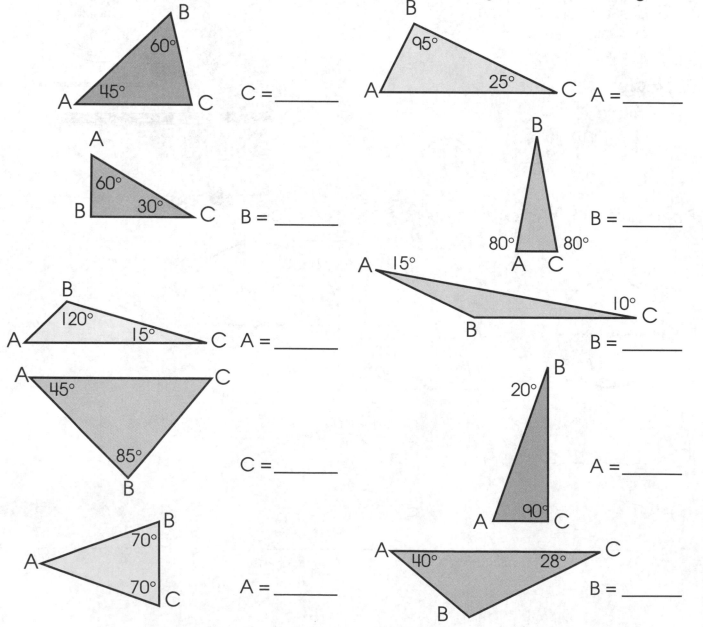

C = _____

A = _____

B = _____

B = _____

A = _____

B = _____

C = _____

A = _____

A = _____

B = _____

# Area of a Triangle

The area of a triangle is found by multiplying $\frac{1}{2}$ times the base times the height. $A = \frac{1}{2} \times b \times h$

**Example:**

$\overline{CD}$ is the height.      4 in.

$\overline{AB}$ is the base.      8 in.

Area $= \frac{1}{2} \times 4 \times 8 = \frac{32}{2} = 16$ sq. in.

**Directions:** Find the area of each triangle.

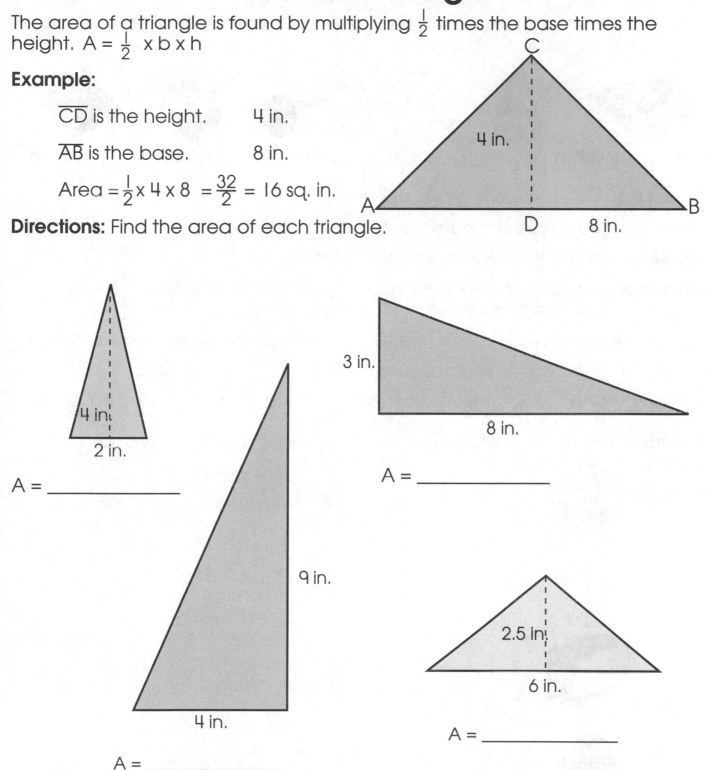

A = _____

A = _____

A = _____

A = _____

# Space Figures

**Space figures** are figures whose points are in more than one plane. Cubes and cylinders are space figures.

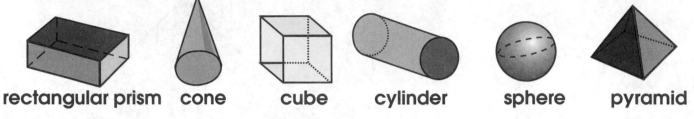

rectangular prism    cone    cube    cylinder    sphere    pyramid

A **prism** has two identical, parallel bases.

All of the faces on a **rectangular prism** are rectangles.

A **cube** is a prism with six identical, square faces.

A **pyramid** is a space figure whose base is a polygon and whose faces are triangles with a common vertex—the point where two rays meet.

A **cylinder** has a curved surface and two parallel bases that are identical circles.

A **cone** has one circular, flat face and one vertex.

A **sphere** has no flat surface. All points are an equal distance from the center.

**Directions:** Circle the name of the figure you see in each of these familiar objects.

cone      sphere      cylinder

cone      sphere      cylinder

cube      rectangular prism      pyramid

cone      pyramid      cylinder

Name _____

# Checking for Congruency

Figures that are **congruent** are the same shape and the same size. Figures are **similar** when they are the same shape but not necessarily the same size.

**Directions:** Label each set of figures below either congruent or similar.

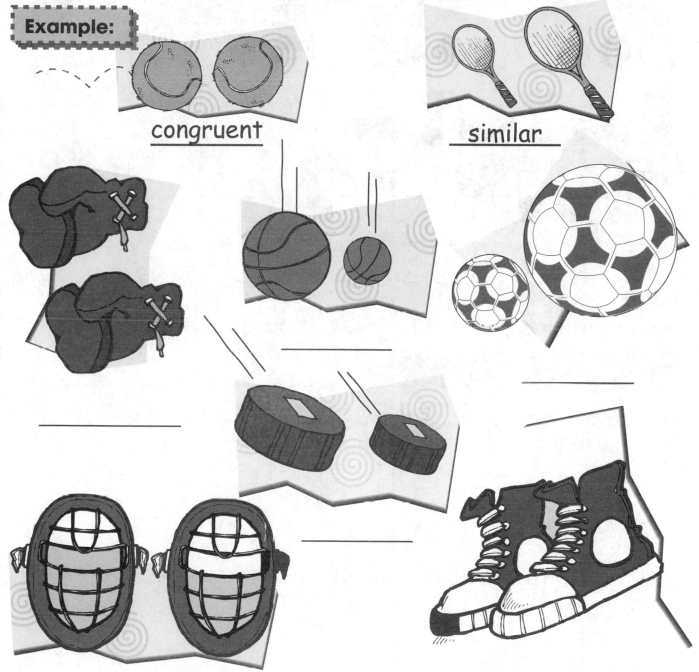

**Example:**

congruent

similar

# Drawing Patterns

**Directions:** Draw the next two shapes in each sequence.

6. How much money would Ginny have if this pattern repeats 4 more times?

| $5 | $1 | $1 | $5 | _____

7. Use a ruler to measure each square.
   Draw the next square in the sequence.

8. Draw your own sequence and have another person complete the next two pictures.

# Venn Diagrams

A **Venn diagram** is a picture that represents a collection. The rectangle always stands for the whole collection. Any circle inside the rectangle stands for a part of it.

This Venn diagram represents all the trucks manufactured by a certain company. Circle R stands for all the red trucks, circle B for all the blue trucks, and circle F for all the four-wheel-drive trucks the company made.

**Directions:** Read each statement about this Venn diagram and identify it as either TRUE or FALSE.

1. All the trucks have four-wheel drive. _____

2. Some of the red trucks have four-wheel drive. _____

3. Some of the four-wheel-drive trucks are blue. _____

4. All of the blue trucks have four-wheel drive. _____

5. None of the red trucks have four-wheel drive. _____

6. All of the four-wheel-drive trucks are either red or blue. _____

7. None of the trucks with four-wheel drive are either red or blue. _____

# Summer Fun

A **pictograph** uses pictures to show information.

**Example:**

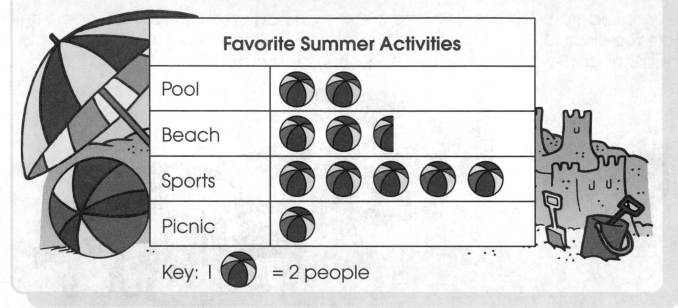

**Directions:** Use this pictograph to answer the questions.

1. What is this graph about? _____

2. How many people does each 🏐 represent? _____

3. How many people like sports best? _____

4. How many people like the beach best? _____

5. Which activity is the least popular? _____

6. How many more people like the beach than the pool? _____

7. How many more people like the pool than a picnic? _____

8. How many people in all were asked about their favorite activities? _____

# Bar Graphs

**Bar graphs** use bars to show information. They are good for showing information that can be easily counted.

**Example:**

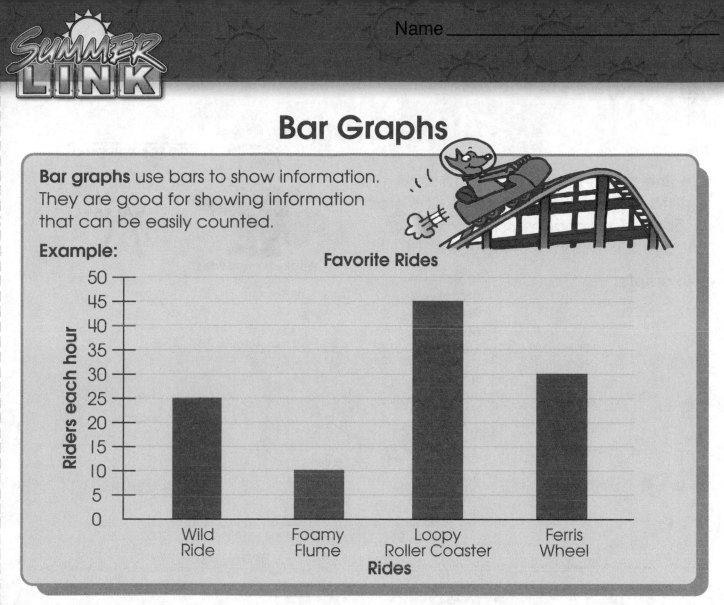

**Favorite Rides**

*Riders each hour*

50
45
40
35
30
25
20
15
10
5
0

Wild Ride | Foamy Flume | Loopy Roller Coaster | Ferris Wheel

**Rides**

**Directions:** Use the bar graph to answer the questions.

1. What is this graph about? _____

2. How many rides are included in the graph? _____

3. How many rode the Wild Ride in one hour? _____

4. How many rode the Foamy Flume in one hour? _____

5. Which ride is the most popular? _____

6. How many more rode the Ferris Wheel than the Wild Ride? _____

7. How many more rode the Loopy Roller Coaster than the Foamy Flume?_____

8. How many altogether rode the rides in one hour? _____

# Line Graphs

A **line graph** is a good way to show data that changes over time. This graph shows the company sales for Wacky Water Slides from 1994 to 2001.

**Example:**

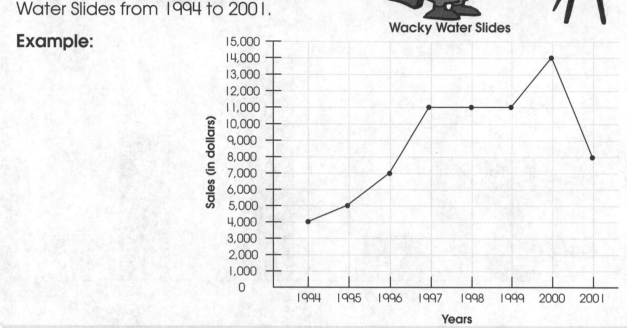

**Wacky Water Slides**

**Directions:** Use the line graph to answer the questions.

1. How many years are covered in the graph? _____

2. How much did the company earn in 1996? _____

3. During which year did the company earn $8,000? _____

4. What was the most money the company ever earned? In what year did this happen? _____

5. How much more did the company earn in 1997 than 1994? _____

6. During which years did sales increase? How does the graph show this?

   _____

   _____

7. During which years did sales stay the same? How does the graph show this? _____

# Ratio

A **ratio** is a comparison of two quantities.

Ratios can be written three ways: 2 to 3, 2 : 3, or $\frac{2}{3}$.
Each ratio is read: two to three.

**Example:**

The ratio of triangles to circles is 2 to 3.
The ratio of circles to triangles is 3 to 2.

**Directions:** Write the ratio that compares these items.

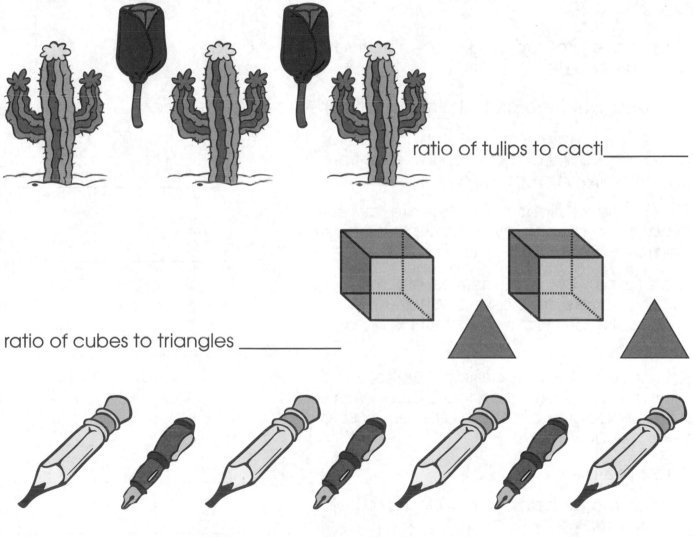

ratio of tulips to cacti _____

ratio of cubes to triangles _____

ratio of pens to pencils _____

# Probability

One thinking skill to get your brain in gear is figuring probability. **Probability** is the likelihood or chance that something will happen. Probability is expressed and written as a ratio.

The probability of tossing heads or tails on a coin is one in two (1:2).

The probability of rolling any number on a die is one in six (1:6).

The probability of getting a red on this spinner is two in four (2:4).

The probability of drawing an ace from a deck of cards is four in fifty-two (4:52).

**Directions:** Write the probability ratios to answer these questions.

1. There are 26 letters in the alphabet. What is the probability of drawing any letter from a set of alphabet cards?

   _____

2. Five of the 26 alphabet letters are vowels. What is the probability of drawing a vowel from the alphabet cards?

   _____

3. Matt takes 10 shots at the basketball hoop. Six of his shots are baskets. What is the probability of Matt's next shot being a basket?

   _____

4. A box contains 10 marbles: 2 white, 3 green, 1 red, 2 orange, and 2 blue. What is the probability of pulling a green marble from the box?

   _____

   A red marble?

   _____

5. What is the probability of pulling a marble that is not blue?

   _____

# Guess the Color

Probability shows the chance that a given event will happen. To show probability, write a fraction. The number of different possibilities is the denominator. The number of times the event could happen is the numerator. (Remember to reduce fractions to the lowest terms.)

Look at the spinner. What is the probability that the arrow will land on . . .

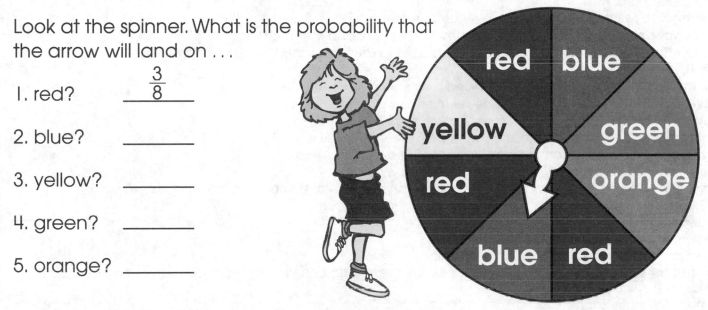

1. red?          $\frac{3}{8}$

2. blue?          _____

3. yellow?          _____

4. green?          _____

5. orange?          _____

Complete the bar graph showing your answers (the data) from above.

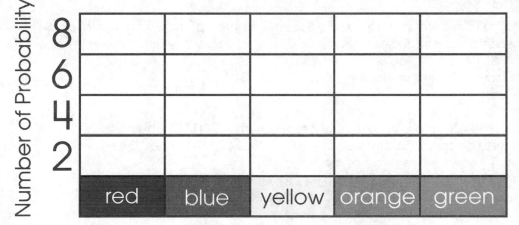

Circle the best title for the above bar graph.
a. Probability of Arrow Landing on a Color
b. Eight Turns of the Spinner
c. Which Color Is the Winner?

# Glossary

**addition:** putting together two or more numbers to find the sum.

**area:** the amount of surface in a given boundary, found by multiplying length times the width.

**bar graph:** displays information by lengths of parallel rectangular bars.

**Celsius:** used to measure temperature in the metric system.

**circumference:** the distance around a circle.

**congruent figures:** have the same shape and size.

**customary measurement:** the standard system for measuring, such as cup, pint, quart, gallon, ounce, pound, inch, foot, yard, mile.

**decimal:** a number with one or more numbers to the right of a decimal point.

**decimal point:** a dot placed between the ones place and the tens place.

**diameter:** a line segment which passes through the center, joining two points on a circle.

**digit:** a numeral.

**dividend:** a number that is to be divided by another number.

**division:** shows how many times one number contains another.

**divisor:** a number by which another number is to be divided.

**estimate:** to give an approximate rather than an exact answer.

**Fahrenheit:** used to measure temperature in the standard system.

**fraction:** stands for part of a whole number.

**geometry:** the branch of mathematics that is concerned with points, lines, and shapes.

**integer:** any positive or negative whole number, including zero.

**line graph:** shows how data changes over time.

**mean:** the most common average.

**median:** the number that falls in the middle.

**metric measurement:** a system of measurement based on counting by tens, such as liter, milliliter, gram, kilogram, centimeter, meter, kilometer.

**mode:** the number that occurs most often in a group.

**multiplication:** taking a number and adding to itself a certain number of times.

**number line:** a line that can be used to compare integers.

**order of operations:** multiplication, division, addition, subtraction.

**ordered pair:** lists the horizontal and the vertical location of the point, such as (3,4).

**parallel lines:** lines that never intersect.

**percent:** a portion of 100 expressed with a % sign.

**perimeter:** the distance around a shape.

**pi:** 3.14 times the diameter.

**pictograph:** uses pictures to show information.

**place value:** the value of a digit, shown by where the numeral is in the number.

**plane figure:** a shape on a flat surface.

**polygon:** a closed figure that has three or more sides.

**probability:** the likelihood or chance that something will happen.

**quotient:** the number received when a number is divided.

**ratio:** a comparison of two quantities.

**ray:** part of a line with one end point.

**rounding:** expressing a number to the nearest ten, hundred, thousand, and so on.

**similar figures:** figures that are the same shape but not necessarily the same size.

**space figures:** figures whose points are in more than one plane.

**subtraction:** "taking away" one number from another to find the difference.

**symmetrical figures:** figures that can be divided equally into two identical parts.

**Venn diagram:** intersecting circles; the portion that overlaps shows characteristics in common, the portion outside shows characteristics that are different.

**volume:** the amount of space a 3-D shape occupies.

## Page 8

### Place Value

Place value is the value of a digit, or numeral, shown by where it is in the number. See the number 1,234,567.

$$1,234,567$$

millions
hundred thousands
ten thousands
thousands
hundreds
tens
ones

**Directions:** Write each numeral in its correct place.

1. The number 8,672,019 has:
   - 2 thousands
   - 8 millions
   - 0 hundreds
   - 1 ten
   - 9 ones
   - 6 hundred thousands
   - 7 ten thousands

2. What number has:
   - 6 ones
   - 7 hundreds
   - 5 hundred thousands
   - 3 millions
   - 4 ten thousands
   - 9 tens
   - 8 thousands

   The number is **3,548,796**.

3. The number 6,792,510 has:
   - 9 ten thousands
   - 0 ones
   - 7 hundred thousands
   - 6 millions
   - 2 thousands
   - 5 hundreds
   - 1 ten

4. What number has:
   - 5 millions
   - 1 hundred
   - 0 hundred thousands
   - 3 tens
   - 8 ten thousands
   - 6 thousands
   - 4 ones

   The number is **5,086,134**.

## Page 9

### More Place Value

**Directions:** Draw a line to connect each number to its correct written form.

1. 791,000 — Three hundred fifty thousand
2. 350,000 — Seventeen million, five hundred thousand
3. 17,600,000 — Seven hundred ninety-one thousand
4. 3,500,000 — Seventy thousand, nine hundred ten
5. 70,910 — Three million, five hundred thousand
6. 35,500,000 — Seventeen billion, five hundred thousand
7. 17,000,500,000 — Thirty-five million, five hundred thousand

**Directions:** Look carefully at this number: 2,071,463,548. Write the numeral for each of the following places.

2,342

8. 6 ten thousands
9. 1 millions
10. 5 hundreds
11. 2 billions
12. 4 hundred thousands
13. 7 ten millions
14. 3 one thousands
15. 0 hundred millions

## Page 10

### Place Value Puzzles

| A3 | 5 | 0 | 9 | | B8 | 6 | 5 | 4 |
| 7 | | C1 | 6 | 2 | | 8 | |
| D7 | 8 | 2 | H2 | 7 | 2 | 5 | 0 |
| 9 | | E5 | 1 | 3 | K2 | 4 | |
| | 2 | | M9 | 6 | 0 | 4 | |
| O0 | 0 | 0 | | 8 | 7 | 0 | |
| | 0 | | 6 | 6 | 4 | 8 | 0 |
| | | 1 | 1 | 1 | | |

**Directions:** Complete the puzzle.

**ACROSS**
A. 3 thousand 5 hundred 9
C. 100 less than 8,754
E. one hundred sixty-two
G. seven hundred eighty-two
I. 100, 150, 200, ___
J. 1, 2, 3, 4, 5 mixed up
L. two
M. 100 less than 9,704
O. three zeros
P. eight
Q. 10,000 more than 56,480
R. one
S. 1 ten, 1 one

**DOWN**
A. 10 more than 3,769
B. ninety-one
C. 28 backwards
D. 5 hundreds, 8 tens, 5 ones
F. 100 less than 773
H. 5, 10, 15, 20, ___
I. ten less than 24,684
K. 2 tens, 9 ones
L. two thousand one
N. 1000, 2000, 3000, ___
P. eight hundreds, 6 tens, 1 one

## Page 11

### Rounding

Rounding a number means to express it to the nearest ten, hundred, thousand, and so on. When rounding a number to the nearest ten, if the number has five or more ones, round up. Round down if the number has four or fewer ones.

**Example:**
Round to the nearest ten: 84 → 80    86 → 90
Round to the nearest hundred: 187 → 200    120 → 100
Round to the nearest thousand: 981 → 1,000    5,480 → 5,000

**Directions:** Round these numbers to the nearest ten.
87 → 90    53 → 50    48 → 50    32 → 30    76 → 80

**Directions:** Round these numbers to the nearest hundred.
168 → 200    243 → 200    591 → 600    743 → 700    493 → 500

**Directions:** Round these numbers to the nearest thousand.
816 → 1,000    3,492 → 3,000    7,621 → 8,000    14,904 → 15,000    62,387 → 62,000

| City Populations | |
|---|---|
| City | Population |
| Cleveland | 492,001 |
| Seattle | 520,947 |
| Omaha | 345,033 |
| Kansas City | 443,878 |
| Atlanta | 396,052 |
| Austin | 514,018 |

**Directions:** Use the city population chart to answer the questions.

Which cities have a population of about 500,000?
**Cleveland, Seattle, Austin**

Which city has a population of about 350,000?
**Omaha**

How many cities have a population of about 400,000? **two**

Which ones? **Kansas City and Atlanta**

## Page 12

### Rounding Off With Roundball

| TEAM | BUILDING | SEATING CAPACITY |
|---|---|---|
| Atlanta Hawks | The Georgia Dome | 34,821 |
| Dallas Mavericks | Reunion Arena | 18,042 |
| Utah Jazz | Delta Center | 19,911 |
| Orlando Magic | Orlando Arena | 17,248 |
| Charlotte Hornets | Charlotte Coliseum | 24,042 |
| Milwaukee Bucks | Bradley Center | 18,717 |
| Houston Rockets | The Summit | 16,285 |
| Portland Trail Blazers | Rose Garden Arena | 21,401 |

**Directions:** Round off the seating capacity of each team's home arena to complete the chart.

| Team | Seating capacity to the nearest... | | |
|---|---|---|---|
| | hundred seats | thousand seats | ten thousand seats |
| Hawks | 34,800 | 35,000 | 30,000 |
| Mavericks | 18,000 | 18,000 | 20,000 |
| Jazz | 19,900 | 20,000 | 20,000 |
| Magic | 17,200 | 17,000 | 20,000 |
| Hornets | 24,000 | 24,000 | 20,000 |
| Bucks | 18,700 | 19,000 | 20,000 |
| Rockets | 16,300 | 16,000 | 20,000 |
| Trail Blazers | 21,400 | 21,000 | 20,000 |

## Page 13

### Estimating

To **estimate** means to give an approximate rather than an exact answer. Rounding each number first makes it easy to estimate an answer.

**Example:**
$93 → 90$, $+48 → +50$, $140$
$321 → 300$, $+597 → +600$, $900$
$1,859 → 2,000$, $-997 → -1,000$, $1,000$

**Directions:** Estimate the sums and differences by rounding the numbers first.

| $68 + 34$ → | $70 + 30 = 100$ | $12 + 98$ → | $10 + 100 = 110$ | $89 + 23$ → | $90 + 20 = 110$ |
|---|---|---|---|---|---|
| $638 - 395$ → | $600 - 400 = 200$ | $281 - 69$ → | $300 - 100 = 200$ | $271 - 126$ → | $300 - 100 = 200$ |
| $1,532 - 998$ → | $2,000 - 1,000 = 1,000$ | $8,312 - 4,789$ → | $8,000 - 5,000$ | $6,341 + 9,286$ → | $6,000 + 9,000 = 15,000$ |

Bonnie has $50 to purchase tennis shoes, a tennis racquet, and tennis balls. Does she have enough money?

___ **yes** ___

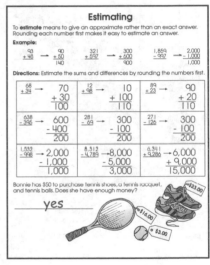

$23.00
$16.00
$3.00

## Page 14

### Estimate by Rounding Numbers

Estimate by rounding numbers to different place values. Use these rules.

**Example:** Round 283 to the nearest hundred.

- Find the digit in the place to be rounded.  283
- Now, look at the digit to its right.  283
- If the digit to the right is less than 5, the digit being rounded remains the same.
- If the digit to the right is 5 or more, the digit being rounded is increased by 1.  283 Rounds to 300
- Digits to the right of the place to be rounded become 0's. Digits to the left remain the same.

**Examples:** Round 4,385 . . .

| to the nearest thousand | to the nearest hundred | to the nearest ten |
|---|---|---|
| 4,385 | 4,385 | 4,385 |
| 3 is less than 5. | 8 is more than 5. | 5 = 5. |
| The 4 stays the same. | The 3 is rounded up to 4. | The 8 is rounded up to 9. |
| 4,000 | 4,400 | 4,390 |

**Directions:** Complete the table.

| NUMBERS TO BE ROUNDED | ROUND TO THE NEAREST THOUSAND | NEAREST HUNDRED | NEAREST TEN |
|---|---|---|---|
| 2,725 | 3,000 | 2,700 | 2,730 |
| 10,942 | 11,000 | 10,900 | 10,940 |
| 6,816 | 7,000 | 6,800 | 6,820 |
| 2,309 | 2,000 | 2,300 | 2,310 |
| 7,237 | 7,000 | 7,200 | 7,240 |
| 959 | 1,000 | 1,000 | 960 |

## Page 15

### What Is the Mode?

**Directions:** There are three kinds of averages: the **mode**, the **median**, and the **mean**. The **mode** is the number that occurs most often. Find the mode.

3, 6, 9, 5, 12, 5, 7, 8 → **5**    11, 7, 9, 11, 3, 8, 9, 10, 11 → **11**

8, 5, 6, 4, 7, 11, 10, 9 → **none**    5, 7, -2, 4, -5, -2, 0, 2, 1 → **-2**

4, 7, 5, 6, 7, 4, 3, 4, 8, 4, 7, 7 → **7, 4**    3, 4, 3, 2, 0, 0, 1, 2, 0, 1 → **0**

3, 3, 3, 3, 3, 3, 3, 3, 3, 3 → **3**    1, 2, 3, 4, 5, 6, 7, 8, 9 → **none**

1, 2, 3, 1, 2, 3, 1, 2, 3, 1, 2, 3 → **1, 2, 3**    13, 12, 10, 15, 12, 14, 12, 11 → **12**

**Directions:** Solve.

1. All of Jill's throws landed 24 feet away. What is the mode? **24 feet**

2. Look at Rob's data for his first ten throws in the first box below. How far would he have to throw the javelin on the the 11th throw so that the data would have two modes? **22 feet**

3. Write a list of 6 numbers that have no mode. **Answers vary**

4. Which javelin thrower had a higher mode, Kate or Adam? **Kate**

| ROB | | | | KATE | ADAM |
|---|---|---|---|---|---|
| Throw | Distance | Throw | Distance | 22 feet | 21 feet |
| 1 | 23 feet | 6 | 20 feet | 23 feet | 20 feet |
| 2 | 26 feet | 7 | 24 feet | 24 feet | 24 feet |
| 3 | 21 feet | 8 | 23 feet | 24 feet | 24 feet |
| 4 | 23 feet | 9 | 22 feet | 21 feet | 21 feet |
| 5 | 25 feet | 10 | 22 feet | 22 feet | 22 feet |
| | | | | 22 feet | 25 feet |

## Page 16

### Jumping the Median

The **median** is another kind of average. When ordering a list of numbers from least to greatest, the median is the number that falls in the middle. Look at Anna's maximum high jumps for the last week.

| Day | Height |
|---|---|
| Monday | 62 inches |
| Tuesday | 64 inches |
| Wednesday | 62 inches |
| Thursday | 64 inches |
| Friday | 60 inches |
| Saturday | 61 inches |
| Sunday | 64 inches |

Order the numbers: 60, 61, 62, **62**, 64, 64, 64. The number 62 falls in the middle. It is the median.

The mode is 64 inches. In some cases, the median and mode are the same number.

If there is an even number of heights, there will be two numbers in the middle. To find the median, add the two middle numbers and divide the sum by 2.

**Example:** 2, 2, 3, 4, 6, 6, 7, 8

The numbers 4 and 6 are both in the middle. $4 + 6 = 10$; $10 \div 2 = 5$. The median is 5. The median does not have to be a number in the list.

MEDIAN
The middle number in an ordered list of numbers

**Directions:** Find the median.

3, 6, 9, 5, 12, 5, 8 → **6**    11, 7, 9, 11, 3, 8, 9, 10 → **9**

11, 6, 4, 7, 5, 9, 11, 10 → **8**    -4, 2, -3, -1, 1, -1, -2 → **-1**

7, 5, 6, 4, 7, 11, 10, 9 → **7**    2, 4, 6, 8, 10, 12, 14, 16 → **9**

3, 3, 3, 3, 3, 3, 3, 3, 3 → **3**    0, 1, 4, -2, 3, -1, -2 → **0**

55, 34, 67, 39, 47, 18, 46, 55, 61 → **47**    2, -2, 1, -1, 3, -4 → **0**

## Page 17

### What Do You Mean?

Probably the most common average is the **mean**. To find the mean, add all the numbers in the list, then divide the sum by the total number of addends.

Suppose a hurdler completes his trials in the following times. Find the mean.

| Trial | Time in Seconds |
|-------|-----------------|
| 1 | 35 |
| 2 | 29 |
| 3 | 34 |
| 4 | 30 |
| 5 | 31 |
| 6 | 33 |

Add the numbers: 35 + 29 + 34 + 30 + 31 + 33 = 192
Divide 192 by 6 because there are 6 numbers in the list: 192 ÷ 6 = 32.
The mean is 32 seconds.

The mean may or may not be a number in the list. The mean may also be different from the median and/or the mode.

**Directions:** Find the mean.

3, 6, 9, 5, 12 ___7___   11, 5, 9, 11, 3, 7, 9, 9 ___8___

3, 1, 0, 2, 0, 0 ___1___   4, 6, -1, -1 ___2___

-3, -2, -3, -1, -1 ___-2___   2, -1, 1, -2 ___0___

3, 3, 3, 3, 3, 3, 3, 3, 3 ___3___   5, 9, 6, 2, 7, 9, 12, 4, 8, 8 ___7___

9, 4, 5, 2, 6, 0, 3, 4, 3 ___4___   6, 7, 3, 6, 4, 2, 7, 5 ___5___

## Page 18

### Weighing In

**Example:**
A **number line** can be used to compare **integers**.
The farther to the right a number is, the greater it is.

3 is greater than -1.
2 is greater than -5.

**Directions:** Circle the greater number in each pair.

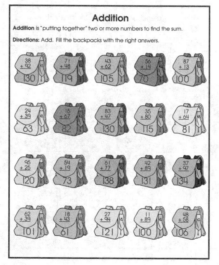

## Page 19

### Counting Puppies

Ty Half-awake has trouble sleeping. His mother suggested that he try counting puppies. So night after night, he lay awake counting puppies.

**Directions:** Each set of three numbers below contains the actual number of puppies Ty counted on a given night and two other numbers. The number he counted will always be the greatest number of the three. Circle the number of puppies in each row that is the greatest number. Then, circle the letter above the greatest number in each group, and use it to spell out the cause of Ty's sleeplessness.

| s 110,001 | l 110,010 | (p) 110,100 |
| l 221,112 | u 222,111 | 212,211 |
| g 523,567 | 523,746 | 523,476 |
| (p) 991,991 | y 919,911 | 991,191 |
| 432,342 | 423,432 | (y) 432,423 |
| m 955,449 | 954,454 | 959,445 |
| 723,327 | a 772,332 | (o) 773,223 |
| s 401,401 | v 410,410 | t 410,401 |
| (e) 883,833 | l 838,388 | r 838,833 |

The cause of Ty's sleeplessness was ___puppy love___

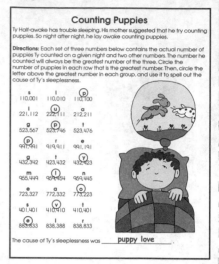

## Page 20

### The Old Ball Park

The fans, hot dogs, the "Wave," and the crack of the bat—these are just a few of the sights, sounds, and smells at the old ball park. American League teams have new parks and old parks, big parks and small parks.

**Directions:** Use the information from the chart to compare the sizes of these parks.

| Team | American League Ball Parks Park | Year Built | Seating |
|------|------|------|------|
| Anaheim Angels | Edison Intnl. Field | 1966 | 45,050 |
| Baltimore Orioles | Camden Yards | 1992 | 48,262 |
| Boston Red Sox | Fenway Park | 1912 | 33,871 |
| Chicago White Sox | Comiskey Park | 1991 | 44,321 |
| Cleveland Indians | Jacobs Field | 1994 | 43,368 |
| Detroit Tigers | Tiger Stadium | 1912 | 46,945 |
| Kansas City Royals | Kauffman Stadium | 1973 | 40,625 |
| Minnesota Twins | Metrodome | 1982 | 48,678 |
| New York Yankees | Yankee Stadium | 1923 | 57,545 |
| Oakland A's | Oakland Coliseum | 1968 | 43,662 |
| Seattle Mariners | Safeco Field | 1999 | 47,000 |
| Tampa Bay Devil Rays | Tropicana Field | 1990 | 44,207 |
| Texas Rangers | The Ballpark | 1994 | 49,166 |
| Toronto Blue Jays | SkyDome | 1989 | 50,516 |

1. What are the two teams that play in stadiums with seating between 50,000 and 60,000? ___Yankees and Blue Jays___

2. There are eleven teams that play in stadiums with seating between 40,000 and 50,000. List them in order from largest to smallest.
   1. Texas Rangers      6. Anaheim Angels
   2. Minnesota Twins      7. Chicago White Sox
   3. Baltimore Orioles      8. Tampa Bay Devil Rays
   4. Seattle Mariners      9. Oakland A's
   5. Detroit Tigers      10. Cleveland Indians
   11. Kansas City Royals

3. Which team plays in the smallest park? ___Boston Red Sox___

## Page 21

### Addition

**Addition** is "putting together" two or more numbers to find the sum.

**Directions:** Add. Fill the backpacks with the right answers.

| 38 +92 = 130 | 71 +48 = 119 | 43 +62 = 105 | 56 +14 = 70 | 87 +13 = 100 |
| 24 +39 = 63 | 15 +67 = 82 | 83 +47 = 130 | 35 +80 = 115 | 17 +64 = 81 |
| 95 +25 = 120 | 54 +19 = 73 | 61 +77 = 138 | 42 +89 = 131 | 37 +97 = 134 |
| 62 +39 = 101 | 18 +43 = 61 | 27 +94 = 121 | 11 +89 = 100 | 48 +58 = 106 |

## Page 22

### Angling Addition Facts

When numbers added in any column equal more than 9, regroup.

| Add the ones. Regroup. | Add the tens. | Add the hundreds. |
|------|------|------|
| **Example:** 486 +109 = 5 | 486 +109 = 95 | 486 +109 = 595 |

**Directions:** Find the sums.

| 852 +137 = 989 | 661 +307 = 968 | 649 +144 = 793 | 953 + 28 = 981 | 537 +253 = 790 |
| 267 +325 = 592 | 807 + 92 = 899 | 366 +324 = 690 | 478 +206 = 684 | 655 +239 = 894 |
| 763 +229 = 992 | 833 +156 = 989 | 581 +309 = 890 | 99 +100 = 199 | |

**Directions:** Solve the problems by using the table.

- How many lures did the shop sell in July and August? ___353 lures___
- How much live bait was sold in July? ___279___
- How many lures were sold in September? ___354___
- How much live bait was sold in August and September? ___1044___

| Dakota Tackle Box Month | Live bait | Lures |
|------|------|------|
| July | 279 | 138 |
| August | 274 | 215 |
| September | 565 | 354 |

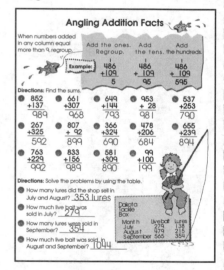

## Page 23

### Underwater Addition

**Directions:** Add.

| 446 +489 = 935 | 476 +527 = 1,003 | 509 +375 = 884 | 251 +368 = 619 |
| | | 708 +507 = 1,215 | 438 +419 = 857 | 334 +278 = 612 |
| 464 +456 = 920 | 589 +322 = 911 | 288 +377 = 665 | 811 +386 = 1,197 | 609 +475 = 1,084 |
| | 531 +249 = 780 | 810 +428 = 1,238 | | |
| 831 +438 = 1,269 | 445 +476 = 921 | 211 +396 = 607 | 230 +284 = 514 | 319 +287 = 606 |
| | 714 +185 = 899 | 767 +246 = 1,013 | 911 +427 = 1,338 | |

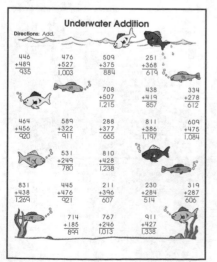

## Page 24

### "Ace"

Why are waiters such good tennis players? To find out, solve each problem. Then, write the matching letter above the answer at the bottom of the page.

| E 19 +23 = 42 | E 46 +37 = 83 | Y 91 +41 = 132 | T 37 +47 = 84 | A 62 +35 = 97 |
| I 346 +127 = 473 | V 861 +123 = 984 | E 673 +135 = 808 | R 492 +329 = 821 | R 647 +135 = 782 |
| A 324 413 +511 = 1,248 | O 613 213 +484 = 1,310 | T 743 135 +856 = 1,734 | O 391 381 +371 = 1,143 | H 421 666 +313 = 1,400 |
| N 4,221 3,113 +5,235 = 12,569 | D 4,671 3,121 +4,781 = 12,573 | G 8,121 1,371 +4,777 = 14,269 | S 1,414 2,336 +2,336 = 6,964 | G 4,171 2,318 +3,117 = 9,606 |

T H E Y   A R E   G O O D
84 1,400 42 132   1,248 782 808   6,964 83 821 984

A T   S E R V I N G
97 1,734   6,964 83 821 984

## Page 25

### Subtraction

**Subtraction** takes away one number from another to find the difference.

| REGROUP (1 ten = 10 ones) | Subtract ones. | Subtract tens. |
|------|------|------|
| 58 -29 | 58 -29 = 9 | 58 -29 = 29 |

**Directions:** Solve these problems.

| 96 -27 = 69 | 35 -19 = 16 | 87 -65 = 22 | 45 -18 = 27 | 74 -47 = 27 |
| 31 -19 = 12 | 86 -58 = 28 | 67 -29 = 38 | 73 -29 = 44 | 92 -52 = 40 |
| 55 -27 = 28 | 81 -69 = 12 | 63 -17 = 46 | 98 -19 = 79 | 42 -16 = 26 |

67 - 28 = ___39___      42 - 23 = ___19___

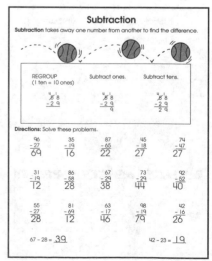

**Page 26**

## Checking Subtraction

You can check your subtraction by using addition.

Example: 34,436  Check: → 22,172
        − 12,264        → + 12,264
        22,172        → 34,436

**Directions:** Subtract. Then check your answers by adding.

| | Check: | | Check: | |
|---|---|---|---|---|
| 15,326 − 11,532 = **3,794** | +11,532 / 15,326 | 28,615 − 25,329 = **3,286** | 3,286 +25,329 / 28,615 | |
| 96,621 − 47,378 = **49,143** | 49,143 +47,378 / 96,621 | 46,496 − 35,877 = **10,619** | 10,619 +35,877 / 46,496 | |
| 77,911 − 63,783 = **14,128** | 14,128 +63,783 / 77,911 | 156,901 − 112,732 = **44,169** | 44,169 +112,732 / 156,901 | |
| 395,638 − 187,569 = **208,069** | 208,069 +187,569 / 395,638 | 67,002 − 53,195 = **13,807** | 13,807 +53,195 / 67,002 | |
| 16,075 − 15,896 = **179** | 179 +15,896 / 16,075 | 39,678 − 19,769 = **19,909** | 19,909 +19,769 / 39,678 | |
| 84,654 − 49,997 = **34,657** | 34,657 +49,997 / 84,654 | 12,335 − 10,697 = **1,638** | 1,638 +10,697 / 12,335 | |

During the summer, 158,941 people visited Yellowstone National Park. During the fall, there were 52,397 visitors. How many more visitors went to the park during the summer than the fall?

**106,544** visitors

**Page 27**

## Subtraction Maze

**Directions:** Solve the problems. Remember to regroup, when needed.

| | | | | | |
|---|---|---|---|---|---|
| 4,172 −1,536 = **2,636** | 6,723 −2,586 = **4,137** | 547 −259 = **288** | 834 −463 = **371** | 562 −325 = **237** | 7,146 −3,498 = **3,648** |
| 9,427 −6,648 = **2,779** | 8,149 −5,372 = **2,777** | 5,389 −1,652 = **3,737** | 421 −275 = **146** | 7,456 −3,724 = **3,732** | 818 −639 = **179** |
| 772 −586 = **186** | 6,524 −4,538 = **1,991** | 5,379 −2,835 = **2,544** | 6,275 −3,761 = **2,514** | 5,612 −1,505 = **4,107** | 8,355 −5,366 = **2,989** |

**Directions:** Shade in the answers from above to find the path.

| | 2,514 | 288 | 186 | 3,732 | 2,989 |
|---|---|---|---|---|---|
| | 2,779 | 156 | 1,901 | 2,414 | 4,137 |
| 3,748 | 3,337 | 2,777 | 371 | 179 | 1,991 |
| 3,048 | 3,737 | 146 | 2,717 | | |
| 679 | 237 | 374 | 4,107 | | |
| 886 | 2,636 | 2,544 | 3,648 | | KITTY |

**Page 28**

## Count the Legs!

**Multiplication** is a quick way to add. For example, count the legs of the horses below. They each have 4 legs. You could add 4 + 4 + 4. But it is quicker to say that there are 3 groups of 4 legs. In multiplication, that is 3 × 4.

**Directions:** Multiply to find the number of legs. Write each problem twice.

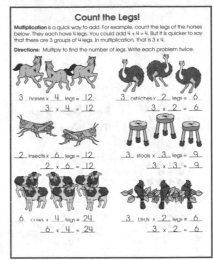

3 horses × 4 legs = 12
3 × 4 = 12

3 ostriches × 2 legs = 6
3 × 2 = 6

2 insects × 6 legs = 12
2 × 6 = 12

3 stools × 3 legs = 9
3 × 3 = 9

6 cows × 4 legs = 24
6 × 4 = 24

3 birds × 2 legs = 6
3 × 2 = 6

**Page 29**

## One-Digit Multiplication

Here's how to do 1-digit multiplication without regrouping.

| Multiply the ones. | Multiply the tens. | Multiply the hundreds and thousands. |
|---|---|---|
| 2,043 × 2 = 6 | 2,043 × 2 = 86 | 2,043 × 2 = 4,086 |

**Directions:** Multiply.

| 41 ×2 = **82** | 33 ×3 = **99** | 103 ×2 = **206** | 122 ×4 = **488** | 101 ×8 = **808** | 1,214 ×2 = **2,428** |
|---|---|---|---|---|---|
| 230 ×3 = **690** | 3,422 ×2 = **6,844** | 689 ×0 = **0** | 3,321 ×3 = **9,963** | 9,738 ×1 = **9,738** | 1,011 ×6 = **6,066** |
| 32 ×3 = **96** | 1,022 ×4 = **4,088** | 5,900 ×1 = **5,900** | 4,413 ×2 = **8,826** | 204 ×2 = **408** | 24 ×2 = **48** |

**Directions:** Write a numeral in each box to make the multiplication problem true.

2 1 ×3 = 6 3

2 5 6 ×1 = 2 5 6

1 0 2 ×2 = 2 0 4

2 3 1 1 ×3 = 6 9 3 3

2 4 1 ×2 = 4 8 2

3 0 3 ×3 = 9 0 9

2 1 3 4 ×2 = 4 2 6 8

8 0 6 3 ×1 = 8 0 6 3

**Page 30**

## Sailing Through Multiplication

**Directions:** For each multiplication problem, color in the matching answer in the picture below.

Example: 33 ×5 = 165

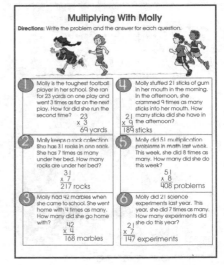

| 24 ×6 = **144** | 97 ×2 = **194** | 82 ×7 = **574** | 76 ×2 = **152** | 54 ×7 = **378** | 62 ×8 = **496** | 42 ×6 = **252** | 23 ×7 = **161** |
|---|---|---|---|---|---|---|---|
| 37 ×3 = **111** | 86 ×2 = **172** | 24 ×5 = **120** | 46 ×2 = **92** | 58 ×4 = **232** | 22 ×8 = **176** | 52 ×4 = **208** | 21 ×8 = **168** |

**Page 31**

## Multiplying With Molly

**Directions:** Write the problem and the answer for each question.

1. Molly is the toughest football player in her school. She ran for 23 yards on one play and went 3 times as far on the next play. How far did she run the second time?
23 ×3 = **69 yards**

2. Molly keeps a rock collection. She has 31 rocks in one sack. She has 7 times as many under her bed. How many rocks are under her bed?
31 ×7 = **217 rocks**

3. Molly had 42 marbles when she came to school. She went home with 4 times as many. How many did she go home with?
42 ×4 = **168 marbles**

4. Molly stuffed 21 sticks of gum in her mouth in the morning. In the afternoon, she crammed 9 times as many sticks into her mouth. How many sticks did she have in the afternoon?
21 ×9 = **189 sticks**

5. Molly did 51 multiplication problems in math last week. This week, she did 8 times as many. How many did she do this week?
51 ×8 = **408 problems**

6. Molly did 21 science experiments last year. This year, she did 7 times as many. How many experiments did she do this year?
21 ×7 = **147 experiments**

**Page 32**

## Multiplication (Two-Digit Multiplier)

**Example A** (no regrouping)
21 ×44 = 84 + 840 = **924**

Step 1 Multiply by ones.
4 × 1 = 4
4 × 2 = 8
Step 2 Multiply by tens.
Add zero in the ones column.
4 × 1 = 4
4 × 2 = 8
Step 3 Add.
84 + 840 = 924

**Example B** (regrouping)
67 ×58 = 536 + 3,350 = **3,886**

Step 1 Multiply by ones.
8 × 7 = 56 (Carry the 5.)
8 × 6 + 5 = 53
Step 2 Multiply by tens.
Add zero in the ones column.
5 × 7 = 35 (Carry the 3.)
5 × 6 + 3 = 33
Step 3 Add.
536 + 3,350 = 3,886

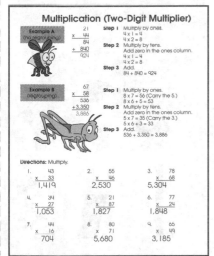

**Directions:** Multiply.

1. 43 ×33 = **1,419**
2. 55 ×46 = **2,530**
3. 78 ×68 = **5,304**
4. 34 ×27 = **1,053**
5. 21 ×87 = **1,827**
6. 77 ×24 = **1,848**
7. 44 ×16 = **704**
8. 80 ×71 = **5,680**
9. 65 ×49 = **3,185**

**Page 33**

## Two-Digit Multiplication With Regrouping

**Example:**
**Steps:**

Multiply by the ones. Carry numbers as needed.
5 3 / 6,074 × 3 8 = 48,592

Multiply by the tens. Carry numbers as needed. Put a zero in the ones place.
6,074 × 3 8 = 48,592 +182,220

Add.
6,074 × 3 8 = 48,592 +182,220 = 230,812

**Directions:** Multiply along each diagonal of the square. Write the answer in the oval.

| 3,807 | | 1,060 | 2,660 | | 4,818 |
|---|---|---|---|---|---|
| | 47 / 53 | | | 95 / 66 | |
| | 20 / 81 | | | 73 / 26 | |
| 1,060 | | 3,807 | 4,818 | | 2,660 |
| 2,704 | | 22,194 | 13,838 | | 15,246 |
| | 26 / 81 | | | 814 / 42 | |
| | 274 / 104 | | | 363 / 17 | |
| 22,194 | | 2,704 | 15,246 | | 13,838 |

What is the pattern of the answers on opposite corners? Why is that so?
**They are the same answer. It doesn't matter which order the numbers are placed.**

**Page 34**

## Multiplication: Two-Digit Numbers Times Three-Digit Numbers

Follow the steps for multiplying a two-digit number by a three-digit number using regrouping.

**Example: Step 1:** Multiply the ones. Regroup.
287 × 43 = 861

**Step 2:** Multiply the tens. Regroup. Add.
287 × 43 = 11,480

287 × 43 = 861 + 11,480 = 12,341

**Directions:** Multiply.

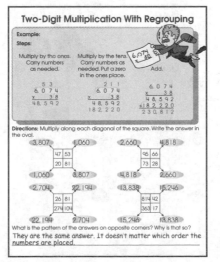

261 ×36 = **9,396**
434 ×48 = **20,832**
357 ×75 = **26,775**
231 ×46 = **10,626**
754 ×65 = **49,010**
614 ×59 = **36,226**
549 ×89 = **48,861**
372 ×94 = **34,968**
458 ×85 = **38,930**
368 ×98 = **36,064**

At the Douglas berry farm, workers pick 378 baskets of peaches each day. Each basket holds 65 peaches. How many peaches are picked each day?
**24,570**

**Summer Link Super Edition Grade 5**

## Page 35

### Backward Multiplication

Division problems are like multiplication problems—just turned around. As you solve 8 ÷ 4, think, "how many groups of 4 make 8?" or "what number 'times' 4 is eight?"

2 × 4 = 8, so 8 ÷ 4 = **2**.

**Directions:** Use the pictures to help you solve these division problems.

9 ÷ 3 = **3**    6 ÷ 2 = **3**

16 ÷ 4 = **4**    10 ÷ 5 = **2**

20 ÷ 1 = **20**    18 ÷ 3 = **6**

## Page 37

### Zeros in the Quotient

Some problems will have a zero in the quotient.

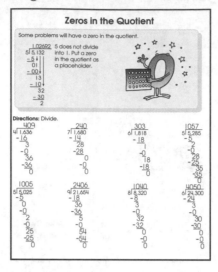

5 does not divide into 1. Put a zero in the quotient as a placeholder.

**Directions:** Divide.

| 409 | 240 | 303 | 1057 |
| 1005 | 2406 | 1040 | 4050 |

## Page 38

### Two-Digit Divisors

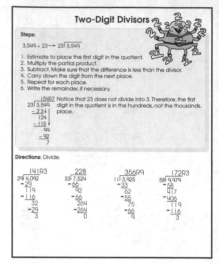

**Steps:**

3,549 ÷ 23 → 23⟌3,549

1. Estimate to place the first digit in the quotient.
2. Multiply the partial product.
3. Subtract. Make sure that the difference is less than the divisor.
4. Carry down the digit from the next place.
5. Repeat for each place.
6. Write the remainder, if necessary.

154R7 Notice that 23 does not divide into 3. Therefore, the first digit in the quotient is in the hundreds, not the thousands, place.

**Directions:** Divide.

| 141R3 | 228 | 356R9 | 172R3 |

## Page 39

### Wisconsin's Nickname

**Directions:** What is Wisconsin known as? To find out, solve the division problems below. Then, find the answers at the bottom of the page and write the corresponding letter on the line above the answer.

T. 14⟌1218 = 87
E. 23⟌1633 = 71
S. 53⟌2756 = 52

A. 38⟌1596 = 42
A. 61⟌5185 = 85
E. 18⟌1764 = 98

T. 22⟌1628 = 74
R. 40⟌2520 = 63
D. 55⟌4400 = 80

G. 31⟌1364 = 44
B. 12⟌780 = 65

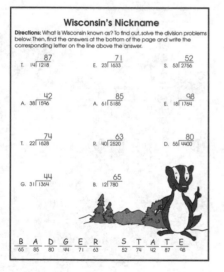

B A D G E R    S T A T E
65 85 80 44 71 63    52 74 42 87 98

## Page 40

### My Dear Aunt Sally

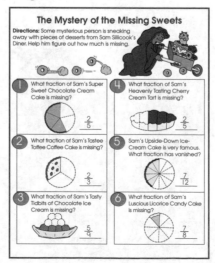

**Example:**
To solve a problem with several operations, follow the rules of My Dear Aunt Sally.

My Dear = Multiplication/Division
Aunt Sally = Addition/Subtraction

Do all multiplication and division steps first, in order from left to right.

Then do all addition and subtraction steps, in order from left to right.

These rules are called the Order of Operations.

4 × 8 + 36 ÷ 6 − 7
32 + 6 − 7
38 − 7
31

**Directions:** Follow the Order of Operations to solve.

4 + 5 × 3 − 6 = 4 + 15 − 6 = 13    4 − 3 + 6 ÷ 2 + 4 × 2 = 1 + 3 + 8 = 12

8 ÷ 4 + 3 × 2 + 2 = 2 + 6 + 2 = 10    5 × 2 − 3 + 5 − 6 + 3 = 10 − 3 + 5 − 2 = 10

2 + 3 × 2 − 4 + 2 × 2 = 2 + 6 − 4 + 4 = 8    6 − 2 + 3 − 2 × 4 + 3 = 4 + 3 − 8 + 3 = 2

4 × 5 − 8 + 2 + 5 × 2 = 20 − 4 + 10 = 26    9 + 3 − 5 − 4 + 2 + 6 = 3 + 5 − 2 + 6 = 12

3 × 3 + 3 − 3 × 3 − 3 = 9 + 3 − 9 − 3 = 0    8 − 4 + 4 × 2 × 3 − 2 = 8 − 1 + 6 − 2 = 11

## Page 41

### Decimals, Fractions, and Percents

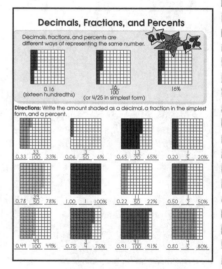

Decimals, fractions, and percents are different ways of representing the same number.

0.16 (sixteen hundredths)    16/100 (or 4/25 in simplest form)    16%

**Directions:** Write the amount shaded as a decimal, a fraction in the simplest form, and a percent.

| 0.33  33/100  33% | 0.06  3/50  6% | 0.65  13/20  65% | 0.20  5  20% |
| 0.78  39/50  78% | 1.00  1  100% | 0.22  11/50  22% | 0.50  1/2  50% |
| 0.49  49/100  49% | 0.75  3/4  75% | 0.91  91/100  91% | 0.80  4/5  80% |

## Page 42

### Percents and Fractions

**Example:**
Steps to change a percent to a fraction, or a fraction to a percent:

PERCENT → FRACTION
67% = 0.67 = 67/100
8% = 0.08 = 8/100 = 2/25
125% = 1.25 = 125/100 = 5/4 = 1 1/4

FRACTION → PERCENT
4/5 = 4 ÷ 5 = 0.8 = 80%
1/3 = 1 ÷ 3 = 0.333 . . . = 33.3%
1 1/2 = 3/2 = 3 ÷ 2 = 1.5 = 150%

**Directions:** Match the percent with the fraction in simplest form. Write the letter on the line.

1. **H** 5%
3. **M** 17%
5. **K** 25%
7. **O** 48%
9. **B** 55%
11. **N** 75%
13. **J** 94%
15. **L** 144%

A. 3/25
C. 1/5
E. 1/2
L. 7/10
K. 1/4
M. 17/100
O. 12/25

B. 11/20
D. 1/5
F. 5/6
H. 1/20
J. 47/50
L. 1 1/25
N. 3/4

2. **A** 12%
4. **G** 20%
6. **C** 33.3%
8. **E** 50%
10. **I** 70%
12. **F** 83.3%
14. **D** 120%

## Page 43

### The Mystery of the Missing Sweets

**Directions:** Some mysterious person is sneaking away with pieces of desserts from Sam Sillicook's Diner. Help him figure out how much is missing.

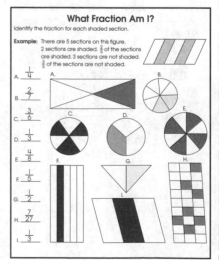

1. What fraction of Sam's Super Sweet Chocolate Cream Cake is missing? 2/5

2. What fraction of Sam's Tastee Toffee Coffee Cake is missing? 2/3

3. What fraction of Sam's Tasty Tidbits of Chocolate Ice Cream is missing? 5/9

4. What fraction of Sam's Heavenly Tasting Cherry Cream Tart is missing? 2/5

5. Sam's Upside-Down Ice-Cream Cake is very famous. What fraction has vanished? 7/12

6. What fraction of Sam's Luscious Licorice Candy Cake is missing? 7/8

## Page 44

### What Fraction Am I?

Identify the fraction for each shaded section.

**Example:** There are 5 sections on this figure. 2 sections are shaded. 2/5 of the sections are shaded. 3 sections are not shaded. 3/5 of the sections are not shaded.

A. 1/4
B. 2/7
C. 3/6
D. 1/3
E. 4/8
F. 1/5
G. 7/27
I. 1/3

## Page 45

**Dare to Compare**

Directions: Compare the fractions below. Write =, <, or > in each box.

$\frac{3}{6}$ < $\frac{2}{3}$   $\frac{3}{4}$ = $\frac{3}{4}$

$\frac{1}{5}$ < $\frac{3}{10}$   $\frac{1}{2}$ > $\frac{1}{3}$

$\frac{1}{2}$ = $\frac{3}{6}$   $\frac{4}{6}$ = $\frac{4}{6}$

$\frac{3}{8}$ < $\frac{6}{8}$   $\frac{3}{8}$ > $\frac{2}{8}$

## Page 46

**Doing Decimals**

Just as a fraction stands for part of a whole number, a decimal also shows part of a whole number. And with decimals, the number is always broken into ten or a power of ten (hundred, thousand, etc.) parts. These place values are named tenths, hundredths, thousandths, etc.

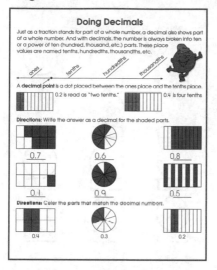

ones   tenths   hundredths   thousandths

A **decimal point** is a dot placed between the ones place and the tenths place.

0.2 is read as "two tenths."   0.4 is four tenths

Directions: Write the answer as a decimal for the shaded parts.

0.7     0.6     0.8

0.1     0.9     0.5

Directions: Color the parts that match the decimal numbers.

0.4     0.3     0.2

## Page 47

**Decimals**

A **decimal** is a number with one or more places to the right of a decimal point.

**Examples:** 6.5 and 2.25

Fractions with denominators of 10 or 100 can be written as decimals.

**Examples.**

$\frac{7}{10}$ = 0.7   $\underline{\quad0\quad}$ ones $\underline{\quad7\quad}$ tenths $\underline{\quad0\quad}$ hundredths

$1\frac{62}{100}$ = 1.62   $\underline{\quad1\quad}$ ones $\underline{\quad5\quad}$ tenths $\underline{\quad2\quad}$ hundredths

Directions: Write the fractions as decimals.

$\frac{5}{10}$ = 0. 5
$\frac{4}{10}$ = 0. 4
$\frac{2}{10}$ = 0. 2
$\frac{6}{10}$ = 0. 6

| | | |
|---|---|---|
| $\frac{63}{100}$ = 0.63 | $2\frac{8}{10}$ = 2.8 | $38\frac{4}{100}$ = 38.04 | $6\frac{13}{100}$ = 6.13 |
| $\frac{1}{4}$ = 0.25 | $\frac{2}{5}$ = 0.4 | $\frac{1}{50}$ = 0.02 | $\frac{100}{200}$ = 0.5 |
| $5\frac{2}{100}$ = 5.02 | $\frac{4}{25}$ = 0.16 | $15\frac{3}{5}$ = 15.6 | $\frac{3}{100}$ = 0.03 |

## Page 48

**More Puzzling Problems**

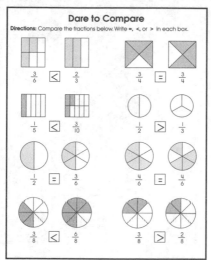

**Across**
3. 7.333 = seven and three hundred thirty-three _____
5. 67.02 = sixty-seven and _____ hundredths
6. 490.1 = four hundred _____ and one tenth
7. 0.512 = five _____ twelve thousandths
9. 8.06 = eight and _____ hundredths
10. 0.007 = _____ thousandths
12. 11.3 = _____ and three tenths
13. 300.12 = _____ hundred and twelve hundredths
15. 62.08 = sixty-two and _____ hundredths
18. 70.009 = _____ and nine thousandths
19. 9.3 = _____ and three tenths
20. 10.51 = _____ and fifty-one hundredths
21. 1,000.02 = one thousand and two _____

**Down**
1. 6.5 = six and five _____
2. 0.428 = four hundred _____ thousandths
3. 8,100.1 = eight _____ one hundred and one tenth
4. 3.02 = three and two _____
8. 0.685 = six hundred _____ thousandths
11. 50.19 = fifty and _____ hundredths
14. 0.015 = _____ thousandths
16. 430.7 = four hundred thirty and seven _____
17. 73.4 = seventy-three and four _____

## Page 49

**Adding Money**

Example:

Steps:
1. Align the decimal points.
2. Add.

$4.32
+ $2.19
$6.51

$10.43
$ 4.25
+ $12.04
$26.72

Directions: Rewrite the problems and align the decimal points. Then, add.

$1.15 + $2.25 = $3.40   $2.09 + $1.46 = $3.55

$1.11 + $5.35 = $6.46   $3.87 + $2.95 = $6.82

$10.42 + $2.54 = $12.96   $8.12 + $3.29 = $11.41

$11.13 + $10.26 = $21.39   $4.03 + $2.99 = $7.02

$42.80 + $103.25 + $32.54 = $178.59   $3.64 + $49.39 + $1.00 = $54.03

## Page 50

**Subtracting Money**

Example:

Steps:
1. Align the decimal points.
2. Subtract.

$14.32
− 5.43
$ 8.89

Directions: Rewrite the problems and align the decimal points. Then, subtract.

$4.15 − $2.25 = $1.90   $2.09 − $1.46 = $0.63

$3.93 − $0.44 = $3.49   $6.06 − $3.85 = $2.21

$7.83 − $2.17 = $5.66   $26.32 − $12.88 = $13.44

$11.13 − $10.26 = $0.87   $4.03 − $2.99 = $1.04

$43.76 − $0.94 = $42.82   $104.65 − $4.87 = $99.78

## Page 51

**Multiplying Money**

Example:
Joey buys 14 paperback books for $1.95 each. How much does he spend?

$1.95
x  14
780
+ 1950
$27.30 ← set decimal point two numbers in from the right

Directions: Rewrite the problems and multiply.

$1.55 x 7 = $10.85   $10.85 x 9 = $97.65

$3.06 x 9 = $27.54   $5.35 x 12 = $64.20

$10.00 x 15 = $150.00   $1.25 x 105 = $131.25

$10.85 x 19 = $206.15   $4.95 x 22 = $108.90

1. Lauren buys wood for bookshelves at a cost of $0.58 per foot. If she buys 27 feet, how much does she spend? $15.66

2. Which costs more: 5 new books for $5.97 each or 12 used books for $2.50 each? the used books

## Page 52

**Dividing Money**

Example:
Six friends earn $63.90 shoveling driveways on a snowy day. If they divide the money evenly, how much does each one earn?

$10.65
6)$63.90
−6
3 9
−3 6
30
−30
0

Directions: Rewrite the problems and divide.

$33.72 ÷ 4 = $8.43   $98.56 ÷ 8 = $12.32

$0.96 ÷ 6 = $0.16   $22.70 ÷ 10 = $2.27

$120.96 ÷ 12 = $10.08   $49.68 ÷ 18 = $2.76

1. Jeremy shovels snow for 4 days and earns the same amount each day. If he earns a total of $23, how much does he earn each day? $5.75

2. Randy is one of 8 people who shares $127.76. Can he buy a poster that costs $16? no; he earns $15.

## Page 53

**The Perfect Sweet-Treat Solution**

Directions: Solve each division problem on a separate sheet of paper. Draw a line from the popcorn (problem) to the correct drink (answer).

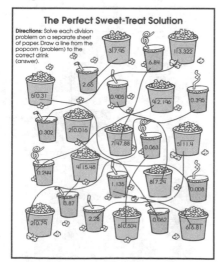

**Summer Link Super Edition Grade 5**

## Page 54

### One-Stop Shopping

**Directions:** Stash McCash is shopping. **Add** to find the total cost of the items. Then, **subtract** to find how much change Stash should receive.

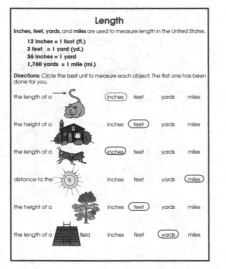

$2.68   $3.36   $0.27   $0.77   $3.15
$3.99
$3.61
$1.54   $1.27
$1.49   $0.88   $4.25   $1.94   $2.55   $2.49

**Example:**

| Stash has $5.00. He buys: | Stash has $8.50. He buys: | Stash has $7.04. He buys: | Stash has $9.00. He buys: |
|---|---|---|---|
| $ 0.88 0.77 + 1.54 $3.19 | $ 1.27 3.99 + 2.68 $7.94 | $ 1.49 3.15 + .27 $4.91 | $ 3.15 3.61 + .88 $7.64 |
| $ 5.00 – 3.19 $ 1.81 Change | $ 8.50 – 7.94 $ .56 Change | $ 7.04 – 4.91 $ 2.13 Change | $ 9.00 – 7.64 $ 1.36 Change |

| Stash has $10.95. He buys: | Stash has $10.00. He buys: | Stash has $9.24. He buys: | Stash has $8.09. He buys: |
|---|---|---|---|
| $ 3.36 2.49 + 4.25 $10.10 | $ 2.55 3.61 + 1.94 $8.10 | $ 4.25 1.27 + 1.54 $7.06 | $ 2.49 2.68 + 1.94 $7.11 |
| $10.95 – 10.10 $ .85 Change | $ 10.00 – 8.10 $ 1.90 Change | $ 9.24 – 7.06 $ 2.18 Change | $ 8.09 – 7.11 $ .98 Change |

## Page 55

### Minute Men

**Directions:** Draw the hour and minute hands on these clocks.

Example:

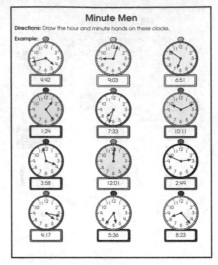

| 4:42 | 9:03 | 6:51 |
| 1:24 | 7:33 | 10:11 |
| 3:58 | 12:01 | 2:49 |
| 4:17 | 5:36 | 8:23 |

## Page 56

### Time to Play Ball

**Directions:** Write the number of the matching clock in front of each sentence.

1. 2. 3. 4.
5. 6. 7. 8.
9. 10.

**9**  Mary's coach says she should be in bed by 9:30 P.M. the night before a game.
**6**  Tom's baseball team practices at 6:15 P.M.
**5**  It was 6:08 P.M. when Mike arrived at practice.
**4**  Coach told the team their next game was tomorrow at 4:45 P.M.
**2**  The National Anthem was played over the loudspeaker at 4:35 P.M.
**3**  Steve and Paul pitch to each other every day at 3:35 P.M.
**10**  Emily went to see her friend Sue's game at 10:21 A.M.
**7**  Coach had us practice running the bases at 2:37 P.M.
**1**  Our game was rained out at 5:51 P.M.
**8**  Sue's game was finished at 12:09 P.M.

## Page 57

### Length

**Inches, feet, yards,** and **miles** are used to measure length in the United States.

12 inches = 1 foot (ft.)
3 feet = 1 yard (yd.)
36 inches = 1 yard
1,760 yards = 1 mile (mi.)

**Directions:** Circle the best unit to measure each object. The first one has been done for you.

| the length of a | (inches) | feet | yards | miles |
| the height of a | inches | (feet) | yards | miles |
| the length of a | (inches) | feet | yards | miles |
| distance to the | inches | feet | yards | (miles) |
| the height of a | inches | (feet) | yards | miles |
| the length of a field | inches | feet | (yards) | miles |

## Page 58

### Length: Metric

**Millimeters, centimeters, meters,** and **kilometers** are used to measure length in the metric system.

1 meter = 39.37 inches
1 kilometer = about ⅝ mile
10 millimeters = 1 centimeter (cm)
100 centimeters = 1 meter (m)
1,000 meters = 1 kilometer (km)

**Directions:** Circle the best unit to measure each object. The first one has been done for you.

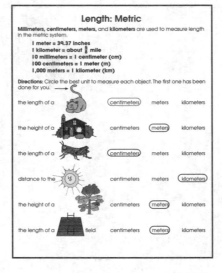

| the length of a | (centimeters) | meters | kilometers |
| the height of a | centimeters | (meters) | kilometers |
| the length of a | (centimeters) | meters | kilometers |
| distance to the | centimeters | meters | (kilometers) |
| the height of a | centimeters | (meters) | kilometers |
| the length of a field | centimeters | (meters) | kilometers |

## Page 59

### Weight

**Ounces, pounds,** and **tons** are used to measure weight in the United States.

16 ounces = 1 pound (lb.)
2,000 pounds = 1 ton (tn.)

**Directions:** Circle the most reasonable estimate for the weight of each object. The first one has been done for you.

| 10 ounces | (10 pounds) | 10 tons |
| 6 ounces | (6 pounds) | 6 tons |
| 2 ounces | 2 pounds | (2 tons) |
| (3 ounces) | 3 pounds | 3 tons |
| 1,800 ounces | (1,800 pounds) | 1,800 tons |
| 20 ounces | 20 pounds | (20 tons) |
| (1 ounce) | 1 pound | 1 ton |

## Page 60

### Weight: Metric

**Grams** and **kilograms** are units of weight in the metric system. A paper clip weighs about 1 gram. A kitten weighs about 1 kilogram.

1 kilogram (kg) = about 2.2 pounds
1,000 grams (g) = 1 kilogram

**Directions:** Circle the best unit to weigh each object.

(kilogram) gram          (kilogram) gram
(kilogram) gram          (kilogram) gram
(kilogram) gram          (kilogram) gram
(kilogram) gram          kilogram (gram)
kilogram (gram)          (kilogram) gram

## Page 61

### Capacity

The **fluid ounce, cup, pint, quart,** and **gallon** are used to measure capacity in the United States.

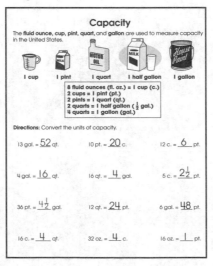

1 cup    1 pint    1 quart    1 half gallon    1 gallon

8 fluid ounces (fl. oz.) = 1 cup (c.)
2 cups = 1 pint (pt.)
2 pints = 1 quart (qt.)
2 quarts = 1 half gallon ( ½ gal.)
4 quarts = 1 gallon (gal.)

**Directions:** Convert the units of capacity.

13 gal. = **52** qt.        10 pt. = **20** c.        12 c. = **6** pt.

4 gal. = **16** qt.        16 qt. = **4** gal.        5 c. = **2½** pt.

36 pt. = **4½** gal.        12 qt. = **24** pt.        6 gal. = **48** pt.

16 c. = **4** qt.        32 oz. = **4** c.        16 oz. = **1** pt.

## Page 62

### Capacity: Metric

**Milliliters** and **liters** are units of capacity in the metric system. A can of soda contains about 350 milliliters of liquid. A large plastic bottle contains 1 liter of liquid. A liter is about a quart.

1,000 milliliters (mL) = 1 liter (L)

**Directions:** Circle the best unit to measure each liquid.

(milliliters) liters          (milliliters) liters
(milliliters) liters          (milliliters) liters
(milliliters) liters          (milliliters) liters
(milliliters) liters          (milliliters) liters
(milliliters) liters          (milliliters) liters

## Page 63

### Temperature: Fahrenheit

Degrees **Fahrenheit** (∞F) is a unit for measuring temperature.

**Directions:** Write the temperature in degrees Fahrenheit (∞F).

**Example:**

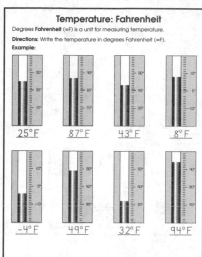

25°F   87°F   43°F   8°F

−4°F   49°F   32°F   94°F

## Page 64

### Temperature: Celsius

Degrees **Celsius** (∞C) is a unit for measuring temperature in the metric system.

**Directions:** Write the temperature in degrees Celsius (∞C).

**Example:**

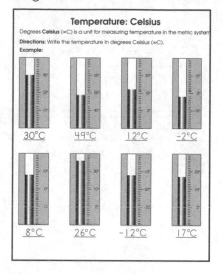

30°C   49°C   12°C   −2°C

8°C   26°C   −12°C   17°C

## Page 65

### Geometry

**Geometry** is the branch of mathematics that has to do with points, lines, and shapes.

**Directions:** Write the word from the box that is described below.

| triangle | square | cube | angle |
| line | ray | segment | rectangle |

a collection of points on a straight path that goes on and on in opposite directions — **line**

a figure with three sides and three corners — **triangle**

a figure with four equal sides and four corners — **square**

part of a line that has one end point and goes on and on in one direction — **ray**

part of a line having two end points — **segment**

a space figure with six square faces — **cube**

two rays with a common end point — **angle**

a figure with four corners and four sides — **rectangle**

## Page 66

### Similar, Congruent, and Symmetrical Figures

**Similar** figures have the same shape but have varying sizes.

Figures that are **congruent** have identical shapes but different orientations. That means they face in different directions.

**Symmetrical** figures can be divided equally into two identical parts.

**Directions:** Cross out the shape that does not belong in each group. Label the two remaining shapes as similar, congruent, or symmetrical.

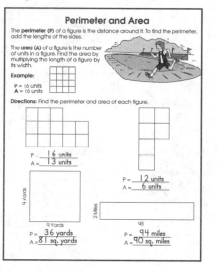

congruent   congruent

congruent   congruent

similar   similar

symmetrical   symmetrical

## Page 67

### Perimeter and Area

The **perimeter (P)** of a figure is the distance around it. To find the perimeter, add the lengths of the sides.

The **area (A)** of a figure is the number of units in a figure. Find the area by multiplying the length of a figure by its width.

**Example:**

P = 16 units
A = 16 units

**Directions:** Find the perimeter and area of each figure.

P = 16 units
A = 13 units

P = 12 units
A = 6 units

9 yards × 9 Yards
P = 36 yards
A = 81 sq. yards

2 Miles × 45
P = 94 miles
A = 90 sq. miles

## Page 68

### Perimeter

The **perimeter** is the distance around a shape.

**Example:**

Find the perimeter of a polygon by adding the lengths of each side.

5 cm   5 cm
6 cm
6 : 6 : 6 = 16 cm

3 in.
3 in.   3 in.
3 in.
3 : 3 : 3 : 3 = 12 in.

3 + 4 + 2 + 3 + 4 + 2 + 2 +
2 + 3 + 2 + 4 + 2 + 2 = 40 cm

**Directions:** Find the perimeter.

3 cm   7 cm
6 cm
16 cm

16 in.
12 in.
56 in.

3.5 ft.
4 ft.
4 ft.
19 ft.

2 mm
2   2
2   2
20 mm

## Page 69

### Figuring Distance

**Directions:** Find the perimeter of each figure.

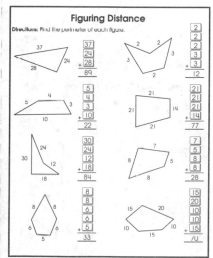

37   37
24   24
28   +28
        89

2
2
2
3
+12

5
4
5   4   3
10   +10
          22

21
21   21   14
21
          77

30   24   12
18
30
24
+18
  84

21
21
21
+14
  77

8   8
8   6
5
8
6
6
+5
  33

15   20
10   10
15
15
20
10
10
+15
  70

## Page 70

### Area

**Example:**

The **area** of a shape is the amount of space it covers. Area is measured in square units, such as square centimeters (cm²) or square inches (in²).

One way to measure the area of a shape is to count the number of square units it covers.

The area of this rectangle is 18 square units.

**Directions:** Find the area of each shape. Write the number of square units.

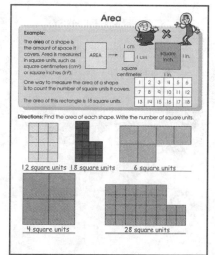

12 square units   18 square units   6 square units

4 square units   28 square units

## Page 71

### Pump Up the Volume!

The **volume** of a 3-D shape is the amount of space it occupies. Volume is measured in cubic units, such as cubic centimeters (cm³) or cubic inches (in³).

Imagine a box filled with unit cubes. The number of cubes is the volume of the box.

The box has a volume of 16 cubic units.

**Directions:** Find the volume of each shape in cubic units.

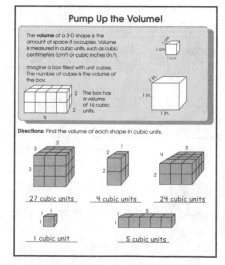

27 cubic units   4 cubic units   24 cubic units

1 cubic unit   5 cubic units

## Page 72

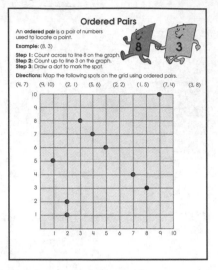

**Ordered Pairs**

An **ordered pair** is a pair of numbers used to locate a point.

**Example:** (8, 3)

**Step 1:** Count across to line 8 on the graph.
**Step 2:** Count up to line 3 on the graph.
**Step 3:** Draw a dot to mark the spot.

**Directions:** Map the following spots on the grid using ordered pairs.

(4, 7)   (9, 10)   (2, 1)   (5, 6)   (2, 2)   (1, 5)   (7, 4)   (3, 8)

## Page 73

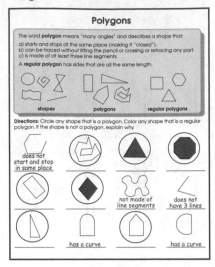

**Polygons**

The word **polygon** means "many angles" and describes a shape that:

a) starts and stops at the same place (making it "closed").
b) can be traced without lifting the pencil or crossing or retracing any part.
c) is made of at least three line segments.

A **regular polygon** has sides that are all the same length.

shapes         polygons         regular polygons

**Directions:** Circle any shape that is a polygon. Color any shape that is a regular polygon. If the shape is not a polygon, explain why.

does not start and stop in same place

not made of line segments

does not have 3 lines

has a curve          has a curve

## Page 74

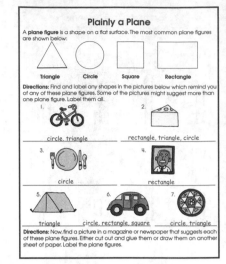

**Plainly a Plane**

A **plane figure** is a shape on a flat surface. The most common plane figures are shown below:

Triangle   Circle   Square   Rectangle

**Directions:** Find and label any shapes in the pictures below which remind you of any of these plane figures. Some of the pictures might suggest more than one plane figure. Label them all.

1. circle, triangle
2. rectangle, triangle, circle
3. circle
4. rectangle
5. triangle
6. circle, rectangle, square
7. circle, triangle

**Directions:** Now, find a picture in a magazine or newspaper that suggests each of these plane figures. Either cut out and glue them or draw them on another sheet of paper. Label the plane figures.

## Page 75

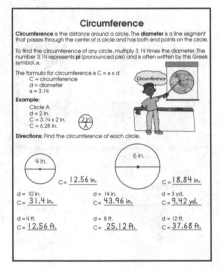

**Circumference**

**Circumference** is the distance around a circle. The **diameter** is a line segment that passes through the center of a circle and has both end points on the circle.

To find the circumference of any circle, multiply 3.14 times the diameter. The number 3.14 represents **pi** (pronounced pie) and is often written by this Greek symbol, $\pi$.

The formula for circumference is $C = \pi \times d$
C = circumference
d = diameter
$\pi$ = 3.14

**Example:**
Circle A
d = 2 in.
C = 3.14 x 2 in.
C = 6.28 in.

**Directions:** Find the circumference of each circle.

4 in.   C = 12.56 in.
6 in.   C = 18.84 in.

d = 10 in.   C = 31.4 in.
d = 14 in.   C = 43.96 in.
d = 3 yd.   C = 9.42 yd.

d = 4 ft.   C = 12.56 ft.
d = 8 ft.   C = 25.12 ft.
d = 12 ft.   C = 37.68 ft.

## Page 76

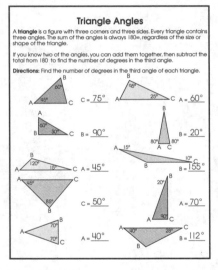

**Triangle Angles**

A **triangle** is a figure with three corners and three sides. Every triangle contains three angles. The sum of the angles is always 180°, regardless of the size or shape of the triangle.

If you know two of the angles, you can add them together, then subtract the total from 180 to find the number of degrees in the third angle.

**Directions:** Find the number of degrees in the third angle of each triangle.

C = 75°
A = 60°
B = 90°
B = 20°
A = 45°
B = 155°
C = 50°
A = 70°
A = 40°
B = 112°

## Page 77

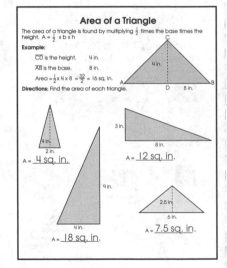

**Area of a Triangle**

The area of a triangle is found by multiplying $\frac{1}{2}$ times the base times the height. $A = \frac{1}{2} \times b \times h$

**Example:**

$\overline{CD}$ is the height.   4 in.
$\overline{AB}$ is the base.   8 in.
Area = $\frac{1}{2} \times 4 \times 8 = \frac{32}{2}$ = 16 sq. in.

**Directions:** Find the area of each triangle.

A = 4 sq. in.
A = 12 sq. in.
A = 18 sq. in.
A = 7.5 sq. in.

## Page 78

**Space Figures**

**Space figures** are figures whose points are in more than one plane. Cubes and cylinders are space figures.

rectangular prism   cone   cube   cylinder   sphere   pyramid

A **prism** has two identical, parallel bases.

All of the faces on a **rectangular prism** are rectangles.

A **cube** is a prism with six identical, square faces.

A **pyramid** is a space figure whose base is a polygon and whose faces are triangles with a common vertex—the point where two rays meet.

A **cylinder** has a curved surface and two parallel bases that are identical circles.

A **cone** has one circular, flat face and one vertex.

A **sphere** has no flat surface. All points are an equal distance from the center.

**Directions:** Circle the name of the figure you see in each of these familiar objects.

cone   (sphere)   cylinder
cone   sphere   (cylinder)
cube   (rectangular prism)   pyramid
(cone)   pyramid   cylinder

## Page 79

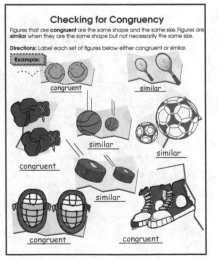

**Checking for Congruency**

Figures that are **congruent** are the same shape and the same size. Figures are **similar** when they are the same shape but not necessarily the same size.

**Directions:** Label each set of figures below either congruent or similar.

**Example:**

congruent          similar

similar

congruent          similar

similar

congruent          congruent

## Page 80

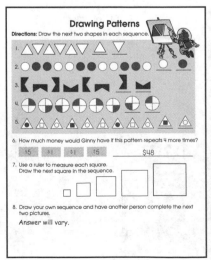

**Drawing Patterns**

**Directions:** Draw the next two shapes in each sequence.

1.
2.
3.
4.
5.

6. How much money would Ginny have if this pattern repeats 4 more times?
$5   $1   $1   $5          $48

7. Use a ruler to measure each square. Draw the next square in the sequence.

8. Draw your own sequence and have another person complete the next two pictures.
Answer will vary.

## Page 81

### Venn Diagrams

A **Venn diagram** is a picture that represents a collection. The rectangle always stands for the whole collection. Any circle inside the rectangle stands for a part of it.

This Venn diagram represents all the trucks manufactured by a certain company. Circle R stands for all the red trucks, circle B for all the blue trucks, and circle F for all the four-wheel-drive trucks the company made.

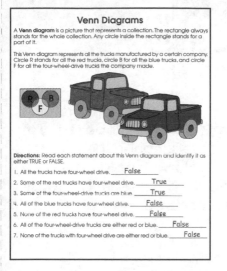

**Directions:** Read each statement about this Venn diagram and identify it as either TRUE or FALSE.

1. All the trucks have four-wheel drive. __False__
2. Some of the red trucks have four-wheel drive. __True__
3. Some of the four-wheel-drive trucks are blue __True__
4. All of the blue trucks have four-wheel drive. __False__
5. None of the red trucks have four-wheel drive. __False__
6. All of the four-wheel-drive trucks are either red or blue. __False__
7. None of the trucks with four-wheel drive are either red or blue. __False__

## Page 82

### Summer Fun

A **pictograph** uses pictures to show information.

**Example:**

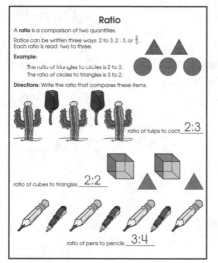

| Favorite Summer Activities | |
|---|---|
| Pool | 🏐🏐 |
| Beach | 🏐🏐🏐 |
| Sports | 🏐🏐🏐🏐🏐 |
| Picnic | 🏐 |

Key: 1 🏐 = 2 people

**Directions:** Use this pictograph to answer the questions.

1. What is this graph about? __favorite summer activities__
2. How many people does each 🏐 represent? __2__
3. How many people like sports best? __10__
4. How many people like the beach best? __5__
5. Which activity is the least popular? __picnicking__
6. How many more people like the beach than the pool? __1__
7. How many more people like the pool than a picnic? __2__
8. How many people in all were asked about their favorite activities? __21__

## Page 83

### Bar Graphs

**Bar graphs** use bars to show information. They are good for showing information that can be easily counted.

**Example:**

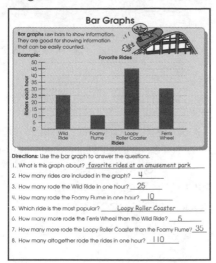

Favorite Rides

**Directions:** Use the bar graph to answer the questions.

1. What is this graph about? __favorite rides at an amusement park__
2. How many rides are included in the graph? __4__
3. How many rode the Wild Ride in one hour? __25__
4. How many rode the Foamy Flume in one hour? __10__
5. Which ride is the most popular? __Loopy Roller Coaster__
6. How many more rode the Ferris Wheel than the Wild Ride? __5__
7. How many more rode the Loopy Roller Coaster than the Foamy Flume? __35__
8. How many altogether rode the rides in one hour? __110__

## Page 84

### Line Graphs

A **line graph** is a good way to show data that changes over time. This graph shows the company sales for Wacky Water Slides from 1994 to 2001.

**Example:**

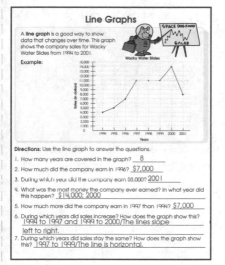

Wacky Water Slides

**Directions:** Use the line graph to answer the questions.

1. How many years are covered in the graph? __8__
2. How much did the company earn in 1996? __$7,000__
3. During which year did the company earn 60,000? __2001__
4. What was the most money the company ever earned? In what year did this happen? __$14,000; 2000__
5. How much more did the company earn in 1997 than 1994? __$7,000__
6. During which years did sales increase? How does the graph show this? __1994 to 1997 and 1999 to 2000/The lines slope left to right.__
7. During which years did sales stay the same? How does the graph show this? __1997 to 1999/The line is horizontal.__

## Page 85

### Ratio

A **ratio** is a comparison of two quantities.
Ratios can be written three ways: 2 to 3, 2 : 3, or $\frac{2}{3}$.
Each ratio is read: two to three.

**Example:**

The ratio of triangles to circles is 2 to 0.
The ratio of circles to triangles is 3 to 2.

**Directions:** Write the ratio that compares these items.

ratio of tulips to cacti __2:3__

ratio of cubes to triangles __2:2__

ratio of pens to pencils __3:4__

## Page 86

### Probability

One thinking skill to get your brain in gear is figuring probability. **Probability** is the likelihood or chance that something will happen. Probability is expressed and written as a ratio.

The probability of tossing heads or tails on a coin is one in two (1:2).

The probability of rolling any number on a die is one in six (1:6).

The probability of getting a red on this spinner is two in four (2:4).

The probability of drawing an ace from a deck of cards is four in fifty-two (4:52).

**Directions:** Write the probability ratios to answer these questions.

1. There are 26 letters in the alphabet. What is the probability of drawing any letter from a set of alphabet cards? __1:26__
2. Five of the 26 alphabet letters are vowels. What is the probability of drawing a vowel from the alphabet cards? __5:26__
3. Matt takes 10 shots at the basketball hoop. Six of his shots are baskets. What is the probability of Matt's next shot being a basket? __6:10__
4. A box contains 10 marbles: 2 white, 3 green, 1 red, 2 orange, and 2 blue. What is the probability of pulling a green marble from the box? __3:10__
   A red marble? __1:10__
5. What is the probability of pulling a marble that is not blue? __8:10__

## Page 87

### Guess the Color

Probability shows the chance that a given event will happen. To show probability, write a fraction. The number of different possibilities is the denominator. The number of times the event could happen is the numerator. (Remember to reduce fractions to the lowest terms.)

Look at the spinner. What is the probability that the arrow will land on . . .

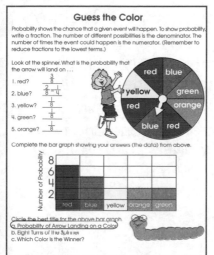

1. red? __$\frac{3}{8}$__
2. blue? __$\frac{2}{8} = \frac{1}{4}$__
3. yellow? __$\frac{1}{8}$__
4. green? __$\frac{1}{8}$__
5. orange? __$\frac{1}{8}$__

Complete the bar graph showing your answers (the data) from above.

Circle the best title for the above bar graph.
a. Probability of Arrow Landing on a Color
b. Eight Turns of the Spinner
c. Which Color Is the Winner?

# Developmental Skills for Fifth Grade Math Success

Parents and educators alike know that the School Specialty name ensures outstanding educational experience and content. Summer Link Math was designed to help your child retain those skills learned during the past school year. With Summer Link Math, your child will be ready to review and master new material with confidence when he or she returns to school in the fall.

Use this checklist—compiled from state curriculum standards—to help your child prepare for proficiency testing. Place a check mark in the box if the appropriate skill has been mastered. If your child needs more work with a particular skill, place an "R" in the box and come back to it for review.

## Math Skills

❑ Understands place value through 999,999.

❑ Uses problem-solving strategies—such as rounding, regrouping, using multiple operations, and Venn diagrams—to solve numerical and word problems.

❑ Compares whole numbers using < > =.

❑ Solves multiple-operation problems using a calculator.

❑ Adds and subtracts proper fractions having like denominators of 12 or less.

❑ Adds and subtracts simple decimals in context of money with and without regrouping.

❑ Tells and writes time shown on traditional and digital clocks.

❑ Uses customary system to measure length, mass, volume, and temperature.

❑ Uses metric system to measure length, mass, volume, and temperature.

❑ Selects the appropriate operational and relational symbols to make an expression true (4 × 3=12).

❑ Recognizes and uses commutative and associative properties of multiplication (5 × 7=35...What is 7 × 5?).

❑ Measures length, width, perimeter, and area to solve numerical and word problems.

❑ Describes, draws, identifies, and analyzes two- and three-dimensional shapes.

❑ Identifies congruent shapes.

❑ Identifies lines of symmetry in shapes.

❑ Recognizes patterns and relationships using a bar graph and locating points on a grid.

❑ Analyzes and solves simple probability problems.

❑ Adds and subtracts with two and three digits, regrouping when necessary.

❑ Multiplies two-digit numbers with regrouping, and divides one and two-digit numbers by divisors of 6 – 10, with and without remainders.

# READING

# Summer Before Grade 5
# Recommended Reading

| | |
|---|---|
| • Autumn Street; Number the Stars; Rabble Starkey | Lois Lowry |
| ✓ Because of Winn-Dixie | Kate Dicamillo |
| • The Birchbark House | Louise Erdich |
| ✓ Black Beauty | Anna Sewell |
| ✓ Bridge to Terabithia | Katherine Paterson |
| • Bud, Not Buddy | Christopher Paul Curtis |
| ✓ ~~Bunnicula~~ | Deborah Howe |
| • Catherine, Called Birdy | Karen Cushman |
| • Chocolate Covered Ants | Stephen Mares |
| • A Corner of the Universe | Ann M. Marker |
| ✓ Crash | Jerry Spinelli |
| ✓ The Cricket in Times Square | George Selden |
| • Dear Mr. Henshaw; ~~Henry and Beezus~~ | Beverly Cleary |
| • Encyclopedia Brown Sets the Pace | Donald J. Sobol |
| ✓ Fly Away Home | Eve Bunting |
| • ~~Frindle~~ | Andrew Clements |
| ✓ ~~Harry Potter Series~~ | J.K. Rowling |
| • Helen Keller's Teacher; Five True Dog Stories | Margaret Davidson |
| • Hoot | Carl Hiaasen |
| • ~~The Indian in the Cupboard~~; Return of the Indian | Lynne Reid Banks |
| • Insectlopedia | Douglas Florian |
| • Little House on the Prairie | Laura Ingalls Wilder |
| • The Magic School Bus Series | Joanna Cole |
| • ~~Matilda~~ | Roald Dahl |
| • Old Yeller | Fred Gipson |
| • Redwall | Brian Jacques |
| • Sounder | William Howard Armstrong |
| • The Thief Lord | Cornelia Funke |
| • A Time to Talk: Poems of Friendship | Myra Cohn Livingston |
| • The Truth About Great White Sharks | Mary M. Cerullo |
| • The Twentieth Century Children's Poetry Treasury | Jack Prelutsky |
| • ~~The Wayside School Series~~ | Louis Sachar |
| • The Wind in the Willows | Kenneth Grahame |

Name _____

# Verbs

A **verb** tells what something does or that something exists.

**Examples:**
Tim **has shared** his apples with us.
Those apples **were** delicious.
I hope Tim **is bringing** more apples tomorrow.
Tim **picked** the apples himself.

**Directions:** Underline the verbs.

1. Gene <u>moved</u> here from Philadelphia.

2. Now he <u>is living</u> in a house on my street.

3. His house is three houses <u>away from</u> mine.

4. I <u>have lived</u> in this house all my life.

5. I hope Gene <u>will like</u> this town.

6. I <u>am helping</u> Gene with his room.

7. He <u>has</u> a lot of stuff!

8. We <u>are painting</u> his walls green.

9. He <u>picked</u> the color himself.

10. I wonder what his parents <u>will say</u>.

**Directions:** Write verbs to complete these sentences.

11. We _____enjoy sharing_____ some paintbrushes.

12. Gene already _____painted with_____ the paint.

13. I _____wore_____ my old clothes.

14. There, _____he had_____ no furniture in his room right now.

15. It _____took_____ several hours to paint his whole room.

# Verb Tense

Not only do verbs tell the action of a sentence but they also tell when the action takes place. This is called the **verb tense**. There are three verb tenses: past, present, and future tense.

**Present-tense verbs** tell what is happening now.

**Example:** Jane **spells** words with long vowel sounds.

**Past-tense verbs** tell about action that has already happened. Past-tense verbs are usually formed by adding **ed** to the verb.

**Example:** stay — stayed.    John **stayed** home yesterday.

Past-tense verbs can also be made by adding helping verbs **was** or **were** before the verb and adding **ing** to the verb.

**Example:** talk — was talking.    Sally **was talking** to her mom.

**Future-tense verbs** tell what will happen in the future. Future-tense verbs are made by putting the word **will** before the verb.

**Example:** paint — will paint.    Susie and Sherry **will paint** the house.

**Directions:** Read the following verbs. Write whether the verb tense is past, present, or future.

| Verb | Tense | Verb | Tense |
|---|---|---|---|
| 1. watches | **present** | 8. writes | present |
| 2. wanted | past | 9. vaulted | past |
| 3. will eat | future | 10. were sleeping | past |
| 4. was squawking | past | 11. will sing | future |
| 5. yawns | present | 12. is speaking | present |
| 6. crawled | past | 13. will cook | future |
| 7. will hunt | future | 14. likes | present |

# Transitive and Intransitive Verbs

An **intransitive verb** can stand alone in the predicate because its meaning is complete. In the following examples, notice that each short sentence is a complete thought. **Examples: Intransitive verbs:** The tree **grows**. The mouse **squeaked**. The deer **will run**.

A **transitive verb** needs a direct object to complete its meaning. The meaning of a sentence with a transitive verb is not complete without a direct object. **Examples: Transitive verbs:** The mouse **wants** seeds. The deer **saw** the hunter. The tree **will lose** its leaves.

The direct object **seeds** tells what the mouse wants. **Leaves** tells what the tree will lose and **hunter** tells what the deer saw.

Both transitive and intransitive verbs can be in the past, present, or future tense.

**Directions:** Underline the verb in each sentence. Write **I** if the sentence has an intransitive verb or **T** if it has a transitive verb.

_____I_____ 1. The snake slid quietly along the ground.

_____T_____ 2. The snake scared a rabbit.

_____I_____ 3. The rabbit hopped quickly back to its hole.

_____I_____ 4. Safe from the snake, the rabbit shivered with fear.

_____T_____ 5. In the meantime, the snake caught a frog.

_____T_____ 6. The frog was watching flies and didn't see the snake.

**Directions:** Complete these sentences with intransitive verbs.

7. Our friends _smiled_____

8. The movie _sucked_____

**Directions:** Complete these sentences with transitive verbs and direct objects.

9. My family _liked bagels_____

10. The lightning _hit our shed_____

**103**          **Summer Link Super Edition Grade 5**

# Subjects and Predicates

The **subject** tells who or what the sentence is about. The **predicate** tells what the subject does, did, is doing, or will do. A complete sentence must have a subject and a predicate.

**Examples:**

| Subject | Predicate |
|---|---|
| Sharon | writes to her grandmother every week. |
| The horse | ran around the track quickly. |
| My mom's car | is bright green. |
| Denise | will be here after lunch. |

**Directions:** Circle the subject of each sentence. Underline the predicate.

1. My sister is a very happy person.

2. I wish we had more holidays in the year.

3. Laura is one of the nicest girls in our class.

4. John is fun to have as a friend.

5. The rain nearly ruined our picnic!

6. My birthday present was exactly what I wanted.

7. Your bicycle is parked beside my skateboard.

8. The printer will need to be filled with paper before you use it.

9. Six dogs chased my cat home yesterday!

10. Anthony likes to read anything he can get his hands on.

11. Twelve students signed up for the dance committee.

12. Your teacher seems to be a reasonable person.

# Compound Subjects and Predicates

**Directions:** Circle the subjects.

1. (Everyone) felt the day had been a great success.
2. (Christina and Andrea) were both happy to take the day off.
3. (No one) really understood why he was crying.
4. (Mr. Winston, Ms. Fuller, and Ms. Landers) took us on a field trip.

**Directions:** Underline the predicates.

5. Who can tell what will happen tomorrow?
6. Mark was a carpenter by trade and a talented painter, too.
7. The animals yelped and whined in their cages.
8. Airplane rides made her feel sick to her stomach.

**Directions:** Combine the sentences to make one sentence with a compound subject.

9. Elizabeth ate everything in sight. George ate everything in sight.

Elizabeth and George ate everything in sight.

10. Wishing something will happen won't make it so. Dreaming something will happen won't make it so.

Wishing or dreaming something will happen won't make it so.

**Directions:** Combine the sentences to make one sentence with a compound predicate.

11. I jumped for joy. I hugged all my friends.

I jumped for joy and hugged all my friends.

12. She ran around the track before the race. She warmed up before the race.

She ran around the track and warmed up before the race.

# Compound Subjects and Predicates

A **compound subject** has two or more nouns or pronouns joined by a conjunction. Compound subjects share the same predicate.

**Examples:**
> **Suki and Spot** walked to the park in the rain.
> **Cars, buses and trucks** splashed water on them.
> **He and I** were glad we had our umbrella.

A **compound predicate** has two or more verbs joined by a conjunction. Compound predicates share the same subject.

**Examples:**
> Suki **went** in the restroom **and wiped** off her shoes.
> Paula **followed** Suki **and waited** for her.

A sentence can have a compound subject and a compound predicate.

**Example: Tina and Maria went** to the mall **and shopped** for an hour.

**Directions:** Circle the compound subjects. Underline the compound predicates.

1. Steve and Jerry went to the store and bought some gum.
2. Police and firefighters worked together and put out the fire.
3. Karen and Marsha did their homework and checked it twice.
4. In preschool, the boys and girls drew pictures and colored them.

**Directions:** Write compound subjects to go with these predicates.

5. _Billy and Brenda_ ate peanut butter sandwiches.
6. _Bob and Buck_ left early.
7. _Fish and crocs_ don't make good pets.
8. _Razzle and Gracie_ found their way home.
9. _Tweedledee and Tweedledum_ are moving to Denver.

**Directions:** Write compound predicates to go with these subjects.

10. A scary book _makes you jump when read._
11. My friend's sister _likes to write and draw_
12. The shadow _is a monster who stalks and screeches_
13. The wind _blew and howled_
14. The runaway car _drifted and accelerated down lanes_

# Conjunctions

**Directions:** Choose the best conjunction from the box to combine the pairs of sentences. Then rewrite the sentences.

| and | but | or | because | when | after | so |
|-----|-----|-----|---------|------|-------|-----|

1. I like Leah. I like Ben.

   _I like Leah and Ben._

2. Should I eat the orange? Should I eat the apple?

   _Should I eat the orange, or the apple?_

3. You will get a reward. You turned in the lost item.

   _You will get a reward, because you turned in the lost item._

4. I really mean what I say! You had better listen!

   _I really mean what I say, so you had better listen!_

5. I like you. You're nice, friendly, helpful, and kind.

   _I like you because you're nice, friendly, helpful, and kind._

6. You can have dessert. You ate all your peas.

   _You can have dessert because you ate all your peas._

7. I like your shirt better. You should decide for yourself.

   _I like your shirt better, but you should decide for yourself._

8. We walked out of the building. We heard the fire alarm.

   _We walked out of the building when we heard the fire alarm._

9. I like to sing folk songs. I like to play the guitar.

   _I like to sing folk songs and play the guitar._

# Capitalization GREAT! and Punctuation

**Directions:** Rewrite the paragraphs below, adding punctuation where it is needed. Capitalize the first word of each sentence and all other words that should be capitalized.

most countries have laws that control advertising in norway no ads at all are allowed on radio or TV in the united states ads for alcoholic drinks, except beer and wine, are not permitted on radio or TV england has a law against advertising cigarettes on TV what do you think about these laws should they be even stricter

Most countries have laws that control advertising. In Norway, no ads at all are allowed on radio or T.V. In the United States, ads for alcoholic drinks, except beer and wine, are not permitted on radio or T.V. England has a law against advertising cigarettes on T.V. What do you think about these laws? Should they be even stricter?

my cousin jeff is starting college this fall he wants to be a medical doctor, so he's going to central university the mayor of our town went there mayor stevens told jeff all about the university our town is so small that everyone knows what everyone else is doing is your town like that

My cousin Jeff is starting college this fall. He wants to be a medical doctor, so he's going to Central University. The mayor of our town went there. Mayor Stevens told Jeff all about the university. Our town is so *small* that everyone knows what everyone else is doing. Is your town like that?

my grandparents took a long vacation last year grandma really likes to go to the atlantic ocean and watch the dolphins my grandfather likes to fish in the ocean my aunt went with them last summer they all had a party on the fourth of july

My grandparents took a long vacation last year. Grandma really likes to go to the Atlantic Ocean and watch the dolphins. My grandfather likes to fish in the ocean. My aunt went with them last summer they all had a party on the fourth of july.

# Commas

**Commas** are used to separate items in a series.
Both examples below are correct. A final comma is optional.

**Examples:**
    The fruit bowl contains oranges, peaches, pears, and apples.
    The fruit bowl contains oranges, peaches, pears and apples.

Commas are also used to separate geographical names and dates.

**Examples:**
    Today's date is January 13, 2000.
    My grandfather lives in Tallahassee, Florida.
    I would like to visit Paris, France.

**Directions:** Place commas where needed in these sentences.

1. I was born on September 21, 1992.
2. John s favorite sports include basketball, football, hockey, and soccer.
3. The ship will sail on November 16, 2004.
4. My family and I vacationed in Salt Lake City, Utah.
5. I like to plant beans, beets, corn, and radishes in my garden.
6. Sandy's party will be held in Youngstown, Ohio.
7. Periods, commas, colons, and exclamation marks are types of punctuation.
8. Cardinals, juncos, blue jays, finches, and sparrows frequent our birdfeeder.
9. My grandfather graduated from high school on June 4, 1962.
10. The race will take place in Burlington, Vermont.

**Directions:** Write a sentence using commas to separate words in a series.

11. I like dark chocolate, milk chocolate, and white chocolate bars.

**Directions:** Write a sentence using commas to separate geographical names.

12. It's humid in Orlando, Florida.

**Directions:** Write a sentence using commas to separate dates.

13. My mom's birthday is June 3, 1988, and my dad's is June 10, 1988.

# Plurals

Some words in the English language do not follow any of the plural rules discussed earlier. These words may not change at all from singular to plural, or they may completely change spellings.

| No Change | Examples: | Complete Change | Examples: |
|---|---|---|---|
| **Singular** | **Plural** | **Singular** | **Plural** |
| deer | deer | goose | geese |
| pants | pants | ox | oxen |
| scissors | scissors | man | men |
| moose | moose | child | children |
| sheep | sheep | leaf | leaves |

**Directions:** Write the singular or plural form of each word. Use a dictionary to help if necessary.

| Singular | Plural | | Singular | Plural |
|---|---|---|---|---|
| 1. moose | moose | | 6. leaf | leaves |
| 2. woman | women | | 7. sheep | sheep |
| 3. deer | deer | | 8. scissors | scissors |
| 4. child | children | | 9. tooth | teeth |
| 5. hoof | hooves | | 10. wharf | wharves |

**Directions:** Write four sentences of your own using two singular and two plural words from above.

The group of moose were happy.
My grandma is a very old woman.
I have many teeth.
The deer frolicked away.

Name _____

# Synonyms and Antonyms

**Directions:** Use the words in the box to write a synonym for each word below. Write it next to the **S**. Next to the **A**, write an antonym. The first one is done for you.

| appear | proud | merry | straight | repair | plain |
| under | melted | unnecessary | late | new | smooth |
| embarrassed | gloomy | bent | break | fancy | above |
| icy | valuable | immediate | old | bumpy | vanish |

5. important
S: Valuable
A: Unnecessary

10. beneath
S: under
A: above

1. crooked
S: **bent**
A: **straight**

6. ashamed
S: embarrassed
A: proud

11. disappear
S: vanish
A: appear

2. frozen
S: icy
A: Melted

7. cheerful
S: merry
A: gloomy

12. ancient
S: old
A: new

3. instant
S: immediate
A: late

8. elegant
S: fancy
A: plain

4. damage
S: break
A: repair

9. rough
S: bumpy
A: smooth

**111**    **Summer Link Super Edition Grade 5**

# Analogies

An **analogy** indicates how different items go together or are similar in some way.

**Examples:**
 **Petal** is to **flower** as **leaf** is to **tree**.
 **Book** is to **library** as **food** is to **grocery**.

If you study the examples, you will see how the second set of objects is related to the first set. A petal is part of a flower, and a leaf is part of a tree. A book can be found in a library, and food can be found in a grocery store.

**Directions:** Fill in the blanks to complete the analogies. The first one has been done for you.

1. Cup is to saucer as glass is to ___coaster___ .

2. Paris is to France as London is to _England_ .

3. Clothes are to hangers as _shoes_ are to boxes.

4. California is to _Pacific Ocean_ as Ohio is to Lake Erie.

5. _Tablecloth_ is to table as blanket is to bed.

6. Pencil is to paper as _paintbrush_ is to canvas.

7. Cow is to _barn_ as child is to house.

8. State is to country as _city_ is to state.

9. Governor is to state as _president_ is to country.

10. _Water_ is to ocean as sand is to desert.

11. Engine is to car as hard drive is to _computer_ .

12. Beginning is to _start_ as stop is to end.

**Directions:** Write three analogies of your own.

_Calf is to cow as lamb is to sheep_
_Beef is to cow as pork is to pig_
_Udder is to cow as teath is to kaneroo_

# Synonym and Antonym Analogies

**Analogies** are a way of comparing items to show how they are related. Analogies can show different types of relationships. Two relationships analogies might show are synonyms or antonyms.

**Examples:**
 **Antonyms:** hot is to cold as happy is to sad
 **Synonyms:** happy is to glad as run is to jog

You can write an analogy this way:
 slow:fast::up:down
You read it this way:
 slow is to fast as up is to down

**Directions:** Write **S** for synonym or **A** for antonym in the blanks in front of each analogy. Then complete the analogies by choosing a word from the box.

| | | | | |
|---|---|---|---|---|
| ~~life~~ | ~~run~~ | ~~comforter~~ | ~~fail~~ | ~~photograph~~ |
| ~~above~~ | ~~feline~~ | ~~play~~ | ~~drape~~ | ~~different~~ |

__S__ 1. dog:canine::cat: _feline_

__S__ 2. coat:parka::curtain: _drape_

__A__ 3. asleep:awake::work: _play_

__A__ 4. ground:sky::below: _above_

__A__ 5. freeze:thaw::stroll: _run_

__S__ 6. dangerous:treacherous::picture: _photograph_

__S__ 7. ancient:old::bedspread: _comforter_

__A__ 8. win:lose::succeed: _fail_

__S__ 9. manmade:artificial::unique: _different_

__A__ 10. wealthy:poor::death: _life_

GREAT!

# Using Conjunctions

**Conjunctions** are joining words that can be used to combine sentences. Words such as **and**, **but**, **or**, **when**, and **after** are conjunctions.

**Examples:**
Sally went to the mall. She went to the movies.
Sally went to the mall, and she went to the movies.

We can have our vacation at home. We can vacation at the beach.
We can have our vacation at home, or we can vacation at the beach.

Mary fell on the playground. She did not hurt herself.
Mary fell on the playground, but she did not hurt herself.

**Note:** The conjunctions **after** or **when** are usually placed at the beginning of the sentence.

**Example:** Marge went to the store. She went to the gas station.
After Marge went to the store, she went to the gas station.

**Directions:** Combine the following sentences using a conjunction.

1. Peter fell down the steps. He broke his foot. (and)
   _Peter fell down and he broke his foot._

2. I visited New York. I would like to see Chicago. (but)
   _I visited New York, but I would like to see Chicago._

3. Amy can edit books. She can write stories. (or) Chicago.
   _Amy can edit books or she can write stories._

4. He played in the barn. John started to sneeze. (when)
   When _He played in the barn when John started to sneeze_

5. The team won the playoffs. They went to the championships. (after) sneeze
   After _The team won the playoffs, after they went to the championships._

**Directions:** Write three sentences of your own using the conjunctions **and**, **but**, **or**, **when**, or **after**.

_The snail goes into it's shell when touched._
_I like pork, but not ham._
_I like pizza and ice cream._

# Proofreading Practice

**Directions:** Circle the six spelling and pronoun mistakes in each paragraph. Write the words correctly on the lines below.

*Excellent!*

Jenna always braged about being ready to meet any challenge or reach any gole. When it was time for our class to elekt it's new officers, Jenna said we should voat for her to be president.

| bragged | challenge | goal |
| elect | its | vote |

Simon wanted to be ours president, too. He tried to coaks everyone to vote for his. He even lowned kids money to get their votes! Well, Jenna may have too much pryde in herself, but I like her in spit of that. At least she didn't try to buy our votes!

| our | coax | him |
| looned | pride | spite |

Its true that Jenna tried other ways to get us to vote for hers. She scrubed the chalkboards even though it was my dayly job for that week. One day, I saw her rinseing out the paintbrushes when it was Peter's turn to do it. Then she made sure we knew about her good deeds so we would praize her.

| it's | her | scrubbed |
| daily | rinsing | praise |

We held the election, but I was shalked when the teacher releesed the results. Simon won! I wondered if he cheeted somehow. I feel like our class was robed! Now Simon is the one who's braging about how great he is. I wish he knew the titel of president doesn't mean anything if no one wants to be around you!

| shocked | released | cheated |
| robbed | bragging | title |

# Check Your Proofreading Skills

**Directions:** Read about the things you should remember when you are revising your writing. Then follow the instructions to revise the paper below.

After you have finished writing your rough draft, you should reread it later to determine what changes you need to make to ensure it's the best possible paper you are capable of writing.

Check yourself by asking the following questions:
**Does my paper stick to the topic?**
**Have I left out any important details?**
**Can I make the writing more lively?**
**Have I made errors in spelling, punctuation or capitalization?**
**Is there any information that should be left out?**

**Directions:** Revise the following story by making changes to correct spelling, punctuation, and capitalization; add details; and cross out words or sentences that do not stick to the topic.

## Hunting for Treasure

No one really believes me when I tell them that I'm a tresure

hunter. But, really, i am. It isn't just any treasure that I like

to hunt, though. I like treasures related to coins. Usually

when I go treasure huting I go alone. I always wear my blue

coat.

One day my good friend Jesse wanted to come with me. Why

would you want to do that?" I said. "Because I like coins, too,"

he replied. What Jesse did not know was that the Coins that I

dig to find are not the coins that just anyone

collects.  The coins i like are special. They are

coins that have been buried in dirt for years!

# Taking Notes

**Taking notes** effectively can help you in many ways with schoolwork. It will help you better understand and remember what you read and hear. It will also help you keep track of important facts needed for reports, essays, and tests.

Each person develops his or her own way of taking notes. While developing your style, keep in mind the following:

► Write notes in short phrases instead of whole sentences.
► Abbreviate words to save time.
  **Examples: pres** for **president** or **&** for **and**
► If you use the same name often in your notes, use initials.
  **Examples: GW** for **George Washington**;  **AL** for **Abraham Lincoln**
► Be brief, but make sure you understand what you write.
► Number your notes, so you can understand where each note starts and stops.
► When taking notes from a long article or book, write down one or two important points per paragraph or chapter.

**Directions:** Reread the story "Hunting for Treasure" on page 116. As you read the story, fill in the note-taking format below with your notes.

Title of Article or Story _____

## Important Points

Paragraph 1      _____

_____

Paragraph 2      _____

_____

# Doing Research

**Directions:** Read about how to do research for a report and answer the questions.

Before starting your report, locate the most likely places to find relevant information for your research. Ask the librarian for help if necessary. A good report will be based on at least three or four sources, so it's important to find references that provide varied information.

Is the topic a standard one, such as a report on the skeletal system? A general encyclopedia, such as World Book, is a good place to begin your research. Remember to use the encyclopedia's index to find related entries. For related entries on the skeletal system, you could check the index for entries on bones, health, and the musculo-skeletal system. The index entry will show which encyclopedia number and pages to read to find information related to each entry topic.

Does your report require current statistics and/or facts? Facts on File and Editorial Research Reports are two sources for statistics. Ask the librarian to direct you to more specialized reference sources, such as The People's Almanac or The New Grove Dictionary of Music and Musicians which are related specifically to your topic.

For current magazine articles, see the Reader's Guide to Periodical Literature, which lists the names and page numbers of magazine articles related to a variety of topics. If you need geographical information about a country, check an atlas such as the Rand McNally Contemporary World Atlas.

1. How many reference sources should you consult before writing your report?
_____

2. What are two references that provide statistics and facts? _____
_____

3. Where will you find a listing of magazine articles? _____
_____

4. Where should you look for geographical information? _____
_____

5. If you're stumped or don't know where to begin, who can help? _____
_____

# Taking Notes

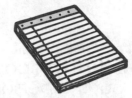

**Directions:** Read about taking notes for your report. Use the "index card" below to write a sample note from one of your reference sources.

When gathering information for a report, it is necessary to take notes. You'll need to take notes when you read encyclopedia entries, books, and magazine or newspaper articles related to your topic.

Before you begin gathering information for a report, organize your thoughts around the who, what, when, where, why, and how questions of your topic. This organized approach will help direct you to the references that best answer these questions. It will also help you select and write in your notes only useful information.

There are different ways of taking notes. Some people use notebook paper. If you write on notebook paper, put a heading on each page. Write only notes related to each heading on specific pages. Otherwise, your notes will be disorganized, and it will be difficult to begin writing your paper.

Many people prefer to put their notes on index cards. Index cards can be easily sorted and organized when you begin writing your report and are helpful when preparing an outline. If you use index cards for your notes, put one fact on each card.

Take several notes from each reference source you use. Having too many notes is better than not having enough information when you start to write your report.

_____

_____

_____

_____

_____

_____

_____

Name _____

# Taking Notes

A **biography** is a written report of a person's life. It is based on facts and actual events. To prepare to write a biographical essay, you could look up information about the person in an encyclopedia.

**Directions:** Select one of the people listed below. Read about that person in an encyclopedia. Take notes to prepare for writing a biographical essay. Then use your notes to answer the questions.

Babe Ruth                    Billie Jean King
Mikhail Baryshnikov          Willie Mays
Golda Meir                   Woodrow Wilson
Dolly Madison                Charles Darwin
Pearl S. Buck                Marie Curie

**My Notes:**

1. Where and when was he or she born? _____

2. If deceased, when did the person die? _____

3. When and why did he or she first become famous? _____
_____
_____

4. What are some important points about this person's career?
_____
_____
_____
_____
_____
_____
_____

# From Grapes to Raisins

**Directions:** Use a piece of paper to cover up the story about how grapes become raisins. Then read the questions.

1. How do grapes become raisins?

2. What happens after the grapes become raisins?

3. Why are raisins brown?

4. In what countries do grapes grow?

**Directions:** Read about how grapes become raisins.

Grapes grow well in places that have lots of sun. In the United States, California is a big producer of grapes and raisins. When grapes are plump and round, they can be picked from their vines to be made into raisins. After the grapes are picked, they are put on big wooden or paper trays. They sit in the sun for many days.

Slowly, the grapes begin to dry and turn into wrinkled raisins. The sun causes them to change colors. Grapes turn brown as they become raisins. Machines take off the stems. Then the raisins are washed. After being dried again, they are put into boxes.

Some places use machines to make raisins dry faster. The grapes are put into ovens that have hot air blowing around inside. These ovens make the grapes shrivel and dry.

Raisins are made in many countries that grow grapes. Besides the United States, countries such as Greece, Turkey, Iran, Spain, and Australia produce a lot of raisins.

**Directions:** Use your notes to answer the four questions at the top of the page. Write your answers on the lines below.

1. _____

2. _____

3. _____

4. _____

# Fact or Opinion?

**Directions:** Read the paragraphs below. Then, in the corresponding numbered blanks, write whether each numbered sentence is a fact or an opinion.

(1) An important rule for stamp collectors to follow is never to handle stamps with their fingers. (2) Instead, to keep the stamps clean, collectors use stamp tongs to pick up stamps. (3) Stamps are stored by being placed on mounts. (4) Stamp mounts are plastic holders that fit around the stamp and keep it clean. (5) The backs of the mounts are sticky, so they can be stuck onto a stamp album page. (6) What a great idea!

(7) The stamps are mounted in stamp albums that have either white or black pages. (8) Some people prefer black pages, claiming that the stamps "show" better. (9) Some people prefer white pages, claiming that they give the album a cleaner look. (10) I think this foolish bickering over page colors is ridiculous!

1. _____

2. _____

3. _____

4. _____

5. _____

6. _____

7. _____

8. _____

9. _____

10. _____

# The Five Senses

**Directions:** Before each sentence, write the sense—hearing, sight, smell, taste, or touch—that is being used. The first one is done for you.

____hearing____    1. The rooster crows outside my window early each morning.

_____    2. After playing in the snow, our fingers and toes were freezing.

_____    3. I could hear sirens in the distance.

_____    4. I think this tree is taller than that one.

_____    5. The delicious salad was filled with fresh, juicy fruits.

_____    6. The odor of the bread baking in the oven was wonderful.

_____    7. There was a rainbow in the sky today.

_____    8. The kitten was soft and fluffy.

_____    9. Her perfume filled the air when she walked by.

_____ 10. An airplane wrote a message in the sky.

_____ 11. The chocolate cake was yummy.

_____ 12. The steamboat whistle frightened the baby.

_____ 13. The sour lemon made my lips pucker.

_____ 14. Her gum-popping got on my nerves.

# A Newspaper Index

An **index** is a listing in a book, magazine, or newspaper that tells where to find items or information.

Newspapers provide many kinds of information. You can read about national events, local news, the weather, and sports. You will also find opinions, feature stories, advice columns, comics, entertainment, recipes, advertisements, and more. A guide that tells you where to find different types of information in a newspaper is called a **newspaper index**. An index of the newspaper usually appears on the front page.

**Directions:** Use the newspaper index to answer the questions.

| | | | |
|---|---|---|---|
| Business | 8 | Local News | 5–7 |
| Classified Ads | 18–19 | National News | 1–4 |
| Comics | 20 | Radio-TV | 17 |
| Editorials | 9 | Sports | 11–13 |
| Entertainment | 14–16 | Weather | 10 |

1. Where would you look for results of last night's basketball games?
   Section: _____ Page(s) _____

2. Where would you find your favorite cartoon strip?
   Section: _____ Page(s) _____

3. Where would you find opinions of upcoming elections?
   Section: _____ Page(s) _____

4. Where would you look to locate a used bicycle to buy?
   Section: _____ Page(s) _____

5. Where would you find out if you need to wear your raincoat tomorrow?
   Section: _____ Page(s) _____

6. Where would you find the listing of tonight's TV shows?
   Section: _____ Page(s) _____

7. Which would be first, a story about the president's trip to Europe or a review of the newest movie? _____

# Help Wanted

**Directions:** Use the following "Help Wanted" ads to answer the questions.

**Baby-sitter.** Caring, responsible person needed to take care of 2 and 4 year old in our home. 25–30 hours per week. Must have own transportation. References required. Call 725-1342 after 7 p.m.

**Clerk/Typist.** Law firm seeks part-time help. Duties include typing, filing, and answering telephone. Monday–Friday, 1–6 p.m. Previous experience preferred. Apply in person.
1392 E. Long St.

**Driver for Disabled.** Van provided. Includes some evenings and Saturdays. No experience necessary. Call Mike at 769-1533.

**Head Nurse.** Join in the bloodmobile team at the American Red Cross. Full- and part-time positions available. Great benefits. Apply Monday thru Friday 9–4. 1495 N. State St.

**Teachers.** For new child-care program. Prefer degree in Early Childhood Development and previous experience. Must be non-smoker. Call 291-5555.

1. For which job would you have to work some evenings and Saturdays?

_____

2. Which job calls for a person who does not smoke?

_____

3. For which job would you have to have your own transportation?

_____

4. For which job must you apply in person?

_____

5. Which ad offers both part-time and full-time positions?

_____

Name _____

# Classified Ads

**Directions:** Write a classified ad for these topics. Include information about the item, a phone number and an eye-catching title.

1. An ad to wash cars

_____

_____

_____

2. An ad for free puppies

_____

_____

_____

3. An ad for something you would like to sell

_____

_____

_____

4. An ad to sell your house

_____

_____

_____

_____

# Cause and Effect

A **cause** is an event or reason which has an effect on something else.

**Example:**
The heavy rains produced flooding in Chicago.
Heavy rains were the **cause** of the flooding in Chicago.

An **effect** is an event that results from a cause.

**Example:**
Flooding in Chicago was due to the heavy rains.
Flooding was the **effect** caused by the heavy rains.

**Directions:** Read the paragraphs. Complete the charts by writing the missing cause (reason) or effect (result).

Club-footed toads are small toads that live in the rainforests of Central and South America. Because they give off a poisonous substance on their skins, other animals cannot eat them.

**Cause:**

They give off a poisonous substance.

**Effect:**

_____

Civets (siv its) are weasel-like animals. The best known of the civets is the mongoose, which eats rats and snakes. For this reason, it is welcome around homes in its native India.

**Cause:**

_____

**Effect:**

It is welcome around homes in its native India.

Bluebirds can be found in most areas of the United States. Like other members of the thrush family of birds, young bluebirds have speckled breasts. This makes them difficult to see and helps them hide from their enemies. The Pilgrims called them "blue robins" because they are much like the English robin. They are the same size and have the same red breast and friendly song as the English robin.

**Cause:**

Young bluebirds have speckled breasts.

_____

**Effect:**

_____

The Pilgrims called them "blue robins."

# "The Boy Who Cried Wolf"

**Directions:** Read the fable "The Boy Who Cried Wolf." Then complete the puzzle.

Once there was a shepherd boy who tended his sheep alone. Sheep are gentle animals. They are easy to take care of. The boy grew bored.

"I can't stand another minute alone with these sheep," he said crossly. He knew only one thing would bring people quickly to him. If he cried, "Wolf!" the men in the village would run up the mountain. They would come to help save the sheep from the wolf.

"Wolf!" he yelled loudly, and he blew on his horn.

Quick as a wink, a dozen men came running. When they realized it was a joke, they were very angry. The boy promised never to do it again. But a week later, he grew bored and cried, "Wolf!" again. Again, the men ran to him. This time they were very, very angry.

Soon afterwards, a wolf really came. The boy was scared. "Wolf!" he cried. "Wolf! Wolf! Wolf!"

He blew his horn, but no one came, and the wolf ate all his sheep.

**Across:**

2. This is where the boy tends sheep.

4. When no one came, the wolf _____ all the sheep.

5. Sheep are _____ and easy to take care of.

**Down:**

1. The people who come are from here.

2. At first, when the boy cries, "Wolf!" the _____ come running.

3. When a wolf really comes, this is how the boy feels.

Name _____

# "The Boy Who Cried Wolf"

**Directions:** Identify the underlined words as a cause or an effect.

1. <u>The boy cries wolf</u> because he is bored.          _____

2. <u>The boy blows his horn</u> and the men come running.     _____

3. No one comes, and <u>the wolf eats all the sheep</u>.        _____

**Directions:** Answer the questions.

4. Why did the shepherd boy blow his horn?

_____

_____

_____

5. Why were the men angry at the shepherd boy?     _____

_____

_____

_____

6. What lesson can be learned from this story?

_____

_____

_____

_____

_____

_____

# Facts and Opinions

**Directions:** Read the articles about cats. List the facts and opinions.

Cats make the best pets. Domestic or house cats were originally produced by crossbreeding several varieties of wild cats. They were used in ancient Egypt to catch rats and mice, which were overrunning bins of stored grain. Today they are still the most useful domestic animal.

**Facts:**

_____

_____

_____

**Opinions:**

_____

_____

It is bad luck for a black cat to cross your path. This is one of the many legends about cats. In ancient Egypt, for example, cats were considered sacred, and often were buried with their masters. During the Middle Ages, cats often were killed for taking part in what people thought were evil deeds. Certainly, cats sometimes do bring misfortune.

**Facts:**

_____

_____

_____

**Opinions:**

_____

_____

# Book Titles

All words in the title of a book are underlined. Underlined words also mean italics.

**Examples:**

The Hunt for Red October was a best-seller!
(The Hunt for Red October)

Have you read Lost in Space? (Lost in Space)

**Directions:** Underline the book titles in these sentences. The first one has been done for you.

1. The Dinosaur Poster Book is for eight year olds.

2. Have you read Lion Dancer by Kate Waters?

3. Baby Dinosaurs and Giant Dinosaurs were both written by Peter Dodson.

4. Have you heard of the book That's What Friends Are For by Carol Adorjan?

5. J.B. Stamper wrote a book called The Totally Terrific Valentine Party Book.

6. The teacher read Almost Ten and a Half aloud to our class.

7. Marrying Off Mom is about a girl who tries to get her widowed mother to start dating.

8. The Snow and The Fire are the second and third books by author Caroline Cooney.

9. The title sounds silly, but Goofbang Value Daze really is the name of a book!

10. A book about space exploration is The Day We Walked on the Moon by George Sullivan.

11. Alice and the Birthday Giant tells about a giant who came to a girl's birthday party.

12. A book about a girl who is sad about her father's death is called Rachel and the Upside Down Heart by Eileen Douglas.

13. Two books about baseball are Baseball Bloopers and Oddball Baseball.

14. Katharine Ross wrote Teenage Mutant Ninja Turtles: The Movie Storybook.

# Clouds

**Directions:** Read about clouds. Then answer the questions.

Have you ever wondered where clouds come from? Clouds are made from billions and billions of tiny water droplets in the air. The water droplets form into clouds when warm, moist air rises and is cooled.

Have you ever seen your breath when you were outside on a very cold day? Your breath is warm and moist. When it hits the cold air, it is cooled. A kind of small cloud is formed by your breath!

Clouds come in many sizes and shapes. On some days, clouds blanket the whole sky. Other times, clouds look like wispy puffs of smoke. There are other types of clouds as well.

Weather experts have named clouds. Big, fluffy clouds that look flat on the bottom are called **cumulus** clouds. **Stratocumulus** is the name for rounded clouds that are packed very close together. You can still see patches of sky, but stratocumulus clouds are thicker than cumulus ones.

If you spot **cumulonimbus** clouds, go inside. These clouds are wide at the bottom and have thin tops. The tops of these clouds are filled with ice crystals. On hot summer days, you may even have seen cumulonimbus clouds growing. They seem to boil and grow as though they are coming from a big pot. A violent thunderstorm usually occurs after you see these clouds. Often, there is hail.

Cumulus, stratocumulus, and cumulonimbus are only three of many types of clouds. If you listen closely, you will hear television weather forecasters talk about these and other clouds. Why? Because clouds are good indicators of weather.

1. How are clouds formed? _____

_____

2. How can you make your own cloud? _____

_____

3. What should you do when you spot cumulonimbus clouds?

_____

4. What often happens after you see cumulonimbus clouds? _____

_____

5. What kind of big fluffy clouds look flat on the bottom? _____

6. What kind of clouds are closely packed? _____

# Jonny's Story

**Directions:** Read the following true story about a little boy. Pay careful attention to the details. As you read, think about the beginning, middle, and end of the story.

Jonny got out of bed. It hurt for him to walk. He could hear his mother calling for him so he limped over to the top of the stairs.

"Jonny, hurry up. I have to get to work," his mom called from the kitchen. When 3 1/2-year-old Jonny didn't hurry down the stairs, his mother went to the door and called again. As she looked up, she noticed that he was moving very slowly. "I guess you will have to eat your breakfast at the sitter's house since we are running so late."

"Mom, my leg hurts," Jonny said. His mother bent down to take a look. Jonny's left ankle was slightly red and swollen.

"I'm sure it does hurt," his mother said as she lifted him up and sat him on the counter to get a closer look. "It feels warm, too. I should call the doctor and try to get an appointment for you today."

It was hard to leave him at the sitter's, but Jonny's mom knew she could call as soon as the doctor's office opened. She left him at the sitter's with an extra big hug and asked the sitter to call if Jonny got any worse.

The appointment was scheduled for later that afternoon. Jonny's mom picked him up from the sitter's and found that Jonny had slept most of the day. He also had a fever. "I'm glad you have an appointment for him at the doctor's," said the sitter.

133         **Summer Link Super Edition Grade 5**

# Jonny's Story

Jonny's mom sat in the busy waiting room as one patient after another was called in to see the doctor. The whole time she sat there, she held him. He slept the whole time. Usually, he was a very busy little boy, so his mom knew he must not be feeling well.

"With his high fever and that swollen ankle, he must have picked up an infection," said the doctor. "This prescription for an antibiotic should have him feeling much better and running around in no time!"

It was quite the opposite, Jonny's family soon discovered. The next morning, Jonny's mom stayed home from work because he was worse, not better. By late afternoon, his fever rose to 105 degrees! "Better bring him into the emergency room," said the doctor.

Jonny was admitted to the hospital and had test after test. Many doctors, some of them specialists, were called in, but no one had an answer. One doctor did have a guess. The pediatrician wondered aloud, "Do you suppose it could be JRA (juvenile rheumatoid arthritis)?"

More tests were done at another hospital, and the pediatrician's diagnosis was confirmed—Jonny did have JRA. This "little boy" is now 29 years old and still has rheumatoid arthritis. He has had many operations and has to take medicine every day for the pain, but he is able to lead a happy, normal life.

Name _____

# Sequencing

**Directions:** Reread the story, if necessary. Then choose an important event from the beginning, middle, and end of the story, and write it below.

Beginning: _____

_____

_____

Middle: _____

_____

_____

End: _____

_____

_____

_____

_____

**Directions:** Number these story events in the order in which they happened.

_____ Jonny's mom called the doctor to get an appointment since Jonny's ankle was red and swollen.

_____ Jonny limped to the top of the stairs.

_____ The pediatrician thought Jonny might have JRA.

_____ The sitter told Jonny's mom that he had slept most of the day.

_____ The doctor gave them a prescription for an antibiotic.

_____ Jonny is now 29 years old.

_____ Jonny told his mom, "My leg hurts."

# Recalling Details

**Directions:** Answer the questions below about "Jonny's Story."

1. How old was Jonny when his ankle began to bother him? _____

2. Why did Jonny's mom stay home from work the second day? _____
   _____

3. What do the letters JRA stand for? _____
   _____

4. When Jonny and his mom were waiting to see the doctor, how did Jonny's
   mom know he must not be feeling well? _____
   _____

5. Where did Jonny's mom take him when she picked him up at the sitter's
   house? _____

**Directions:** Write the letter of the definition beside the word it
defines. If you need help, use a dictionary, or check the
context of the story.

a. strong medicine used to treat infections
b. found to be true
c. doctor that specializes in child care
d. not yet an adult
e. did not walk correctly

_____ pediatrician

_____ antibiotic

_____ confirmed

_____ limped

_____ juvenile

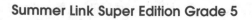

# Context Clues

When you read, you may confuse words that look alike. You can tell when you read a word incorrectly because it doesn't make sense. You can tell from the **context** (the other words in the sentence or the sentences before or after) what the word should be. These **context clues** can help you figure out the meaning of a word by relating it to other words in the sentence.

**Directions:** Circle the correct word for each sentence below. Use the context to help you.

1. We knew we were in trouble as soon as we heard the crash.

   The baseball had gone (through, thought) the picture window!

2. She was not able to answer my question because her (month, mouth) was full of pizza.

3. Asia is the largest continent in the (world, word).

4. I'm not sure I heard the teacher correctly. Did he say what I (through, thought) he said?

5. I was not with them on vacation so I don't know a (think, thing) about what happened.

6. My favorite (month, mouth) of the year is July because I love fireworks and parades!

7. You will do better on your book report if you (think, thing) about what you are going to say.

# Newspapers

**Directions:** Write the answers.

1. What is the name of your daily local newspaper?
   _____

2. List the sections included in your local newspaper.
   _____

3. What sections of the newspaper do you read on a regular basis?
   _____

4. Ask a parent which sections he or she reads on a regular basis.
   _____

5. Find the editorial section of your newspaper. An editorial is the opinion of one person. Write the main idea of one editorial. _____
   _____
   _____
   _____

6. If you could work at a newspaper, which job would you like? Why?
   _____
   _____
   _____

**Directions:** Read a copy of USA Today. You can find a copy in most libraries. Compare it to your local paper.

7. How are they alike? _____
   _____

8. How are they different? _____
   _____

# Desert Plants

**Directions:** Read the information about desert plants. Use context clues to determine the meaning of the bold words. Check the correct answers.

Desert plants have special features, or adaptations, that allow them to **survive** the harsh conditions of the desert. A cactus stores water in its tissues when it rains. It then uses this supply of water during the long dry season. The tiny needles on some kinds of **cacti** may number in the tens of thousands. These sharp thorns protect the cactus. They also form tiny shadows in the sunlight that help keep the plant from getting too hot.

Other plants are able to live by dropping their leaves. This cuts down on the **evaporation** of their water supply in the hot sun. Still other plants survive as seeds, protected from the sun and heat by tough seed coats. When it rains, the seeds **sprout** quickly, bloom, and produce more seeds that can **withstand** long dry spells.

Some plants spread their roots close to the Earth's surface to quickly gather water when it does rain. Other plants, such as the mesquite, have roots that grow 50 or 60 feet below the ground to reach underground water supplies.

1. Based on the other words in the sentence, what is the correct definition of **survive**?
   ____ continue to live
   ____ bloom in the desert
   ____ flower

2. Based on the other words in the sentence, what is the correct definition of **evaporation**?
   ____ water loss from heat
   ____ much-needed rainfall
   ____ boiling

3. Based on the other words in the sentence, what is the correct definition of **withstand**?
   ____ put up with
   ____ stand with another
   ____ take from

4. Based on the other words in the sentence, what is the correct definition of **cacti**?
   ____ a type of sand dune
   ____ more than one cactus
   ____ a caravan of camels

5. Based on the other words in the sentence, what is the correct definition of **sprout**?
   ____ a type of bean that grows only in the desert
   ____ begin to grow
   ____ a small flower

# Lizards

**Directions:** Read the information about lizards. Then answer the questions.

Lizards are reptiles, related to snakes, turtles, alligators, and crocodiles. Like other reptiles, lizards are cold-blooded. This means their body temperature changes with that of their surroundings. However, by changing their behavior throughout the day they can keep their temperature fairly constant.

Lizards are among the many animals that live in deserts. They usually come out of their burrows early in the morning. Most lizards lie in the sun to get warm before starting their daily activities. In mid-morning, they hunt for food. If it becomes too hot, lizards can raise their tails and bodies off the ground to help cool off. At mid-day, they return to their burrows or crawl under rocks for several hours. Late in the day, they again lie in the sun to absorb heat before the chilly desert night falls.

Like all animals, lizards have ways of protecting themselves. Some types of lizards have developed a most unusual defense. If a hawk or other animal grabs one of these lizards by its tail, the tail will break off. The tail will continue to wiggle around to distract the attacker while the lizard runs away. A month or two later, the lizard grows a new tail.

There are about 3,000 kinds of lizards, and all of them can bite, but only two types of lizards are poisonous: the Gila monster of the southwestern United States and the Mexican bearded lizard. Both are short-legged, thick-bodied reptiles with fat tails. These lizards do not attack people and will not bite them unless they are attacked.

1. What can a lizard do if it becomes too hot? _____

   _____

2. What is an unusual defense some lizards have developed to protect themselves?

   _____

3. What two types of lizards are poisonous? _____

   _____

# The Arctic Circle

**Directions:** Read the article about the Arctic Circle. Then answer the questions.

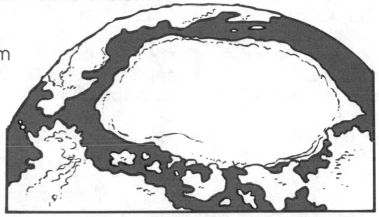

On the other side of the globe from Antarctica, at the northernmost part of the Earth, is another icy land. This is the Arctic Circle. It includes the North Pole itself and the northern fringes of three continents— Europe, Asia and North America, including the state of Alaska— as well as Greenland and other islands.

The seasons are opposite at the two ends of the Earth. When it is summer in Antarctica, it is winter in the Arctic Circle. In both places, there are very long periods of sunlight in summer and very long nights in the winter. On the poles themselves, there are six full months of sunlight and six full months of darkness each year.

Compared to Antarctica, the summers are surprisingly mild in some areas of the Arctic Circle. Much of the snow cover may melt, and temperatures often reach 50 degrees in July. Antarctica is covered by water—frozen water, of course—so nothing can grow there. Plant growth is limited in the polar regions not only by the cold, but also by wind, lack of water, and the long winter darkness.

In the far north, willow trees grow but only become a few inches high! The annual rings, the circles within the trunk of a tree that show its age and how fast it grows, are so narrow in those trees that you need a microscope to see them.

A permanently frozen layer of soil, called "permafrost," keeps roots from growing deep enough into the ground to anchor a plant. Even if a plant could survive the cold temperatures, it could not grow roots deep enough or strong enough to allow the plant to get very big.

1. What three continents have land included in the Arctic Circle?

   _____     _____     _____

2. Is the Arctic Circle generally warmer or colder than Antarctica?

   _____

3. What is "permafrost"?_____

4. Many tall pine trees grow in the Arctic Circle.          True          False

# News Services

**Directions:** Read the information about news services. Then answer the questions.

When people read daily newspapers, they expect to see current news from all over the world. Some newspapers have offices or reporters in Washington, D.C. and other major cities around the world. Most newspapers rely on news services for international news. News services are organizations that gather and sell news to papers, radio, and television stations. They are sometimes referred to as "wire services," because they originally sent stories over telegraph or Teletype lines, or "wires."

The two largest news services are the Associated Press and United Press International. Stories sent by these services have their initials—AP or UPI—at the beginning of the article. All large American newspapers are members of either the AP or UPI service.

At one time, people had to wait for messengers to arrive by foot, horse, or ship to learn the news. By the time it reached a newspaper, news could be months old.

Gathering news from around the world became much faster after the invention of the telegraph, Teletype, telephone, and transatlantic cable. Today, satellites, computers, and fax machines can send stories, pictures, and even videos around the world in seconds.

1. What is another name for news service organizations?

_____

2. What are the two largest news service organizations?

_____

3. What are three inventions that have speeded up worldwide news-gathering?

_____

_____

4. Why do newspapers use news services?

_____

5. How was news delivered before the invention of modern communication
   devices? _____

# Newspaper Jobs

**Directions:** Read the information about jobs at a newspaper. Then answer the questions.

It takes an army of people to put out one of the big daily newspapers. Three separate departments are needed to make a newspaper operate smoothly: editorial, mechanical, and business.

The editorial department is the one most people think about first. That is the news-gathering part of the newspaper. The most familiar job in this department is that of the reporter—the person who obtains information for a story and writes it. A photographer takes pictures to go along with the reporter's story.

Editors are the decision-makers. There are many editors at a large newspaper. They assign stories to reporters, read the stories to be certain they are correct and decide where and if the stories should appear in the paper. The most important stories go on the front page. There are also photo editors who choose which pictures will appear in the paper. Other workers in the editorial department include artists, copy editors, proofreaders and cartoonists.

The biggest job in the mechanical department is printing the paper. Most large newspapers have their own printing presses. Some small papers send their work to outside printing shops. After an issue, or edition, is printed, it is ready to be sold or "circulated" to the public.

Circulation of the paper is one of the jobs of the business department. This department also sells advertising space. This is very important for newspapers. Many papers make more money selling advertising space than selling newspapers. The business department also takes care of normal business jobs, like paying employees, paying bills and keeping records.

1. What are the three main departments at a newspaper?

    _____

2. Who gets the information for a story and writes it? _____

3. Who are the decision-makers at a newspaper? _____

4. What is the biggest job for the mechanical department?

    _____

5. What is the most important job of the business department?

    _____

# Valuable Stamps

Most people collect stamps as a hobby. They spend small sums of money to get the stamps they want, or they trade stamps with other collectors. They rarely make what could be considered "big money" from their philately hobby.

A few collectors are in the business of philately as opposed to the hobby. To the people who can afford it, some stamps are worth big money. For example, a U.S. airmail stamp with a face value of 24 cents when it was issued in 1918 is now worth more than $35,000 if a certain design appears on the stamp. Another stamp, the British Guiana, an ugly stamp that cost only a penny when it was issued, later sold for $280,000!

The Graf Zeppelin is another example of an ugly stamp that became valuable. Graf Zeppelin is the name of a type of airship, similar to what we now call a "blimp," invented around the turn of the century. Stamps were issued to mark the first roundtrip flight the Zeppelin made between two continents. A set of three of these stamps cost $4.55 when they were issued. The stamps were ugly and few of them sold. The postal service destroyed the rest. Now, because they are rare, each set of the Graf Zeppelin stamps is worth hundreds of dollars.

**Directions:** Answer these questions about valuable stamps.

1. What is the most valuable stamp described? _____

2. For how much did this stamp originally sell? _____

3. What did a collector later pay for it? _____

4. The Graf Zeppelin stamps originally sold for $4.55 for a set of

☐ four.          ☐ six.          ☐ three.

5. Which stamp did the postal service destroy because it didn't sell?

☐ British Guiana          ☐ Graf Zeppelin          ☐ British Zeppelin

# Chickens

Have you ever heard the expression "pecking order"? In the pecking order of a school, the principal is at the top of the order. Next comes the assistant principal, then the teachers and students.

In the pecking order of chickens, the most aggressive chicken is the leader. The leader is the hen that uses her beak most often to peck the chickens she bosses. These chickens, in turn, boss other chickens by pecking them, and so on. Chickens can peck all others who are "below" them in the pecking order. They never peck "above" themselves by pecking their bosses.

**Directions:** Answer these questions about chickens.

1. Put this pecking order of four chickens in order.

   _____ This chicken pecks numbers 3 and 4 but never 1.

   _____ No one pecks this chicken. She's the top boss.

   _____ This chicken can't peck anyone.

   _____ This chicken pecks chicken number 4.

2. Use context clues to figure out the definition of **aggressive**. _____

   _____

   _____

3. Who is at the top of the pecking order in a school? _____

   _____

# No Kidding About Goats

Goats are independent creatures. Unlike sheep, which move easily in herds, goats cannot be driven along by a goatherd. They must be moved one or two at a time. Moving a big herd of goats can take a long time, so goatherds must be patient people.

Both male and female goats can have horns, but some goats don't have them at all. Male goats have beards but females do not. Male goats also have thicker and shaggier coats than females. During breeding season, when goats mate to produce babies, male goats have a very strong smell.

Goats are kept in paddocks with high fences. The fences are high because goats are good jumpers. They like to nibble on hedges and on the tips of young trees. They can cause a lot of damage this way! That is why many farmers keep their goats in a paddock.

Baby goats are called "kids," and two or three at a time are born to the mother goat. Farmers usually begin to bottle-feed kids when they are a few days old. They milk the mother goat and keep the milk. Goat's milk is much easier to digest than cow's milk, and many people think it tastes delicious.

**Directions:** Answer these questions about goats.

1. Use context clues to choose the correct definition of **goatherd**.

   ☐ person who herds goats     ☐ goats in a herd     ☐ person who has heard of goats

2. Use context clues to choose the correct definition of **paddock**.

   ☐ pad     ☐ fence     ☐ pen

3. Use context clues to choose the correct definition of **nibble**.

   ☐ take small bites     ☐ take small drinks     ☐ take little sniffs

4. Use context clues to choose the correct definition of **delicious**.

   ☐ delicate     ☐ tasty     ☐ terrible

# "The Man and the Snake"

**Directions:** Read the fable "The Man and the Snake." Then, number the events In order.

Once, a kind man saw a snake in the road. It was winter and the poor snake was nearly frozen. The man began to walk away, but he could not.

"The snake is one of Earth's creatures, too," he said. He picked up the snake and put it in a sack. "I will take it home to warm up by my fire. Then I will set it free."

The man stopped for lunch at a village inn. He put his coat and his sack on a bench by the fireplace. He planned to sit nearby, but the inn was crowded, so he had to sit across the room.

He soon forgot about the snake. As he was eating his soup, he heard screams. Warmed by the fire, the snake had crawled from the bag. It hissed at the people near the fire.

The man jumped up and ran to the fireplace. "Is this how you repay the kindness of others?" he shouted.

He grabbed a stick used for stirring the fire and chased the snake out of the inn.

\_\_\_\_\_ The man puts his bag down by the fireplace.

\_\_\_\_\_ The man chases the snake.

\_\_\_\_\_ A kind man rescues the snake.

\_\_\_\_\_ The snake warms up and crawls out of the bag.

\_\_\_\_\_ The man plans to take the snake home.

\_\_\_\_\_ The man eats a bowl of soup.

\_\_\_\_\_ The snake hisses at people.

\_\_\_\_\_ A snake is nearly frozen in the road.

\_\_\_\_\_ The man grabs a stick from the fireplace.

# "The Sly Fox"

**Directions:** Read the legend "The Sly Fox." Then answer the questions.

One evening, Fox met Wolf in the forest. Wolf was in a terrible mood. He felt hungry, too. So he said to Fox, "Don't move! I'm going to eat you this minute."

As he spoke, Wolf backed Fox up against a tree. Fox realized she couldn't run away.

"I will have to use my wits instead of my legs," she thought to herself.

Aloud to Wolf, Fox said calmly, "I would have made a good dinner for you last year. But I've had three little babies since then. I spend all my time looking for food to feed them."

Before she could go on, Wolf interrupted. "I don't care how many children you have! I'm going to eat you right now." Wolf began closing in on Fox.

"Stop!" shouted Fox. "Look how skinny I am. I ran off all my fat looking for food for my children. But I know where you can find something that's good and fat!" Wolf backed off to listen.

"There's a well near here. In the bottom of it is a big fat piece of cheese. I don't like cheese, so it's of no use to me. Come, I'll show you."

Wolf trotted off after Fox, making sure she could not run away.

"See," said Fox when they got to the well.

Inside was what looked like a round yellow piece of cheese. It was really the moon's reflection, but Wolf didn't know this. Wolf leaned over the well, wondering how to get the cheese. Fox jumped up quickly and pushed Wolf in.

"I am a sly, old thing," Fox chuckled as she trotted home to her children. And to this day, that's why foxes are sly.

1.  What is the main idea of this legend? (Check one.)

    _____ Fox is cornered but uses her wits to outsmart Wolf and save her own life.

    _____ Wolf is in a terrible mood and wants to eat Fox.

    _____ Wolf thinks the moon was made of cheese.

2.  Why did Fox say she will not make a good meal for Wolf? _____

    _____

    _____

3.  What happens to Wolf at the end? _____

    _____

# "The Sly Fox"

**Directions:** Review the legend "The Sly Fox." Then, answer the questions.

1. What are three events in the story that show Wolf's bad mood?

_____

_____

_____

2. What does Fox say she will have to use to get away from Wolf?_____

3. Where does Fox tell Wolf he can find a nice fat meal? _____

_____

4. How does Fox finally rid herself of Wolf? _____

5. What does Fox say as she trots home? _____

6. Have you ever been in a situation where you used words to solve a problem instead of fighting with someone? Write about it.

_____

_____

_____

7. In addition to teaching why foxes are sly, what other lesson does this story teach?

_____

_____

_____

_____

_____

# "Grasshopper Green"

**Directions:** Read the poem "Grasshopper Green." Then answer the questions.

Grasshopper Green is a comical guy,
He lives on the best of fare.
Bright little trousers, jacket and cap,
These are his summer wear.

Out in the meadow he loves to go,
Playing away in the sun.
It's hopperty, skipperty, high and low,
Summer's the time for fun.

Grasshopper Green has a cute little house,
He stays near it every day.
It's under the hedge where he is safe,
Out of the gardener's way.

Gladly he's calling the children to play
Out in the beautiful sun
It's hopperty, skipperty, high and low,
Summer's the time for fun.

1. What does **comical** mean in this poem? _____

2. What are three things Grasshopper Green wears in the summer?

_____

3. Where does he love to go and play? _____

4. Whom does Grasshopper Green call to play? _____

5. What is summer the time for? _____

6. Use a dictionary. What does **fare** mean in this poem? _____

7. You won't find the words **hopperty** and **skipperty** in a dictionary. Based on the poem, write your own definitions of these words.

_____

# Oceans

If you looked at Earth from up in space, you would see a planet that is mostly blue. This is because more than two-thirds of Earth is covered with water. You already know that this is what makes our planet different from the others, and what makes life on Earth possible. Most of this water is in the four great oceans: Pacific, Atlantic, Indian, and Arctic. The Pacific is by far the largest and the deepest. It is more than twice as big as the Atlantic, the second largest ocean.

The water in the ocean is salty. This is because rivers are always pouring water into the oceans. Some of this water picks up salt from the rocks it flows over. It is not enough salt to make the rivers taste salty. But the salt in the oceans has been building up over millions of years. The oceans get more and more salty every century.

The ocean provides us with huge amounts of food, especially fish. There are many other things we get from the ocean, including sponges and pearls. The oceans are also great "highways" of the world. Ships are always crossing the oceans, transporting many goods from country to country.

The science of studying the ocean is called oceanography. Today, oceanographers have special equipment to help them learn about the oceans and seas. Electronic instruments can be sent deep below the surface to make measurements. The newest equipment uses sonar or echo-sounding systems that bounce sound waves off the sea bed and use the echoes to make pictures of the ocean floor.

**Directions:** Answer these questions about the oceans.

1. How much of the Earth is covered by water? _____

2. Which is the largest and deepest ocean? _____

3. What is the science of studying the ocean? _____

4. What new equipment do oceanographers use? _____

_____

# Your Five Senses

Your senses are very important to you. You depend on them every day. They tell you where you are and what is going on around you. Your senses are sight, hearing, touch, smell, and taste.

Try to imagine for a minute that you were suddenly unable to use your senses. Imagine, for instance, that you are in a cave and your only source of light is a candle. Without warning, a gust of wind blows out the flame.

Your senses are always at work. Your eyes let you read this book. Your nose brings the scent of dinner cooking. Your tongue helps you taste dinner later. Your hand feels the softness as you stroke a puppy. Your ears tell you that a storm is approaching.

Your senses also help keep you from harm. They warn you if you touch something that will burn you. They keep you from looking at a light that is too bright, and they tell you if a car is coming up behind you. Each of your senses collects information and sends it as a message to your brain. The brain is like the control center for your body. It sorts out the messages sent by your senses and acts on them.

**Directions:** Answer these questions about the five senses.

1. Circle the main idea:

   Your senses keep you from harm.

   Your senses are important to you in many ways.

2. Name the five senses.

   a. _____

   b. _____

   c. _____

   d. _____

   e. _____

3. Which part of your body acts as the "control center"?

   _____

Name_____

# Hearing

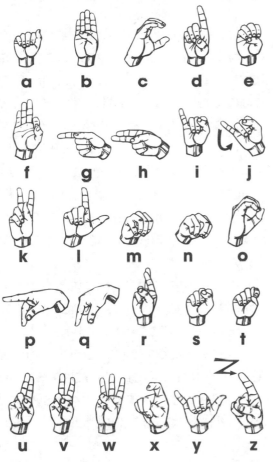

Every sound you hear is made by the movement of air. These movements, called vibrations, spread out in waves. Your outer ear collects these "sound waves" and sends them down a tube to the inner ear. The vibrations hit the eardrum, a flap of skin stretched across the inner end of the tube. As the eardrum vibrates, a tiny bone called the hammer moves back and forth. This helps the vibrations move to three small bones and then to the cochlea, where they are changed to nerve impulses. The impulses travel to the brain where they are recognized as sounds.

Some people have trouble hearing or cannot hear at all. This is called being deaf. Some deaf people can understand what you are saying by watching how your lips move. They use their eyes as their ears. Sometimes a hearing aid can help improve hearing. It is like a tiny radio that fits into the ear. Sounds enter the hearing aid and are made much louder.

Deaf people also have difficulty learning to speak because they cannot hear how to say words. Many deaf people "talk" by making pictures with their hands. This kind of talking is called sign language. Every letter of the alphabet has a sign. These signs are shown above.

**Directions:** Answer these questions about the sense of hearing.

1. Sound is made by movements of the air called _____ .

2. The flap of skin stretched over the inner end of the tube inside your ear is
   called the _____ .

3. People who cannot hear are said to be _____ .

4. The language of making pictures
   with your hands is called _____ .

5. Read this word in sign language.
   It says _____ .

# Taste

The senses of taste and smell work very closely together. If you can't smell your food, it is difficult to recognize the taste. You may have noticed this when you've had a bad cold with a stuffed-up nose.

Tasting is the work of your tongue. All over your tongue are tiny taste sensors called taste buds. If you look at your tongue in a mirror, you can see small groups of taste buds. They are what give your tongue its rough appearance. Each taste bud has a small opening in it. Tiny pieces of food and drink enter this opening. There taste sensors gather information about the taste and send messages to your brain. Your brain decides what the taste is.

Taste buds located in different areas of your tongue recognize different tastes. There are only four tastes your tongue can recognize: sweet, sour, bitter, and salty. All other flavors are a mixture of taste and smell.

**Directions:** Answer these questions about the sense of taste.

1. It is difficult to taste your food if you can't _____ .

2. The tiny taste sensors on your tongue are called _____ .

3. The four tastes that your tongue can recognize are _____

   _____ .

4. All other flavors are a mixture of _____ .

Name _____

# Deep-Sea Diving

One part of the world is still largely unexplored. It is the deep sea. Over the years, many people have explored the sea. But the first deep-sea divers wanted to find sunken treasure. They weren't really interested in studying the creatures or life there. Only recently have they begun to learn some of the mysteries of the sea.

It's not easy to explore the deep sea. A diver must have a way of breathing under water. He must be able to protect himself from the terrific pressure. The pressure of air is about 15 pounds on every square inch. But the pressure of water is about 1,300 pounds on every square inch!

The first diving suits were made of rubber. They had a helmet of brass with windows in it. The shoes were made of lead and weighed 20 pounds each! These suits let divers go down a few hundred feet, but they were no good for exploring very deep waters. With a metal diving suit, a diver could go down 700 feet. Metal suits were first used in the 1930s.

In 1937, a diver named William Beebe wanted to explore, deeper than anyone had ever gone before. He was not interested in finding treasure. He wanted to study deep-sea creatures and plants. He invented a hollow metal ball called the bathysphere. It weighed more than 5,000 pounds, but in it Beebe went down 3,028 feet. He saw many things that had never been seen by humans before.

**Directions:** Answer these questions about early deep-sea diving.

1. What were the first deep-sea divers interested in? _____

2. What are two problems that must be overcome in deep-sea diving?

    a. _____

    b. _____

3. How deep could a diver go wearing a metal suit? _____

4. Who was the deep-sea explorer who invented the bathysphere?

_____

# Dolphins and Porpoises

Dolphins and porpoises are members of the whale family. In fact, they are the most common whales. If they have pointed or "beaked" faces, they are dolphins. If they have short faces, they are porpoises. Sometimes large groups of more than 1,000 dolphins can be seen.

Dolphins and porpoises swim in a special way called "porpoising." They swim through the surface waters, diving down and then leaping up—sometimes into the air. As their heads come out of the water, they breathe in air. Dolphins are acrobatic swimmers, often spinning in the air as they leap.

Humans have always had a special relationship with dolphins. Stories dating back to the ancient Greeks talk about dolphins as friendly, helpful creatures. There have been reports over the years of people in trouble on the seas who have been rescued and helped by dolphins.

**Directions:** Answer these questions about dolphins and porpoises.

1. The small members of the
   whale family with the pointed faces are _____ .

2. Those members of the
   whale family with short faces are _____ .

3. What do you call the special
   way dolphins and porpoises swim? _____ .

4. Do dolphins breathe with lungs or gills? _____

5. How did ancient Greeks describe dolphins?_____

6. Where have dolphins been reported to help people?_____

# Giraffes

**Directions:** Read about giraffes. Then answer the questions.

Giraffes are tall, beautiful, and graceful animals that live in Africa. When they are grown, male giraffes are about 18 feet tall. Adult females are about 14 feet tall.

Giraffes are not fat animals, but because they are so big, they weigh a lot. The average male weighs 2,800 pounds. Females weigh about 400 pounds less. Giraffes reach their full height when they are four years old. They continue to gain weight until they are about eight years old.

If you have ever seen giraffes, you know their necks and legs are very long. They are not awkward, though! Giraffes can move very quickly. They like to jump over fences and streams. They do this gracefully. They do not trip over their long legs.

If they are frightened, they can run 35 miles an hour. When giraffes gallop, all four feet are sometimes off the ground! Usually, young and old giraffes pace along at about 10 miles an hour.

Giraffes are strong. They can use their back legs as weapons. A lion can run faster than a giraffe, but a giraffe can kill a lion with one quick kick from its back legs.

Giraffes do not look scary. Their long eyelashes make them look gentle. They usually have a curious look on their faces. Many people think they are cute. Do you?

1.  What is the weight of a full-grown male giraffe? _____

2.  What is the weight of an adult female? _____

3.  When does a giraffe run 35 miles an hour? _____

4.  What do giraffes use as weapons? _____

5.  For how long do giraffes continue to gain weight?

    _____

6.  When do giraffes reach their full height?

    _____

7.  Use a dictionary. What does **gallop** mean?

    _____

# A California Tribe

**Directions:** Read about the Yuma. Then answer the questions.

California was home to many Native Americans. The weather was warm, and food was plentiful. California was an ideal place to live.

One California tribe that made good use of the land was the Yuma. The Yuma farmed and gathered roots and berries. They harvested dozens of wild plants. They gathered acorns, ground them up, and used them in cooking. The Yuma mixed acorns with flour and water to make a kind of oatmeal. They fished in California's rich waters. They hunted deer and small game. The Yuma made the most of what Mother Nature offered.

The Yuma lived in huts. The roofs were made of dirt. The walls were made of grass. Some Yuma lived together in big round buildings made with poles and woven grasses. As many as 50 people lived in these large homes.

Like other tribes, the Yuma made crafts. Their woven baskets were especially beautiful. The women also wove cradles, hats, bowls and other useful items for the tribe.

When it was time to marry, a boy's parents chose a 15-year-old girl for him. The girl was a Yuma, too, but from another village. Except for the chief, each man took only one wife.

When a Yuma died, a big ceremony was held. The Yumas had great respect for death. After someone died, his or her name was never spoken again.

1.  What were two reasons why California was an ideal place to live?

    _____

2.  What did the Yuma use acorns for?_____

    _____

3.  What was a beautiful craft made by the Yuma?  _____

4.  How old was a Yuma bride?  _____

5.  What types of homes did the Yuma live in?  _____

6.  How did the Yuma feel about death?  _____

    _____

# The Yuma

**Directions:** Review what you read about the Yuma. Write the answers.

1. How did the Yuma make good use of the land?

   _____

   _____

2. How were the Yuma like the Pueblo people?_____

   _____

   _____

3. How were they different?_____

   _____

   _____

4. Why did the Yuma have homes different than those of the Pueblo tribes?

   _____

   _____

5. When it was time for a young Yuma man to marry, his parents selected a fifteen-year-old bride for him from another tribe. Do you think this is a good idea? Why or why not?

   _____

   _____

6. Why do you suppose the Yuma never spoke a person's name after he or she died?

   _____

   _____

7. Do you think this would be an easy thing to do? Explain your answer.

   _____

   _____

# "Over the Hills and Far Away"

**Directions:** Read "Over the Hills and Far Away." Then answer the questions.

Tom, Tom the piper's son,
Learned to play when he was one,
But the only tune that he could play
Was "Over the Hills and Far Away."

Now Tom with his pipe made such a noise
That he pleased the girls and he pleased the boys,
And they all danced when they heard him play
"Over the Hills and Far Away."

Tom played his pipe with such great skill,
Even pigs and dogs could not keep still.
The dogs would wag their tails and dance,
The pigs would oink and grunt and prance.

Yes, Tom could play, his music soared—
But soon the pigs and dogs got bored.
The children, too, thought it was wrong,
For Tom to play just one dull song.

1. How old is Tom when he learns to play? _____

2. What tune does Tom play? _____

   _____

3. What do the dogs do when Tom plays? _____

   _____

4. Why does everyone get tired of Tom's music? _____

   _____

5. What do the pigs do when Tom plays? _____

   _____

6. What instrument does Tom play? _____

# Helen Keller

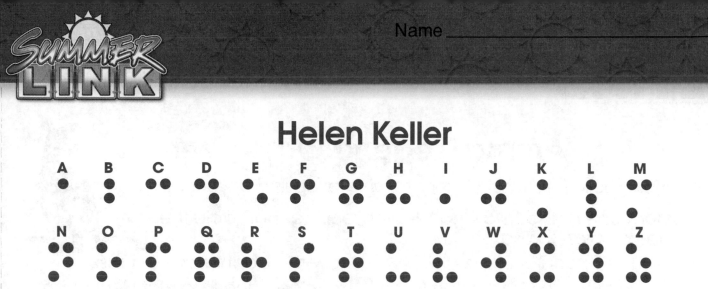

The story of Helen Keller has given courage and hope to many people. Helen had many problems, but she used her life to do great things.

When Helen Keller was a child, she often behaved in a wild way. She was very bright and strong, but she could not tell people what she was thinking or feeling. And she didn't know how others thought or felt. Helen was blind and deaf.

Helen was born with normal hearing and sight, but this changed when she was 1 year old. She had a serious illness with a very high fever. After that, Helen was never able to see or hear again.

As a child, Helen was angry and lonely. But when she was 6 years old, her parents got a teacher for her. They brought a young woman named Anne Sullivan to stay at their house and help Helen. After much hard work, Helen began to learn sign language. Anne taught Helen many important things, such as how to behave like other children. Because Helen was so smart, she learned things very quickly. She learned how to read Braille. By the time she was 8 years old, she was becoming very famous. People were amazed at what she could do.

Helen continued to learn. She even learned how to speak. When she was 20 years old, she went to college. Helen did so well in college that a magazine paid her to write the story of her life. After college, she earned money by writing and giving speeches. She traveled all around the world. She worked to get special schools and libraries for the blind and deaf. She wrote many books, including one about her teacher, Anne Sullivan.

Here is how "Helen" is written in Braille:

**Directions:** Answer these questions about Helen Keller.

1. What caused Helen to be blind and deaf? _____

   _____

2. What happy thing happened when Helen was 6 years old? _____

   _____

3. What was her teacher's name? _____

# Animal Legend Organizer

**Directions:** Follow the instructions to write a legend of your own.

1. Select one of the following titles for your legend. Circle the one you plan to use.

   How the Tiger Got Stripes      How the Elephant Got a Tusk

   How the Giraffe Got a Long Neck      How the Kangaroo Got Her Pouch

   How the Gazelle Got Twisty Horns      Why the Pig Has a Short Tail

   How the Elephant Got Big Ears      Why Birds Fly

   Why Rabbits Are Timid      How the Giraffe Got a Long Neck

   How the Mouse Got a Long Tail      Why Fish Swim

2. Briefly explain the type of conflict that will be in your legend. _____

   _____

   _____

3. Write words and phrases to show events you plan to include in your legend.

   _____

   _____

4. Summarize how you plan to settle the conflict or solve the problem. _____

   _____

   _____

**Directions:** Write your legend. Give it a title. Illustrate it if you like.

_____

_____

_____

_____

_____

_____

# Kanati's Son

A **legend** is a story or group of stories handed down through generations. Legends are usually about an actual person.

**Directions:** Read about Kanati's son. Then number the events in order.

This legend is told by a tribe called the Cherokee (chair-oh-key).

Long ago, soon after the world was made, a hunter and his wife lived on a big mountain with their son. The father's name was Kanati (kah-na-tee), which means "lucky hunter." The mother's name was Selu (see-loo), which means "corn." No one remembers the son's name.

The little boy used to play alone by the river each day. One day, elders of the tribe told the boy's parents they had heard two children playing. Since their boy was the only child around, the parents were puzzled. They told their son what the elders had said.

"I do have a playmate," the boy said. "He comes out of the water. He says he is the brother that mother threw in the river."

Then Selu knew what had happened.

"He is formed from the blood of the animals I washed in the river," she told Kanati. "After you kill them, I wash them in the river before I cook them."

Here is what Kanati told his boy: "Tomorrow when the other boy comes, wrestle with him. Hold him to the ground and call for us."

The boy did as his parents told him. When he called, they came running and grabbed the wild boy. They took him home and tried to tame him. The boy grew up with magic powers. The Cherokee called this "adawehi" (ad-da-we-hi). He was always getting into mischief! But he saved himself with his magic.

_____ Selu and Kanati try to tame the boy from the river.

_____ The little boy tells Selu and Kanati about the other boy.

_____ The little boy's parents are puzzled.

_____ The new boy grows up with magic powers.

_____ The elders tell Selu and Kanati they heard two children playing.

_____ The little boy wrestles his new playmate to the ground.

Summer Link Super Edition Grade 5

# "Hickory, Dickory, Dock"

**Directions:** Read the poem "Hickory, Dickory, Dock." Then answer the questions.

Hickory, dickory, dock,
The mouse ran up the clock.
The clock struck one,
And down he run,
Hickory, dickory, dock.

Dickory, dickory, dare,
The pig flew in the air.
The man in brown
Soon brought him down,
Dickory, dickory, dare.

*Hickory*
*Dickory*
*Dock*

1.    What is the main idea? (Check one.)

_____ Mice and pigs can cause a lot of problems
to clocks and men in brown suits.

_____ There is no main idea. This poem is just for fun.

_____ Beware of mice in your clocks and flying pigs.

2.    Why do you think the mouse runs down the clock? _____

_____

**Directions:** Number these events in order.

_____ The clock strikes one.

_____ The mouse runs back down the clock.

_____ The mouse runs up the clock.

_____ The man in brown brings the pig down.

_____ The pig flies in the air.

# "Mr. Nobody"

**Directions:** After reading the poem "Mr. Nobody," number in order the things people blame him for.

I know a funny little man
As quiet as a mouse,
Who does the mischief that is done
In everybody's house!
No one ever sees his face.
And yet we all agree
That every plate we break was cracked
By Mr. Nobody.

It's he who always tears out books,
Who leaves the door ajar,
He pulls the buttons from our shirts,
And scatters pins afar;
That squeaking door will always squeak,
The reason is, you see,
We leave the oiling to be done
By Mr. Nobody.

The finger marks upon the wall
By none of us are made;
We never leave the blinds unclosed
To let the carpet fade.
The bowl of soup we do not spill,
It's not our fault, you see
These mishaps—every one is caused
By Mr. Nobody.

_____ Putting finger marks on walls       _____ Scattering pins

_____ Leaving the door ajar               _____ Breaking plates

_____ Spilling soup                       _____ Pulling buttons off shirts

_____ Tearing out books                   _____ Squeaking doors

_____ Leaving the blinds open

# Recipes

**Sequencing** is putting items or events in logical order.

**Directions:** Read the recipe. Then number the steps in order for making brownies.

Preheat the oven to 350 degrees. Grease an 8-inch square baking dish.

In a mixing bowl, place two squares (2 ounces) of unsweetened chocolate and 1/3 cup butter. Place the bowl in a pan of hot water and heat it to melt the chocolate and the butter.

When the chocolate is melted, remove the pan from the heat. Add 1 cup sugar and two eggs to the melted chocolate and beat it. Next, stir in 3/4 cup sifted flour, 1/2 teaspoon baking powder and 1/2 teaspoon salt. Finally, mix in 1/2 cup chopped nuts.

Spread the mixture in the greased baking dish. Bake for 30 to 35 minutes. The brownies are done when a toothpick stuck in the center comes out clean. Let the brownies cool. Cut them into squares.

_____ Stick a toothpick in the center of the brownies to make sure they are done.

_____ Mix in chopped nuts.

_____ Melt chocolate and butter in a mixing bowl over a pan of hot water.

_____ Cool brownies and cut into squares.

_____ Beat in sugar and eggs.

_____ Spread mixture in a baking dish.

_____ Stir in flour, baking powder and salt.

_____ Bake for 30 to 35 minutes.

_____ Turn oven to 350 degrees and grease pan.

# Summarizing

A **summary** includes the main points from an article, book, or speech.

**Example:**
   Tomb robbing was an important business in ancient Egypt. Often entire families participated in the plunder of tombs. These robbers may have been laborers, officials, tomb architects, or guards, but they all probably had one thing in common. They were involved in the building or designing of the tomb or they wouldn't have had the knowledge necessary to successfully rob the burial sites. Not only did tomb robbing ensure a rich life for the robbers but it also enabled them to be buried with many riches themselves.

**Summary:**
   Tomb robbing occurred in ancient Egypt. The robbers stole riches to use in their present lives or in their burials. Tomb robbers usually had some part in the building or design of the tomb. This allowed them to find the burial rooms where the treasures were stored.

**Directions:** Read about life in ancient Egypt. Then write a three- to five-sentence summary.

   Egyptologists have learned much from the pyramids and mummies of ancient Egypt from the items left by grave robbers.
   Women of ancient Egypt wore makeup to enhance their features. Dark colored minerals called *kohl* were used as eyeliner and eye shadow. Men also wore eyeliner. Women used another mineral called *ocher* on their cheeks and lips to redden them. Henna, a plant which produces an orange dye, tinted the fingernails, the palms of their hands, and the soles of their feet.
   Perfume was also important in ancient Egypt. Small cones made of wax were worn on top of the head. These cones contained perfume oils. The sun slowly melted the wax, and the perfume would scent the hair, head, and shoulders.

_____

_____

_____

_____

_____

# Writing a Summary

**Directions:** Read the following selection. Then, write a summary of the selection.

## Man's First Flights

In the first few years of the 20th century, the majority of people strongly believed that man could not and would not ever be able to fly. There were a few daring individuals who worked to prove the public wrong.

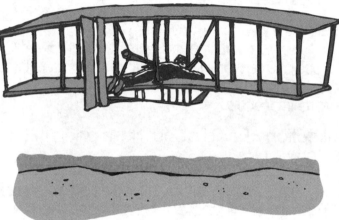

On December 8, 1903, Samuel Langley attempted to fly his version of an airplane from the roof of a houseboat on the Potomac River. Langley happened to be the secretary of the Smithsonian Institution, so his flight was covered not only by news reporters but also by government officials. Unfortunately, his trip met with sudden disaster when his aircraft did a nose dive into the river.

Nine days later, brothers Orville and Wilbur Wright attempted a flight. They had assembled their aircraft at their home in Dayton, Ohio, and shipped it to Kitty Hawk, North Carolina. On December 17, the Wright brothers made several flights, the longest one lasting an incredible 59 seconds. Since the Wright brothers had kept their flight attempts secret, their miraculous flight was only reported by two newspapers in the United States.

_____

_____

_____

_____

_____

_____

_____

# Using an Outline to Write an Essay

Outlines help you organize information and notes into a manageable form. Outlines also help you prepare to write reports and essays by keeping your thoughts in a logical order or sequence. Once you have a good outline, converting it to paragraph form is easy.

To convert an outline to an essay, add your own words to expand the words and phrases in the outline into sentence form. Information from the first main topic becomes the first paragraph.

    I. Painting the tree house
        A. Choose a color of paint
        B. Choose a kind of paint
            1. Cans of paint
            2. Spray paint

Information from the second and third main topics become the second and third paragraphs of the essay.

    II. Putting furniture in the tree house
        A. Tables
        B. Chairs
    III. Making a visitors' policy
        A. Who can visit?
            1. Friends
            2. Sisters and brothers
            3. Parents
        B. When can they visit?

To write an essay, remember to indent each paragraph, begin each paragraph with a topic sentence, and include supporting details.

**Directions:** Read the beginning of the essay. Then finish it on another sheet of paper using your own words and information from the outline.

### Finishing Touches

    Finishing a tree house takes a lot of thought and planning. First, it needs to be painted. The paint will help protect the wood from rain and snow. The best kind of paint for finishing the wood would be in cans. It would brush on easily, smoothly and quickly. Green would be a great color for the tree house because it would blend in with the green leaves of the trees.

# Making an Outline

An outline will help you organize your ideas before you begin writing your report.

    Title
  I. First Main Idea
    A. A supporting idea or fact
    B. Another supporting idea or fact
      1. An example or related fact
      2. An example or related fact
  II. Second Main Idea
    A. A supporting idea or fact
    B. Another supporting idea or fact
  III. Third Main Idea
    A. A supporting idea or fact
    B. Another supporting idea or fact

**Directions:** Use information from your notes to write an outline for your report. Follow the above format, but expand your outline to include as many main ideas, facts, and examples as necessary.

_____

_____

_____

_____

_____

_____

_____

_____

_____

# Building a Tree House

**Directions:** Study the sample outline for building a house. Then use words and phrases from the box to fill in the missing parts of the outline on how to build a tree house.

I. Find land
   A. On a hill
   B. By a lake
   C. In the city
II. Gather materials
   A. Buy wood
   B. Buy nails
   C. Buy tools
     1. Hammer
     2. Screwdriver
     3. Drill
     4. Saw
III. Build the house
   A. Who will use the tools?
   B. Who will carry the wood?

> Collect wood scraps
> Who will hold the boards?
> Who will use the hammer?
> Gather tools
> Can we climb it easily?
> Saw
> How will we get things off the ground?

I. Find a tree
   A. Is it sturdy?

   B. _____

II. Gather supplies
   A. _____

   B. _____

     1. Hammer and nails

     2. _____

III. Build the tree house
   A. _____

   B. _____

   C. _____

# Writing the Paper

**Directions:** Read more about writing a report. Then write your report.

Before you begin, be certain you clearly understand what is expected. How long should your report be? Must it be typed? Can it be written in pen? Should it be double-spaced?

Begin the first draft of your report with a general introduction of your topic. In the introduction, briefly mention the main points you will write about. One paragraph is usually enough to introduce your paper.

Next, comes the body of your report. Start a new paragraph for each main point. Include information that supports that point. If you are writing a long report, you may need to write a new paragraph for each supporting idea and/or each example. Follow your outline to be certain you cover all points. Depending on the number of words required to cover your topic, the body of the report will be anywhere from three or four paragraphs to several pages long.

In one or two concluding paragraphs, briefly summarize the main points you wrote about in the body of the report and state any conclusions you have drawn as a result of your research.

Once you finish the first draft, you will need to edit and rewrite your report to make it read smoothly and correct errors. You may need to rewrite your report more than once to make it the best it can be.

If possible, put the report aside for a day or two before you rewrite it so you can look at it with fresh eyes and a clear mind. Professional writers often write several drafts, so don't be discouraged about rewrites! Rewriting and editing are the keys to good writing—keys that every writer, no matter how old or experienced, relies on.

**Directions:** Circle the words in the puzzle related to writing a report.

```
K K N K T O P I C D T B
L D O B T T O D P T D O
I N T R O D U C T I O N
E N E R G D E E O O O N
D W S R G E Y C P C X R
S A F E A T T E I E Y O
R W A Q U B W P C D G F
L I C O N C L U S I O N
O U T L I N E U T T E D
R E S E A R C H R E S E
```

topic
facts
outline
introduction
body
conclusion
notes
research
edit

# Author's Purpose

Authors write to fulfill one of three purposes: to **inform**, to **entertain**, or to **persuade**.

Authors who write to inform are providing facts for the reader in an informational context. **Examples:** Encyclopedia entries and newspaper articles

Authors who write to entertain are hoping to provide enjoyment for the reader. **Examples:** Funny stories and comics

Authors who write to persuade are trying to convince the reader to believe as they believe. **Examples:** Editorials and opinion essays

**Directions:** Read each paragraph. Write **inform, entertain**, or **persuade** on the line to show the author's purpose.

1. The whooping crane is a migratory bird. At one time, this endangered bird was almost extinct. These large white cranes are characterized by red faces and trumpeting calls. Through protection of both the birds and their habitats, the whooping crane is slowly increasing in number.

_____

2. It is extremely important that all citizens place bird feeders in their yards and keep them full for the winter. Birds that spend the winter in this area are in danger of starving due to lack of food. It is every citizen's responsibility to ensure the survival of the birds.

_____

3. Imagine being able to hibernate like a bear each winter! Wouldn't it be great to eat to your heart's content all fall? Then, sometime in late November, inform your teacher that you will not be attending school for the next few months because you'll be resting and living off your fat? Now, that would be the life!

_____

4. Bears, woodchucks and chipmunks are not the only animals that hibernate. The queen bumblebee also hibernates in winter. All the other bees die before winter arrives. The queen hibernates under leaves in a small hole. She is cold-blooded and therefore is able to survive slightly frozen.

_____

# Alliterative Poetry

**Alliteration** is the repetition of a consonant sound in a group of words.

**Example:** Barney Bear bounced a ball.

Alliterative story poems can be fun to read and write. Any of several rhyming patterns can be used. Possibilities include:
   Every two lines rhyme.
   Every other line rhymes.
   The first line rhymes with the last line and the two middle lines rhyme with
      each other.
   All four lines rhyme.

**Example:**
   Thomas Tuttle tries to dine,
   On turkey, tea and treats so fine.
   Thomas eats tomatoes and tortellini,
   He devours tuna and tettrazini.

   When tempting tidbits fill the table,
   Thomas tastes as much as he is able,
   He stuffs himself from top to toes,
   Where he puts it, goodness knows!

**Directions:** Write an alliterative story poem using any rhyming pattern listed above. Your poem should be at least four lines long.

_____

_____

_____

_____

_____

_____

_____

# Haiku

**Haiku** is a form of unrhymed Japanese poetry. A haiku poem has only three lines. Each line has a specific number of syllables.

Haiku poems usually describe a season or something in nature. Sometimes haiku are written about feelings.

**The Haiku pattern:**
Line 1 — 5 syllables
Line 2 — 7 syllables
Line 3 — 5 syllables

**Example haiku:**
Winter snow slides from
The eave. Drops—plop—on my head,
As I walk under.                — *D.S. Underwood*

When writing haiku you do not count words per line. Count only the number of syllables.

**Directions:** To prepare for writing your poem, think of words about a snowy day. Write them on the lines. After each word, write the number of syllables in the word.

<u>frosty     (2)</u>     <u>white  (1)</u>   <u>snowflakes (2)</u>

_____     _____   _____

_____     _____   _____

_____     _____   _____

When writing any type of poetry, it is a good idea to start on scrap paper so you can write, erase, cross out, and rewrite.

**Directions:** Write a haiku poem about a snowy day on scrap paper. When you are satisfied with your poem, rewrite it below. At the end of each line, write the number of syllables in the line.

_____     _____

_____     _____

_____     _____

**Directions:** Select one of the topics in the box. Prewrite your poem on scrap paper. Write it on good paper when you are satisfied with it.

| | | | |
|---|---|---|---|
| rainy day | summer | spring | fall |
| a sparrow | joy | sadness | friendship |

# Tankas

Haiku poems are given to friends as gifts. A **tanka** is a poem written in response to haiku. If a person receives a haiku, he or she is supposed to send a tanka in reply! A tanka is much like a haiku but has two more lines.

**The tanka pattern:**
Line 1 — 5 syllables
Line 2 — 7 syllables
Line 3 — 5 syllables
Line 4 — 7 syllables
Line 5 — 7 syllables

**Example tanka:**
The snow on your head
It did plop—slop and slide down
Your neck to your socks.
The winter wind blew, gave you
A chill, now you sneeze—Ah choo!
— *D.S. Underwood*

Remember to count syllables per line.

**Directions:** Write a tanka in response to one of the two haiku poems you wrote. Prewrite on scrap paper. When you are satisfied with your tanka, rewrite it below. At the end of each line, write the number of syllables in the line.

_____   \_\_\_\_\_

_____   \_\_\_\_\_

_____   \_\_\_\_\_

_____

_____

**Directions:** Trade your haiku with a partner. Write a tanka in response to your partner's haiku.

_____

_____

_____

_____

_____

# Commands, Requests, and Exclamations

A **command** is a sentence that orders someone to do something. It ends with a period or an exclamation mark (!).

A **request** is a sentence that asks someone to do something. It ends with a period or a question mark (?).

An **exclamation** is a sentence that shows strong feeling. It ends with an exclamation mark (!).

**Examples:**
    **Command:**    Stay in your seat.
    **Request:**      Would you please pass the salt?
                      Please pass the salt.
    **Exclamation:**  Call the police!

In the first and last two sentences in the examples, the subject is not stated. The subject is understood to be **you**.

**Directions:** Write **C** if the sentence is a command, **R** if it is a request, and **E** if it is an exclamation. Put the correct punctuation at the end of each sentence.

_____ 1. Look both ways before you cross the street

_____ 2. Please go to the store and buy some bread for us

_____ 3. The house is on fire

_____ 4. Would you hand me the glue

_____ 5. Don't step there

_____ 6. Write your name at the top of the page

_____ 7. Please close the door

_____ 8. Would you answer the phone

_____ 9. Watch out

_____ 10. Take one card from each pile

# Run-On Sentences

A **run-on sentence** occurs when two or more sentences are joined together without the correct punctuation. A run-on sentence must be divided into two or more separate sentences.

**Example:**

**Run-on:** On Tuesday my family went to the amusement park but unfortunately it rained and we got wet and it took hours for our clothes to dry.

**Correct:** On Tuesday, my family went to the amusement park. Unfortunately, it rained and we got wet. It took hours for our clothes to dry.

**Directions:** Rewrite these run-on sentences correctly.

1. I have a dog named Boxer and a cat named Phoebe and they are both well-behaved and friendly.

_____

_____

2. Jacob's basketball coach makes the team run for 20 minutes each practice and then he makes them play a full game and afterwards he makes them do 50 push-ups and 100 sit-ups.

_____

_____

_____

3. My family members each enjoy different hobbies Mom likes to paint Dad likes to read I like to play sports and my younger sister likes to build model airplanes although I think they are too hard.

_____

_____

_____

_____

# Writing: Topic Sentences

The topic sentence in a paragraph usually comes first. Sometimes, however, the topic sentence can come at the end or even in the middle of a paragraph. When looking for the topic sentence, try to find the one that tells the main idea of a paragraph.

**Directions:** Read the following paragraphs and underline the topic sentence in each.

The maple tree sheds its leaves every year. The oak and elm trees shed their leaves, too. Every autumn, the leaves on these trees begin changing color. Then, as the leaves gradually begin to die, they fall from the trees. Trees that shed their leaves annually are called deciduous trees.

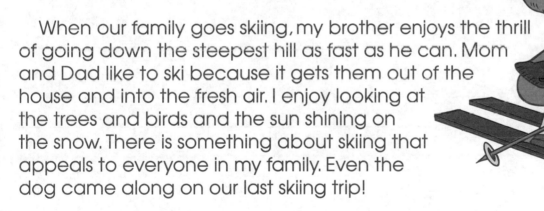

When our family goes skiing, my brother enjoys the thrill of going down the steepest hill as fast as he can. Mom and Dad like to ski because it gets them out of the house and into the fresh air. I enjoy looking at the trees and birds and the sun shining on the snow. There is something about skiing that appeals to everyone in my family. Even the dog came along on our last skiing trip!

If you are outdoors at night and there is traffic around, you should always wear bright clothing so that cars can see you. White is a good color to wear at night. If you are riding a bicycle, be sure it has plenty of reflectors, and if possible, headlamps as well. Be especially careful when crossing the street, because sometimes drivers cannot see you in the glare of their headlights. Being outdoors at night can be dangerous, and it is best to be prepared!

# Four Kinds of Sentences

**Directions:** For each pair of words, write two kinds of sentences (any combination of question, command, statement, or exclamation). Use one or both words in each sentence. Name each kind of sentence you wrote.

**Example:** pump     crop

Question: <u>What kind of crops did you plant</u>?

Command:  <u>Pump the water as fast as you can</u>.

> exclamation
> question
> command
> statement

1. pinch    health

_____ : _____
_____ : _____

2. fond    fact

_____ : _____
_____ : _____

3. insist    hatch

_____ : _____
_____ : _____

exclamation    command    statement    question

# Glossary of Reading and Language Arts Terms

**adjective:** a describing word that tells more about a noun

**adverb:** tells when, where, or how about the verb of a sentence

**antonym:** words with opposite, or nearly opposite, meanings

**articles:** any one of the words *a, an,* or *the* used to modify a noun

**autobiography:** a written account of your life

**base word (also called root word):** the word left after you take off a prefix or a suffix

**character:** a person, animal, or object that a story is about

**climax:** the most thrilling part of the story where the problem will or will not be solved

**compound word:** a word formed by two or more words

**conclusion:** a final decision about something, or the part of a story that tells what happens to the characters

**conjunction:** words that join other words, phrases, and sentences

**contraction:** shortened forms of two words often using an apostrophe to show where letters are missing

**dialogue:** a conversation between two or more people

**digraph:** two consonants pronounced as one sound

**diphthongs:** two vowels together that make a new sound

**fact:** something known to be true

**fiction:** stories that are made up

**homophone:** a word with the same pronunciation as another, but with a different meaning, and often a different spelling, such as *son–sun*

**idiom:** a figure of speech or phrase that means something different than what the words actually say, such as "He changed his bad habits and *turned over a new leaf*"

**inference:** an educated guess

**metaphor:** a direct comparison that does not use *like* or *as*

**mood:** the atmosphere one gets from strong, descriptive language

**nonfiction:** stories that are true

**noun:** a word that names a person, place, or thing

**opinion:** a belief based on what a person thinks instead of what is known to be true

**plot:** explains the events in a story that create a problem

**plural:** a form of a word that names or refers to more than one person or thing

**point of view:** the attitude a person has about a particular topic

**prefix:** a part that is added to the beginning of a word that changes the word's meaning

**preposition:** a word that comes before a noun or pronoun, showing the relationship of that noun or pronoun to another word in the sentence

**pronoun:** a word that is used in place of a noun

**proofreading:** reading to find and correct errors

**punctuation:** the marks that qualify sentences, such as a period, comma, question mark, exclamation point, and apostrophe

**reading strategies:** main idea, supporting details, context clues, fact/opinion

**resolution:** tells how the characters solve the story problem

**setting:** the place and time that a story happens

**simile:** a comparison using *like* or *as*

**suffix:** a part added to the end of a word to change the word's meaning

**synonym:** words that mean the same, or almost the same, thing

**theme:** a message or central idea of the story

**verb:** a word that can show action

**verb tense:** tells whether the action is happening in the past, present, or future

## Page 101

### Verbs

A **verb** tells what something does or that something exists.

**Examples:**
Tim **has shared** his apples with us.
Those apples **were** delicious.
I hope Tim **is bringing** more apples tomorrow.
Tim **picked** the apples himself.

**Directions:** Underline the verbs.

1. Gene moved here from Philadelphia.
2. Now he is living in a house on my street.
3. His house is three houses away from mine.
4. I have lived in this house all my life.
5. I hope Gene will like this town.
6. I am helping Gene with his room.
7. He has a lot of stuff!
8. We are painting his walls green.
9. He picked the color himself.
10. I wonder what his parents will say.

**Directions:** Write verbs to complete these sentences.

11. We ______ some paintbrushes.
12. Gene already ______ the paint.
13. I ______ thes.
14. Ther ______ no furniture in his room right now.
15. It ______ several hours to paint his whole room.

Answers will vary.

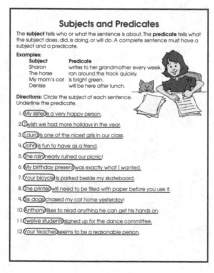

## Page 102

### Verb Tense

Not only do verbs tell the action of a sentence but they also tell when the action takes place. This is called the **verb tense**. There are three verb tenses: past, present, and future tense.

**Present-tense verbs** tell what is happening now.

**Example:** Jane **spells** words with long vowel sounds.

**Past-tense verbs** tell about action that has already happened. Past-tense verbs are usually formed by adding **ed** to the verb.

**Example:** stay — stayed. John **stayed** home yesterday.

Past-tense verbs can also be made by adding helping verbs **was** or **were** before the verb and adding **ing** to the verb.

**Example:** talk — was talking. Sally **was talking** to her mom.

**Future-tense verbs** tell what will happen in the future. Future-tense verbs are made by putting the word **will** before the verb.

**Example:** paint — will paint. Susie and Sherry **will paint** the house.

**Directions:** Read the following verbs. Write whether the verb tense is past, present, or future.

| Verb | Tense | Verb | Tense |
|---|---|---|---|
| 1. watches | present | 8. writes | present |
| 2. wanted | past | 9. vaulted | past |
| 3. will eat | future | 10. were sleeping | past |
| 4. was squawking | past | 11. will sing | future |
| 5. yawns | present | 12. is speaking | present |
| 6. crawled | past | 13. will cook | future |
| 7. will hunt | future | 14. likes | present |

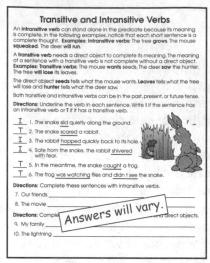

## Page 103

### Transitive and Intransitive Verbs

An **intransitive verb** can stand alone in the predicate because its meaning is complete. In the following examples, notice that each short sentence is a complete thought. **Examples: Intransitive verbs:** The tree **grows**. The mouse **squeaked**. The deer **will run**.

A **transitive verb** needs a direct object to complete its meaning. The meaning of a sentence with a transitive verb is not complete without a direct object. **Examples: Transitive verbs:** The mouse **wants** seeds. The deer **saw** the hunter. The tree **will lose** its leaves.

The direct object **seeds** tells what the mouse wants. **Leaves** tells what the tree will lose and **hunter** tells what the deer saw.

Both transitive and intransitive verbs can be in the past, present, or future tense.

**Directions:** Underline the verb in each sentence. Write **I** if the sentence has an intransitive verb or **T** if it has a transitive verb.

I 1. The snake slid quietly along the ground.
T 2. The snake scared a rabbit.
I 3. The rabbit hopped quickly back to its hole.
I 4. Safe from the snake, the rabbit shivered with fear.
T 5. In the meantime, the snake caught a frog.
T 6. The frog was watching flies and didn t see the snake.

**Directions:** Complete these sentences with intransitive verbs.

7. Our friends ______
8. The movie ______

**Directions:** Comple ... direct objects.

9. My family ______
10. The lightning ______

Answers will vary.

## Page 104

### Subjects and Predicates

The **subject** tells who or what the sentence is about. The **predicate** tells what the subject does, did, is doing, or will do. A complete sentence must have a subject and a predicate.

**Examples:**

| Subject | Predicate |
|---|---|
| Sharon | writes to her grandmother every week. |
| The horse | ran around the track quickly. |
| My mom's car | is bright green. |
| Denise | will be here after lunch. |

**Directions:** Circle the subject of each sentence. Underline the predicate.

1. My sister is a very happy person.
2. I wish we had more holidays in the year.
3. Laura is one of the nicest girls in our class.
4. John is fun to have as a friend.
5. The rain nearly ruined our picnic!
6. My birthday present was exactly what I wanted.
7. Your bicycle is parked beside my skateboard.
8. The printer will need to be filled with paper before you use it.
9. Six dogs chased my cat home yesterday!
10. Anthony likes to read anything he can get his hands on.
11. Twelve students signed up for the dance committee.
12. Your teacher seems to be a reasonable person.

## Page 105

### Compound Subjects and Predicates

**Directions:** Circle the subjects.

1. Everyone felt the day had been a great success.
2. Christina and Andrea were both happy to take the day off.
3. No one really understood why he was crying.
4. Mr. Winston, Ms. Fuller, and Ms. Landers took us on a field trip.

**Directions:** Underline the predicates.

5. Who can tell what will happen tomorrow?
6. Mark was a carpenter by trade and a talented painter, too.
7. The animals yelped and whined in their cages.
8. Airplane rides made her feel sick to her stomach.

**Directions:** Combine the sentences to make one sentence with a compound subject.

9. Elizabeth ate everything in sight. George ate everything in sight.
Elizabeth and George ate everything in sight.
10. Wishing something will happen won t make it so. Dreaming something will happen won t make it so.
Wishing and dreaming something will happen won't make it so.

**Directions:** Combine the sentences to make one sentence with a compound predicate.

11. I jumped for joy. I hugged all my friends.
I jumped for joy and hugged all my friends.
12. She ran around the track before the race. She warmed up before the race.
She ran around the track and warmed up before the race.

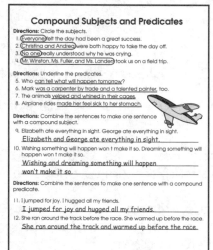

## Page 106

### Compound Subjects and Predicates

A **compound subject** has two or more nouns or pronouns joined by a conjunction. Compound subjects share the same predicate.

**Examples:**
**Suki and Spot** walked to the park in the rain.
**Cars, buses and trucks** splashed water on them.
**He and I** were glad we had our umbrella.

A **compound predicate** has two or more verbs joined by a conjunction. Compound predicates share the same subject.

**Examples:**
Suki **went** in the restroom **and wiped** off her shoes.
Paula **followed** Suki **and waited** for her.

A sentence can have a compound subject and a compound predicate.

**Example: Tina and Maria went** to the mall **and shopped** for an hour.

**Directions:** Circle the compound subjects. Underline the compound predicates.

1. Steve and Jerry went to the store and bought some gum.
2. Police and firefighters worked together and put out the fire.
3. Karen and Marsha did their homework and checked it twice.
4. In preschool, the boys and girls drew pictures and colored them.

**Directions:** Write compound subjects to go with these predicates.

5. ______ ate peanut butter sandwiches.
6. ______ left early.
7. ______ pets.
8. ______ me.
9. ______ Denver.

**Directions:** ... to go with these subjects.

10. A scary ______
11. My friend ______
12. The shadow ______
13. The wind ______
14. The runaway car ______

Answers will vary.

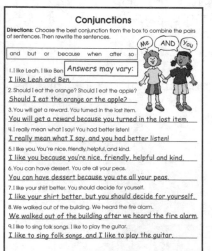

## Page 107

### Conjunctions

**Directions:** Choose the best conjunction from the box to combine the pairs of sentences. Then rewrite the sentences.

| and | but | or | because | when | after | so |
|---|---|---|---|---|---|---|

Answers may vary:

1. I like Leah. I like Ben.
I like Leah and Ben.
2. Should I eat the orange? Should I eat the apple?
Should I eat the orange or the apple?
3. You will get a reward. You turned in the lost item.
You will get a reward because you turned in the lost item.
4. I really mean what I say! You had better listen!
I really mean what I say, and you had better listen!
5. I like you. You're nice, friendly, helpful, and kind.
I like you because you're nice, friendly, helpful and kind.
6. You can have dessert. You ate all your peas.
You can have dessert because you ate all your peas.
7. I like your shirt better. You should decide for yourself.
I like your shirt better, but you should decide for yourself.
8. We walked out of the building. We heard the fire alarm.
We walked out of the building after we heard the fire alarm.
9. I like to sing folk songs. I like to play the guitar.
I like to sing folk songs, and I like to play the guitar.

## Page 108

### Capitalization and Punctuation

**Directions:** Rewrite the paragraphs below, adding punctuation where it is needed. Capitalize the first word of each sentence and all other words that should be capitalized.

most countries have laws that control advertising in norway no ads at all are allowed on radio or TV in the united states ads for alcoholic drinks, except beer and wine, are not permitted on radio or TV england has a law against advertising cigarettes on TV what do you think about these laws should they be even stricter

Most countries have laws that control advertising. In Norway, no ads at all are allowed on radio or TV. In the United States, ads for alcoholic drinks, except beer and wine, are not permitted on radio or TV. England has a law against advertising cigarettes on TV. What do you think about these laws? Should they be even stricter?

my cousin jeff is starting college this fall he wants to be a medical doctor, so he's going to central university the mayor of our town went there mayor stevens told jeff all about the university our town is so small that everyone knows what everyone else is doing is your town like that

My cousin, Jeff, is starting college this fall. He wants to be a medical doctor, so he's going to Central University. The mayor of our town went there. Mayor Stevens told Jeff all about the university. Our town is so small that everyone knows what everyone else is doing. Is your town like that?

my grandparents took a long vacation last year grandma really likes to go to the atlantic ocean and watch the dolphins my grandfather likes to fish in the ocean my aunt went with them last summer they all had a party on the fourth of july

My grandparents took a long vacation last year. Grandma really likes to go to the Atlantic Ocean and watch the dolphins. My grandfather likes to fish in the ocean. My aunt went with them last summer. They all had a party on the Fourth of July.

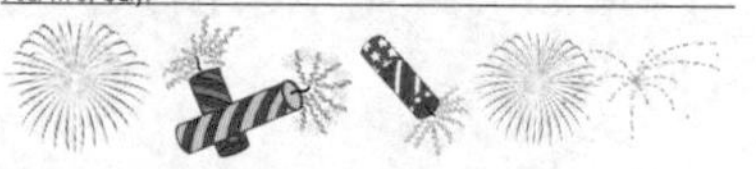

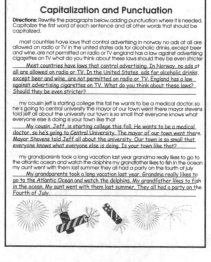

## Page 109

### Commas

**Commas** are used to separate items in a series.
Both examples below are correct. A final comma is optional.

**Examples:**
The fruit bowl contains oranges, peaches, pears, and apples.
The fruit bowl contains oranges, peaches, pears and apples.

Commas are also used to separate geographical names and dates.

**Examples:**
Today's date is January 13, 2000.
My grandfather lives in Tallahassee, Florida.
I would like to visit Paris, France.

**Directions:** Place commas where needed in these sentences.

1. I was born on September 21,1992.
2. John's favorite sports include basketball, football, hockey and soccer.
3. The ship will sail on November 16, 2004.
4. My family and I vacationed in Salt Lake City, Utah.
5. I like to plant beans, beets, corn and radishes in my garden.
6. Sandy's party will be held in Youngstown, Ohio.
7. Periods, commas, colons and exclamation marks are types of punctuation.
8. Cardinals, juncos, blue jays, finches and sparrows frequent our birdfeeder.
9. My grandfather graduated from high school on June 4, 1962.
10. The race will take place in Burlington, Vermont.

**Directions:** Write a sentence using commas to separate words in a series.

11. ______

**Directions:** Write a sentence using ... geographical names.

12. ______

**Directions:** Write a ... commas to separate dates.

13. ______

Sentences will vary.

## Page 110

### Plurals

Some words in the English language do not follow any of the plural rules discussed earlier. These words may not change at all from singular to plural, or they may completely change spellings.

| No Change Examples: | | Complete Change Examples: | |
|---|---|---|---|
| Singular | Plural | Singular | Plural |
| deer | deer | goose | geese |
| pants | pants | ox | oxen |
| scissors | scissors | man | men |
| moose | moose | child | children |
| sheep | sheep | leaf | leaves |

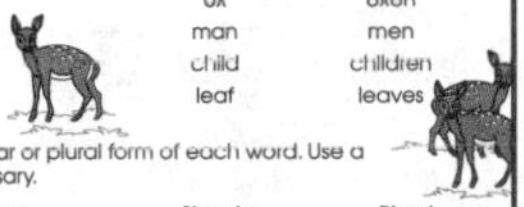

**Directions:** Write the singular or plural form of each word. Use a dictionary to help if necessary.

| Singular | Plural | Singular | Plural |
|---|---|---|---|
| 1. moose | moose | 6. leaf | leaves |
| 2. woman | women | 7. sheep | sheep |
| 3. deer | deer | 8. scissors | scissors |
| 4. child | children | 9. tooth | teeth |
| 5. hoof | hooves | 10. wharf | wharves or wharfs |

**Directions:** Write four sentences of your own using two singular and two plural words from above.

Sentences will vary.

## Page 111

### Synonyms and Antonyms

**Directions:** Use the words in the box to write a synonym for each word below. Write it next to the **S.** Next to the **A.** write an antonym. The first one is done for you.

| | | | | | |
|---|---|---|---|---|---|
| appear | proud | merry | straight | repair | plain |
| under | melted | unnecessary | late | new | smooth |
| embarrassed | gloomy | bent | break | fancy | above |
| icy | valuable | immediate | old | bumpy | vanish |

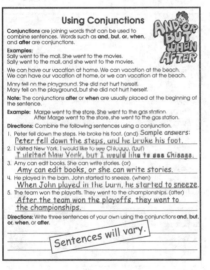

5. important S: valuable A: unnecessary
10. beneath S: under A: above
1. crooked S: bent A: straight
6. ashamed S: embarrassed A: proud
11. disappear S: vanish A: appear
2. frozen S: icy A: melted
7. cheerful S: merry A: gloomy
12. ancient S: old A: new
3. instant S: immediate A: late
8. elegant S: fancy A: plain
4. damage S: break A: repair
9. rough S: bumpy A: smooth

## Page 112

### Analogies

An **analogy** indicates how different items go together or are similar in some way.

**Examples:**
**Petal** is to **flower** as **leaf** is to **tree**.
**Book** is to **library** as **food** is to **grocery**.

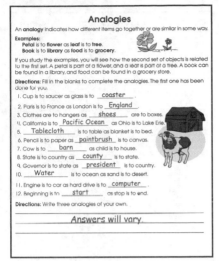

If you study the examples, you will see how the second set of objects is related to the first set. A petal is part of a flower, and a leaf is part of a tree. A book can be found in a library, and food can be found in a grocery store.

**Directions:** Fill in the blanks to complete the analogies. The first one has been done for you.

1. Cup is to saucer as glass is to coaster.
2. Paris is to France as London is to England.
3. Clothes are to hangers as shoes are to boxes.
4. California is to Pacific Ocean as Ohio is to Lake Erie.
5. Tablecloth is to table as blanket is to bed.
6. Pencil is to paper as paintbrush is to canvas.
7. Cow is to barn as child is to house.
8. State is to country as county is to state.
9. Governor is to state as president is to country.
10. Water is to ocean as sand is to desert.
11. Engine is to car as hard drive is to computer.
12. Beginning is to start as stop is to end.

**Directions:** Write three analogies of your own.

Answers will vary.

## Page 113

### Synonym and Antonym Analogies

**Analogies** are a way of comparing items to show how they are related. Analogies can show different types of relationships. Two relationships analogies might show are synonyms or antonyms.

**Examples:**
**Antonyms:** hot is to cold as happy is to sad
**Synonyms:** happy is to glad as run is to jog

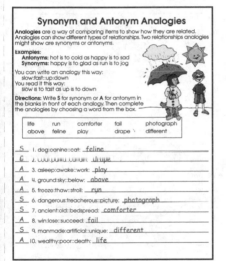

You can write an analogy this way:
slow:fast::up:down
You read it this way:
slow is to fast as up is to down

**Directions:** Write **S** for synonym or **A** for antonym in the blanks in front of each analogy. Then complete the analogies by choosing a word from the box.

| | | | | |
|---|---|---|---|---|
| life | run | comforter | fail | photograph |
| above | feline | play | drape | different |

S 1. dog:canine::cat: feline
S 2. couch:sofa::curtain: drape
A 3. asleep:awake::work: play
A 4. ground:sky::below: above
A 5. freeze:thaw::stroll: run
S 6. dangerous:treacherous::picture: photograph
S 7. ancient:old::bedspread: comforter
A 8. win:lose::succeed: fail
S 9. manmade:artificial::unique: different
A 10. wealthy:poor::death: life

## Page 114

### Using Conjunctions

**Conjunctions** are joining words that can be used to combine sentences. Words such as **and**, **but**, **or**, **when**, and **after** are conjunctions.

**Examples:**
Sally went to the mall. She went to the movies.
Sally went to the mall, and she went to the movies.

We can have our vacation at home. We can vacation at the beach.
We can have our vacation at home, or we can vacation at the beach.

Mary fell on the playground. She did not hurt herself.
Mary fell on the playground, but she did not hurt herself.

**Note:** The conjunctions **after** or **when** are usually placed at the beginning of the sentence.

**Example:** Marge went to the store. She went to the gas station.
After Marge went to the store, she went to the gas station.

**Directions:** Combine the following sentences using a conjunction.

1. Peter fell down the steps. He broke his foot. (and) Sample answers:
Peter fell down the steps, and he broke his foot.
2. I visited New York. I would like to see Chicago. (but)
I visited New York, but I would like to see Chicago.
3. Amy can edit books. She can write stories. (or)
Amy can edit books, or she can write stories.
4. He played in the barn. John started to sneeze. (when)
When John played in the barn, he started to sneeze.
5. The team won the playoffs. They went to the championships. (after)
After the team won the playoffs, they went to the championships.

**Directions:** Write three sentences of your own using the conjunctions **and**, **but**, **or**, **when**, or **after**.

Sentences will vary.

## Page 115

### Proofreading Practice

**Directions:** Circle the six spelling and pronoun mistakes in each paragraph. Write the words correctly on the lines below.

Jenna always braged about being ready to meet any chalenge or reach any gole. When it was time for our class to elekt new officers, Jenna said we should voat for her to be president.

bragged, challenge, goal, elect, its, vote

Simon wanted to be ours president, too. He tried to coax everyone to vote for his. He even owned kids money to get their votes! Well, Jenna may have too much pryde in herself, but I like her in spit of that. At least she didn't try to buy our votes!

our, coax, him, loaned, pride, spite

Its true that Jenna tried other ways to get us to vote for her. She scrubed the chalkboards even though it was my dayly job for that week. One day, I saw her rinseing out the paintbrushes when it was Peter's turn to do it. Then she made sure we knew about her good deeds so we would praize her.

It's, her, scrubbed, daily, rinsing, praise

We held the election, but I was shalked when the teacher releesed the results. Simon won! I wondered if he cheeted somehow. I feel like our class was robed. Now Simon is the one who's braging about how great he is. I wish he knew the tite of president doesn't mean anything if no one wants to be around you!

shocked, released, cheated, robbed, bragging, title

## Page 116

### Check Your Proofreading Skills

**Directions:** Read about the things you should remember when you are revising your writing. Then follow the instructions to revise the paper below.

After you have finished writing your rough draft, you should reread it later to determine what changes you need to make to ensure it's the best possible paper you are capable of writing.

Check yourself by asking the following questions:
**Does my paper stick to the topic?**
**Have I left out any important details?**
**Can I make the writing more lively?**
**Have I made errors in spelling, punctuation or capitalization?**
**Is there any information that should be left out?**

**Directions:** Revise the following story by making changes to correct spelling, punctuation, and capitalization; add details; and cross out words or sentences that do not stick to the topic.

**Hunting for Treasure** Answers may vary.

No one really believes me when I tell them that I'm a ~~tresure~~ treasure hunter. But, really, I am. It isn't just any treasure that I like to hunt, though. I like treasures related to coins. Usually, when I go treasure ~~huting~~ hunting, I go alone. ~~I always wear my blue coat.~~

One day, my good friend Jesse wanted to come with me. "Why would you want to do that?" I said. "Because I like coins, too," he replied. What Jesse did not know was that the coins that I dig ~~to find~~ are not the coins that just anyone collects. The coins I like are special. They are coins that have been buried in dirt for years!

## Page 117

### Taking Notes

**Taking notes** effectively can help you in many ways with schoolwork. It will help you better understand and remember what you read and hear. It will also help you keep track of important facts needed for reports, essays, and tests.

Each person develops his or her own way of taking notes. While developing your style, keep in mind the following:

- Write notes in short phrases instead of whole sentences.
- Abbreviate words to save time.
  **Examples: pres** for **president** or **&** for **and**
- If you use the same name often in your notes, use initials.
  **Examples: GW** for **George Washington; AL** for **Abraham Lincoln**
- Be brief, but make sure you understand what you write.
- Number your notes, so you can understand where each note starts and stops.
- When taking notes from a long article or book, write down one or two important points per paragraph or chapter.

**Directions:** Reread the story "Hunting for Treasure" on page 116. As you read the story, fill in the note-taking format below with your notes.

Title of Article or Story: Hunting for Treasure

Important Points

Paragraph 1

Paragraph 2

Answers will vary.

## Page 118

### Doing Research

**Directions:** Read about how to do research for a report and answer the questions.

Before starting your report, locate the most likely places to find relevant information for your research. Ask the librarian for help if necessary. A good report will be based on at least three or four sources, so it's important to find references that provide varied information.

Is the topic a standard one, such as a report on the skeletal system? A general encyclopedia, such as *World Book*, is a good place to begin your research. Remember to use the encyclopedia's index to find related entries. For related entries on the skeletal system, you could check the index for entries on bones, health, and the musculo-skeletal system. The index entry will show which encyclopedia number and pages to read to find information related to each entry topic.

Does your report require current statistics and/or facts? *Facts on File* and *Editorial Research Reports* are two sources for statistics. Ask the librarian to direct you to more specialized reference sources, such as *The People's Almanac* or *The New Grove Dictionary of Music and Musicians* which are related specifically to your topic.

For current magazine articles, see the *Reader's Guide to Periodical Literature*, which lists the names and page numbers of magazine articles related to a variety of topics. If you need geographical information about a country, check an atlas such as the *Rand McNally Contemporary World Atlas*.

1. How many reference sources should you consult before writing your report? 3–4
2. What are two references that provide statistics and facts? *Facts on File*, *Editorial Research Reports*
3. Where will you find a listing of magazine articles? *Reader's Guide to Periodical Literature*
4. Where should you look for geographical information? *Rand McNally Contemporary World Atlas*
5. If you're stumped or don't know where to begin, who can help? the librarian

## Page 119

### Taking Notes

**Directions:** Read about taking notes for your report. Use the "index card" below to write a sample note from one of your reference sources.

When gathering information for a report, it is necessary to take notes. You'll need to take notes when you read encyclopedia entries, books, and magazine or newspaper articles related to your topic.

Before you begin gathering information for a report, organize your thoughts around the who, what, when, where, why, and how questions of your topic. This organized approach will help direct you to the references that best answer these questions. It will also help you select and write in your notes only useful information.

There are different ways of taking notes. Some people use notebook paper. If you write on notebook paper, put a heading on each page. Write only notes related to each heading on specific pages. Otherwise, your notes will be disorganized, and it will be difficult to begin writing your paper.

Many people prefer to put their notes on index cards. Index cards can be easily sorted and organized when you begin writing your report and are helpful when preparing an outline. If you use index cards for your notes, put one fact on each card.

Take several notes from each reference source you use. Having too many notes is better than not having enough information when you start to write your report.

*Answers will vary.*

## Page 120

### Taking Notes

A **biography** is a written report of a person's life. It is based on facts and actual events. To prepare to write a biographical essay, you could look up information about the person in an encyclopedia.

**Directions:** Select one of the people listed below. Read about that person in an encyclopedia. Take notes to prepare for writing a biographical essay. Then use your notes to answer the questions.

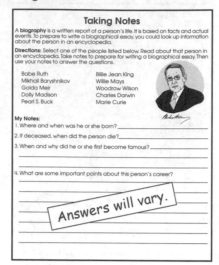

Babe Ruth
Mikhail Baryshnikov
Golda Meir
Dolly Madison
Pearl S. Buck

Billie Jean King
Willie Mays
Woodrow Wilson
Charles Darwin
Marie Curie

**My Notes:**

1. Where and when was he or she born? _____
2. If deceased, when did the person die? _____
3. When and why did he or she first become famous? _____
4. What are some important points about this person's career? _____

*Answers will vary.*

## Page 121

### From Grapes to Raisins

**Directions:** Use a piece of paper to cover up the story about how grapes become raisins. Then read the questions.

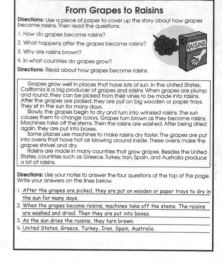

1. How do grapes become raisins?
2. What happens after the grapes become raisins?
3. Why are raisins brown?
4. In what countries do grapes grow?

**Directions:** Read about how grapes become raisins.

Grapes grow well in places that have lots of sun. In the United States, California is a big producer of grapes and raisins. When grapes are plump and round, they can be picked from their vines to be made into raisins. After the grapes are picked, they are put on big wooden or paper trays. They sit in the sun for many days.

Slowly, the grapes begin to dry and turn into wrinkled raisins. The sun causes them to change colors. Grapes turn brown as they become raisins. Machines take off the stems. Then the raisins are washed. After being dried again, they are put into boxes.

Some places use machines to make raisins dry faster. The grapes are put into ovens that have hot air blowing around inside. These ovens make the grapes shrivel and dry.

Raisins are made in many countries that grow grapes. Besides the United States, countries such as Greece, Turkey, Iran, Spain, and Australia produce a lot of raisins.

**Directions:** Use your notes to answer the four questions at the top of the page. Write your answers on the lines below.

1. After the grapes are picked, they are put on wooden or paper trays to dry in the sun for many days.
2. When the grapes become raisins, machines take off the stems. The raisins are washed and dried. Then they are put into boxes.
3. As the sun dries the raisins, they turn brown.
4. United States, Greece, Turkey, Iran, Spain, Australia

## Page 122

### Fact or Opinion?

**Directions:** Read the paragraphs below. Then, in the corresponding numbered blanks, write whether each numbered sentence is a fact or an opinion.

(1) An important rule for stamp collectors to follow is never to handle stamps with their fingers. (2) Instead, to keep the stamps clean, collectors use stamp tongs to pick up stamps. (3) Stamps are stored by being placed on mounts. (4) Stamp mounts are plastic holders that fit around the stamp and keep it clean. (5) The backs of the mounts are sticky, so they can be stuck onto a stamp album page. (6) What a great idea!

(7) The stamps are mounted in stamp albums that have either white or black pages. (8) Some people prefer black pages, claiming that the stamps "show" better. (9) Some people prefer white pages, claiming that they give the album a cleaner look. (10) I think this foolish bickering over page colors is ridiculous!

1. fact
2. fact
3. fact
4. fact
5. fact
6. opinion
7. fact
8. opinion
9. opinion
10. opinion

## Page 123

### The Five Senses

**Directions:** Before each sentence, write the sense—hearing, sight, smell, taste, or touch—that is being used. The first one is done for you.

| | |
|---|---|
| hearing | 1. The rooster crows outside my window early each morning. |
| touch | 2. After playing in the snow, our fingers and toes were freezing. |
| hearing | 3. I could hear sirens in the distance. |
| sight | 4. I think this tree is taller than that one. |
| taste | 5. The delicious salad was filled with fresh, juicy fruits. |
| smell | 6. The odor of the bread baking in the oven was wonderful. |
| sight | 7. There was a rainbow in the sky today. |
| touch | 8. The kitten was soft and fluffy. |
| smell | 9. Her perfume filled the air when she walked by. |
| sight | 10. An airplane wrote a message in the sky. |
| taste | 11. The chocolate cake was yummy. |
| hearing | 12. The steamboat whistle frightened the baby. |
| taste | 13. The sour lemon made my lips pucker. |
| hearing | 14. Her gum-popping got on my nerves. |

## Page 124

### A Newspaper Index

An **index** is a listing in a book, magazine, or newspaper that tells where to find items or information.

Newspapers provide many kinds of information. You can read about national events, local news, the weather, and sports. You will also find opinions, feature stories, advice columns, comics, entertainment, recipes, advertisements, and more. A guide that tells you where to find different types of information in a newspaper is called a **newspaper index**. An index of the newspaper usually appears on the front page.

**Directions:** Use the newspaper index to answer the questions.

| | | | |
|---|---|---|---|
| Business | 8 | Local News | 5—7 |
| Classified Ads | 18—19 | National News | 1—4 |
| Comics | 20 | Radio-TV | 17 |
| Editorials | 9 | Sports | 11—13 |
| Entertainment | 14—16 | Weather | 10 |

1. Where would you look for results of last night's basketball games?
   Section: **Sports**          Page(s) **11-13**
2. Where would you find your favorite cartoon strip?
   Section: **Comics**          Page(s) **20**
3. Where would you find opinions of upcoming elections?
   Section: **Editorials**          Page(s) **9**
4. Where would you look to locate a used bicycle to buy?
   Section: **Classified Ads**          Page(s) **18-19**
5. Where would you find out if you need to wear your raincoat tomorrow?
   Section: **Weather**          Page(s) **10**
6. Where would you find the listing of tonight's TV shows?
   Section: **Radio-TV**          Page(s) **17**
7. Which would be first, a story about the president's trip to Europe or a review of the newest movie? **the president's trip to Europe**

## Page 125

### Help Wanted

**Directions:** Use the following "Help Wanted" ads to answer the questions.

**Baby-sitter.** Caring, responsible person needed to take care of 2 and 4 year old in our home. 25—30 hours per week. Must have own transportation. References required. Call 725-1342 after 7 p.m.

**Clerk/Typist.** Law firm seeks part-time help. Duties include typing, filing, and answering telephone. Monday–Friday, 1—6 p.m. Previous experience preferred. Apply in person. 1392 E. Long St.

**Driver for Disabled.** Van provided. Includes some evenings and Saturdays. No experience necessary. Call Mike at 769-1533.

**Head Nurse.** Join in the bloodmobile team at the American Red Cross. Full- and part-time positions available. Great benefits. Apply Monday thru Friday 9—4. 1495 N. State St.

**Teachers.** For new child-care program. Prefer degree in Early Childhood Development and previous experience. Must be non-smoker. Call 291-5555.

1. For which job would you have to work some evenings and Saturdays?
   Driver for Disabled
2. Which job calls for a person who does not smoke?
   Teacher
3. For which job would you have to have your own transportation?
   Baby-sitter
4. For which job must you apply in person?
   Clerk/Typist
5. Which ad offers both part-time and full-time positions?
   Head Nurse

## Page 126

### Classified Ads

**Directions:** Write a classified ad for these topics. Include information about the item, a phone number and an eye-catching title.

1. An ad to wash cars

2. An ad for free puppies

3. An ad for something you would like to sell

4. An ad to sell your house

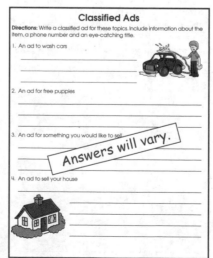

*Answers will vary.*

## Page 127

### Cause and Effect

A **cause** is an event or reason which has an effect on something else.

**Example:**
The heavy rains produced flooding in Chicago.
Heavy rains were the **cause** of the flooding in Chicago.

An **effect** is an event that results from a cause.

**Example:**
Flooding in Chicago was due to the heavy rains.
Flooding was the **effect** caused by the heavy rains.

**Directions:** Read the paragraphs. Complete the charts by writing the missing cause (reason) or effect (result).

Club-footed toads are small toads that live in the rainforests of Central and South America. Because they give off a poisonous substance on their skins, other animals cannot eat them.

| Cause: | Effect: |
|---|---|
| They give off a poisonous substance. | Other animals cannot eat them. |

Civets (siv its) are weasel-like animals. The best known of the civets is the mongoose, which eats rats and snakes. For this reason, it is welcome around homes in its native India.

| Cause: | Effect: |
|---|---|
| They eat rats and snakes. | It is welcome around homes in its native India. |

Bluebirds can be found in most areas of the United States. Like other members of the thrush family of birds, young bluebirds have speckled breasts. This makes them difficult to see and helps them hide from their enemies. The Pilgrims called them "blue robins" because they are much like the English robin. They are the same size and have the same red breast and friendly song as the English robin.

| Cause: | Effect: |
|---|---|
| Young bluebirds have speckled breasts. | It helps them hide from enemies. |
| They are like the English robin. | The Pilgrims called them "blue robins." |

## Page 128

### "The Boy Who Cried Wolf"

**Directions:** Read the fable "The Boy Who Cried Wolf." Then complete the puzzle.

Once there was a shepherd boy who tended his sheep alone. Sheep are gentle animals. They are easy to take care of. The boy grew bored.

"I can't stand another minute alone with these sheep," he said crossly. He knew only one thing would bring people quickly to him. If he cried, "Wolf!" the men in the village would run up the mountain. They would come to help save the sheep from the wolf.

"Wolf!" he yelled loudly, and he blew on his horn.

Quick as a wink, a dozen men came running. When they realized it was a joke, they were very angry. The boy promised never to do it again. But a week later, he grew bored and cried, "Wolf!" again. Again, the men ran to him. This time they were very, very angry.

Soon afterwards, a wolf really came. The boy was scared. "Wolf!" he cried. Wolf! Wolf! Wolf!"

He blew his horn, but no one came, and the wolf ate all his sheep.

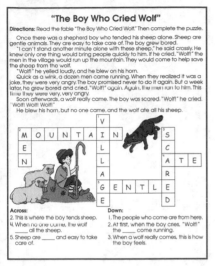

Crossword puzzle:
- M O U N T A I N (with V-I-L-L-A-G-E down, S-C-A-T-E)
- M E N
- G E N T L E

**Across:**
2. This is where the boy tends sheep.
4. When no one comes, the wolf _____ all the sheep.
5. Sheep are _____ and easy to take care of.

**Down:**
1. The people who come are from here.
2. At first, when the boy cries, "Wolf!" the _____ come running.
3. When a wolf really comes, this is how the boy feels.

## Page 129

### "The Boy Who Cried Wolf"

**Directions:** Identify the underlined words as a cause or an effect.

1. The boy cries wolf because he is bored. _____ effect
2. The boy blows his horn and the men come running. _____ effect
3. No one comes, and the wolf eats all the sheep. _____ effect

**Directions:** Answer the questions.

4. What lesson can be learned from this story?
   Sample answer:
   Always tell the truth.

5. How is this story like the two other fables you read?

6. Is the boy in the story more like the fox or _____?

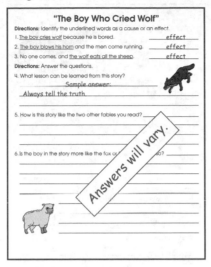

*Answers will vary.*

## Page 130

### Facts and Opinions

**Directions:** Read the articles about cats. List the facts and opinions.

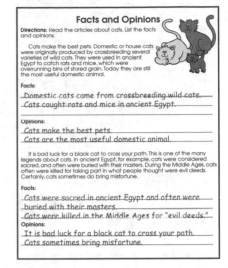

Cats make the best pets. Domestic or house cats were originally produced by crossbreeding several varieties of wild cats. They were used in ancient Egypt to catch rats and mice, which were overrunning bins of stored grain. Today they are still the most useful domestic animal.

**Facts:**
Domestic cats came from crossbreeding wild cats.
Cats caught rats and mice in ancient Egypt.

**Opinions:**
Cats make the best pets.
Cats are the most useful domestic animal.

It is bad luck for a black cat to cross your path. This is one of the many legends about cats. In ancient Egypt, for example, cats were considered sacred, and often were buried with their masters. During the Middle Ages, cats often were killed for taking part in what people thought were evil deeds. Certainly, cats sometimes do bring misfortune.

**Facts:**
Cats were sacred in ancient Egypt and often were buried with their masters.
Cats were killed in the Middle Ages for "evil deeds."

**Opinions:**
It is bad luck for a black cat to cross your path.
Cats sometimes bring misfortune.

## Page 131

### Book Titles

All words in the title of a book are underlined. Underlined words also mean italics.

**Examples:**
The Hunt for Red October was a best-seller!
(The Hunt for Red October)
Have you read Lost in Space? (Lost in Space)

**Directions:** Underline the book titles in these sentences. The first one has been done for you.

1. The Dinosaur Poster Book is for eight year olds.
2. Have you read Lion Dancer by Kate Waters?
3. Baby Dinosaurs and Giant Dinosaurs were both written by Peter Dodson.
4. Have you heard of the book That's What Friends Are For by Carol Adorjan?
5. J.B. Stamper wrote a book called The Totally Terrific Valentine Party Book.
6. The teacher read Almost Ten and a Half aloud to our class.
7. Marrying Off Mom is about a girl who tries to get her widowed mother to start dating.
8. The Snow and The Fire are the second and third books by author Caroline Cooney.
9. The title sounds silly, but Goofbang Value Daze really is the name of a book!
10. A book about space exploration is The Day We Walked on the Moon by George Sullivan.
11. Alice and the Birthday Giant tells about a giant who came to a girl's birthday party.
12. A book about a girl who is sad about her father's death is called Rachel and the Upside Down Heart by Eileen Douglas.
13. Two books about baseball are Baseball Bloopers and Oddball Baseball.
14. Katharine Ross wrote Teenage Mutant Ninja Turtles: The Movie Storybook.

## Page 132

### Clouds

**Directions:** Read about clouds. Then answer the questions.

Have you ever wondered where clouds come from? Clouds are made from billions and billions of tiny water droplets in the air. The water droplets form into clouds when warm, moist air rises and is cooled.

Have you ever seen your breath when you were outside on a very cold day? Your breath is warm and moist. When it hits the cold air, it is cooled. A kind of small cloud is formed by your breath!

Clouds come in many sizes and shapes. On some days, clouds blanket the whole sky. Other times, clouds look like wispy puffs of smoke. There are other types of clouds as well.

Weather experts have named clouds. Big, fluffy clouds that look flat on the bottom are called cumulus clouds. Stratocumulus is the name for rounded clouds that are packed very close together. You can still see patches of sky, but stratocumulus clouds are thicker than cumulus ones.

If you spot cumulonimbus clouds, go inside. These clouds are wide at the bottom and have thin tops. The tops of these clouds are filled with ice crystals. On hot summer days, you may even have seen cumulonimbus clouds growing. They seem to boil and grow as though they are coming from a big pot. A violent thunderstorm usually occurs after you see these clouds. Often, there is hail.

Cumulus, stratocumulus and cumulonimbus are only three of many types of clouds. If you listen closely, you will hear television weather forecasters talk about these and other clouds. Why? Because clouds are good indications of weather.

1. How are clouds formed? Water droplets in the air form clouds when warm, moist air rises and cools.

2. How can you make your own cloud? by breathing outside on a cold day

3. What should you do when you spot cumulonimbus clouds?
   go inside

4. What often happens after you see cumulonimbus clouds?
   violent thunderstorms, sometimes hail

5. What kind of big fluffy clouds look flat on the bottom? cumulus

6. What kind of clouds are closely packed? stratocumulus

## Page 135

### Sequencing

**Directions:** Reread the story, if necessary. Then choose an important event from the beginning, middle, and end of the story, and write it below.

Beginning: _____

Middle: _____

End: _____

*Answers will vary.*

**Directions:** Number these story events in the order in which they happened.

3  Jonny's mom called the doctor to get an appointment since Jonny's ankle was red and swollen.

1  Jonny limped to the top of the stairs.

6  The pediatrician thought Jonny might have JRA.

4  The sitter told Jonny's mom that he had slept most of the day.

5  The doctor gave them a prescription for an antibiotic.

7  Jonny is now 29 years old.

2  Jonny told his mom, "My leg hurts."

## Page 136

### Recalling Details

**Directions:** Answer the questions below about "Jonny's Story."

1. How old was Jonny when his ankle began to bother him? 3 1/2 years

2. Why did Jonny's mom stay home from work the second day? Because Jonny was feeling worse.

3. What do the letters JRA stand for? juvenile rheumatoid arthritis

4. When Jonny and his mom were waiting to see the doctor, how did Jonny's mom know he must not be feeling well? Because he slept the whole time.

5. Where did Jonny's mom take him when she picked him up at the sitter's house? to the doctor's office.

**Directions:** Write the letter of the definition beside the word it defines. If you need help, use a dictionary, or check the context of the story.

a. strong medicine used to treat infections
b. found to be true
c. doctor that specializes in child care
d. not yet an adult
e. did not walk correctly

C  pediatrician
A  antibiotic
B  confirmed
E  limped
D  juvenile

## Page 137

### Context Clues

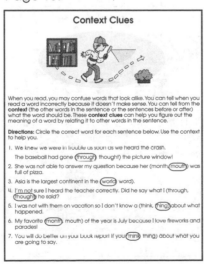

When you read, you may confuse words that look alike. You can tell when you read a word incorrectly because it doesn't make sense. You can tell from the context (the other words in the sentence or the sentences before or after) what the word should be. These context clues can help you figure out the meaning of a word by relating it to other words in the sentence.

**Directions:** Circle the correct word for each sentence below. Use the context to help you.

1. We knew we were in trouble as soon as we heard the crash. The baseball had gone (through) thought) the picture window!

2. She was not able to answer my question because her (month (mouth)) was full of pizza.

3. Asia is the largest continent in the (world) word).

4. I'm not sure I heard the teacher correctly. Did she say what I (through, (though) he said?

5. I was not with them on vacation so I don't know a (think, (thing) about what happened.

6. My favorite (month) mouth) of the year is July because I love fireworks and parades!

7. You will do better on your book report if you (think) thing) about what you are going to say.

## Page 138

### Newspapers

**Directions:** Write the answers.

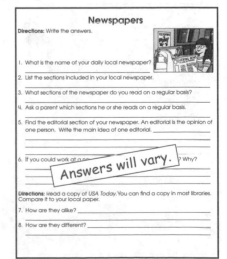

1. What is the name of your daily local newspaper?

2. List the sections included in your local newspaper.

3. What sections of the newspaper do you read on a regular basis?

4. Ask a parent which sections he or she reads on a regular basis.

5. Find the editorial section of your newspaper. An editorial is the opinion of one person. Write the main idea of one editorial. _____

6. If you could work at a _____ ? Why?

*Answers will vary.*

**Directions:** Read a copy of USA Today. You can find a copy in most libraries. Compare it to your local paper.

7. How are they alike? _____

8. How are they different? _____

Summer Link Super Edition Grade 5

## Page 139

### Desert Plants

**Directions:** Read the information about desert plants. Use context clues to determine the meaning of the bold words. Check the correct answers.

Desert plants have special features, or adaptations, that allow them to **survive** the harsh conditions of the desert. A cactus stores water in its tissues when it rains. It then uses this supply of water during the long dry season. The tiny needles on some kinds of **cacti** may number in the tens of thousands. These sharp thorns protect the cactus. They also form tiny shadows in the sunlight that help keep the plant from getting too hot.

Other plants are able to live by dropping their leaves. This cuts down on the **evaporation** of their water supply in the hot sun. Still other plants survive as seeds, protected from the sun and heat by tough seed coats. When it rains, the seeds **sprout** quickly, bloom, and produce more seeds that can **withstand** long dry spells.

Some plants spread their roots close to the Earth's surface to quickly gather water when it does rain. Other plants, such as the mesquite, have roots that grow 50 or 60 feet below the ground to reach underground water supplies.

1. Based on the other words in the sentence, what is the correct definition of **survive**?
   - ✓ continue to live
   - ___ bloom in the desert
   - ___ flower
2. Based on the other words in the sentence, what is the correct definition of **evaporation**?
   - ✓ water loss from heat
   - ___ much-needed rainfall
   - ___ boiling
3. Based on the other words in the sentence, what is the correct definition of **withstand**?
   - ✓ put up with
   - ___ stand with another
   - ___ take from
4. Based on the other words in the sentence, what is the correct definition of **cacti**?
   - ___ a type of sand dune
   - ✓ more than one cactus
   - ___ a caravan of camels
5. Based on the other words in the sentence, what is the correct definition of **sprout**?
   - ___ a type of bean that grows only in the desert
   - ✓ begin to grow
   - ___ a small flower

## Page 140

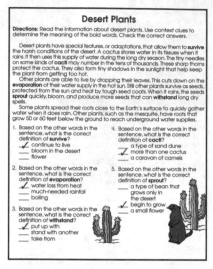

### Lizards

**Directions:** Read the information about lizards. Then answer the questions.

Lizards are reptiles, related to snakes, turtles, alligators, and crocodiles. Like other reptiles, lizards are cold-blooded. This means their body temperature changes with that of their surroundings. However, by changing their behavior throughout the day they can keep their temperature fairly constant.

Lizards are among the many animals that live in deserts. They usually come out of their burrows early in the morning. Most lizards lie in the sun to get warm before starting their daily activities. In mid-morning, they hunt for food. If it becomes too hot, lizards can raise their tails and bodies off the ground to help cool off. At mid-day, they return to their burrows or crawl under rocks for several hours. Late in the day, they again lie in the sun to absorb heat before the chilly desert night falls.

Like all animals, lizards have ways of protecting themselves. Some types of lizards have developed a most unusual defense. If a hawk or other animal grabs one of these lizards by its tail, the tail will break off. The tail will continue to wiggle around to distract the attacker while the lizard runs away. A month or two later, the lizard grows a new tail.

There are about 3,000 kinds of lizards, and all of them can bite, but only two types of lizards are poisonous: the Gila monster of the southwestern United States and the Mexican bearded lizard. Both are short-legged, thick-bodied reptiles with fat tails. These lizards do not attack people and will not bite them unless they are attacked.

1. What can a lizard do if it becomes too hot? raise its tail and body off the ground, crawl in burrows or under rocks
2. What is an unusual defense some lizards have developed to protect themselves? tails will break off and distract predators
3. What two types of lizards are poisonous? Gila monster and Mexican bearded lizard

## Page 141

### The Arctic Circle

**Directions:** Read the article about the Arctic Circle. Then answer the questions.

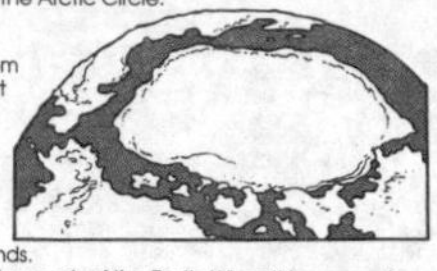

On the other side of the globe from Antarctica, at the northernmost part of the Earth, is another icy land. This is the Arctic Circle. It includes the North Pole itself and the northern fringes of three continents—Europe, Asia and North America, including the state of Alaska—as well as Greenland and other islands.

The seasons are opposite at the two ends of the Earth. When it is summer in Antarctica, it is winter in the Arctic Circle. In both places, there are very long periods of sunlight in summer and very long nights in the winter. On the poles themselves, there are six full months of sunlight and six full months of darkness each year.

Compared to Antarctica, the summers are surprisingly mild in some areas of the Arctic Circle. Much of the snow cover may melt, and temperatures often reach 50 degrees in July. Antarctica is covered by water—frozen water, of course—so nothing can grow there. Plant growth is limited in the polar regions not only by the cold, but also by wind, lack of water, and the long winter darkness.

In the far north, willow trees grow but only become a few inches high! The annual rings, the circles within the trunk of a tree that show its age and how fast it grows, are so narrow in those trees that you need a microscope to see them.

A permanently frozen layer of soil, called "permafrost," keeps roots from growing deep enough into the ground to anchor a plant. Even if a plant could survive the cold temperatures, it could not grow roots deep enough or strong enough to allow the plant to get very big.

1. What three continents have land included in the Arctic Circle? Europe, Asia, North America
2. Is the Arctic Circle generally warmer or colder than Antarctica? warmer
3. What is "permafrost"? a permanently frozen layer of soil
4. Many tall pine trees grow in the Arctic Circle. True (False) — False circled

## Page 142

### News Services

**Directions:** Read the information about news services. Then answer the questions.

When people read daily newspapers, they expect to see current news from all over the world. Some newspapers have offices or reporters in Washington, D.C. and other major cities around the world. Most newspapers rely on news services for international news. News services are organizations that gather and sell news to papers, radio, and television stations. They are sometimes referred to as "wire services," because they originally sent stories over telegraph or Teletype lines, or "wires."

The two largest news services are the Associated Press and United Press International. Stories sent by these services have their initials—AP or UPI—at the beginning of the article. All large American newspapers are members of either the AP or UPI service.

At one time, people had to wait for messengers to arrive by foot, horse, or ship to learn the news. By the time it reached a newspaper, news could be months old.

Gathering news from around the world became much faster after the invention of the telegraph, Teletype, telephone, and transatlantic cable. Today, satellites, computers, and fax machines can send stories, pictures, and even videos around the world in seconds.

1. What is another name for news service organizations? wire services
2. What are the two largest news service organizations? Associated Press (AP) and United Press International (UPI)
3. What are three inventions that have speeded up worldwide news-gathering? telegraph, Teletype, telephone, transatlantic cable, satellites, computers, fax machines
4. Why do newspapers use news services? to obtain news from all over the world
5. How was news delivered before the invention of modern communication devices? by messengers on foot, horse or ship

## Page 143

### Newspaper Jobs

**Directions:** Read the information about jobs at a newspaper. Then answer the questions.

It takes an army of people to put out one of the big daily newspapers. Three separate departments are needed to make a newspaper operate smoothly: editorial, mechanical, and business.

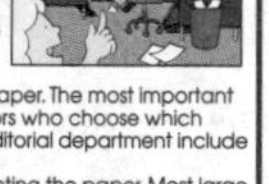

The editorial department is the one most people think about first. That is the news-gathering part of the newspaper. The most familiar job in this department is that of the reporter—the person who obtains information for a story and writes it. A photographer takes pictures to go along with the reporter's story.

Editors are the decision-makers. There are many editors at a large newspaper. They assign stories to reporters, read the stories to be certain they are correct and decide where and if the stories should appear in the paper. The most important stories go on the front page. There are also photo editors who choose which pictures will appear in the paper. Other workers in the editorial department include artists, copy editors, proofreaders and cartoonists.

The biggest job in the mechanical department is printing the paper. Most large newspapers have their own printing presses. Some small papers send their work to outside printing shops. After an issue, or edition, is printed, it is ready to be sold or "circulated" to the public.

Circulation of the paper is one of the jobs of the business department. This department also sells advertising space. This is very important for newspapers. Many papers make more money selling advertising space than selling newspapers. The business department also takes care of normal business jobs, like paying employees, paying bills and keeping records.

1. What are the three main departments at a newspaper? editorial, mechanical, business
2. Who gets the information for a story and writes it? reporter
3. Who are the decision-makers at a newspaper? editors
4. What is the biggest job for the mechanical department? ______
5. What is the most important job of the business department? selling advertising space

## Page 144

### Valuable Stamps

Most people collect stamps as a hobby. They spend small sums of money to get the stamps they want, or they trade stamps with other collectors. They rarely make what could be considered "big money" from their philately hobby.

A few collectors are in the business of philately as opposed to the hobby. To the people who can afford it, some stamps are worth big money. For example, a U.S. airmail stamp with a face value of 24 cents when it was issued in 1918 is now worth more than $35,000 if a certain design appears on the stamp. Another stamp, the British Guiana, an ugly stamp that cost only a penny when it was issued, later sold for $280,000!

The Graf Zeppelin is another example of an ugly stamp that became valuable. Graf Zeppelin is the name of a type of airship, similar to what we now call a "blimp," invented around the turn of the century. Stamps were issued to mark the first roundtrip flight the *Zeppelin* made between two continents. A set of three of these stamps cost $4.55 when they were issued. The stamps were ugly and few of them sold. The postal service destroyed the rest. Now, because they are rare, each set of the Graf Zeppelin stamps is worth hundreds of dollars.

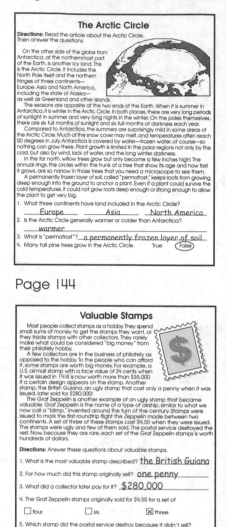

**Directions:** Answer these questions about valuable stamps.

1. What is the most valuable stamp described? the British Guiana
2. For how much did this stamp originally sell? one penny
3. What did a collector later pay for it? $280,000
4. The Graf Zeppelin stamps originally sold for $4.55 for a set of
   - ☐ four.
   - ☐ six.
   - ☒ three.
5. Which stamp did the postal service destroy because it didn't sell?
   - ☐ British Guiana
   - ☒ Graf Zeppelin
   - ☐ British Zeppelin

## Page 145

### Chickens

Have you ever heard the expression "pecking order"? In the pecking order of a school, the principal is at the top of the order. Next comes the assistant principal, then the teachers and students.

In the pecking order of chickens, the most aggressive chicken is the leader. The leader is the hen that uses her beak most often to peck the chickens she bosses. These chickens, in turn, boss other chickens by pecking them, and so on. Chickens can peck all others who are "below" them in the pecking order. They never peck "above" themselves by pecking their bosses.

**Directions:** Answer these questions about chickens.

1. Put this pecking order of four chickens in order.
   - 2 This chicken pecks numbers 3 and 4 but never 1.
   - 1 No one pecks this chicken. She's the top boss.
   - 4 This chicken can't peck anyone.
   - 3 This chicken pecks chicken number 4.
2. Use context clues to figure out the definition of **aggressive**. Answers will vary.
3. Who is at the top of the pecking order in a school? Answers may include: principal

## Page 146

### No Kidding About Goats

Goats are independent creatures. Unlike sheep, which move easily in herds, goats cannot be driven along by a goatherd. They must be moved one or two at a time. Moving a big herd of goats can take a long time, so goatherds must be patient people.

Both male and female goats can have horns, but some goats don't have them at all. Male goats have beards but females do not. Male goats also have thicker and shaggier coats than females. During breeding season, when goats mate to produce babies, male goats have a very strong smell.

Goats are kept in paddocks with high fences. The fences are high because goats are good jumpers. They like to nibble on hedges and on the tips of young trees. They can cause a lot of damage this way! That is why many farmers keep their goats in a paddock.

Baby goats are called "kids," and two or three at a time are born to the mother goat. Farmers usually begin to bottle-feed kids when they are a few days old. They milk the mother goat and keep the milk. Goat's milk is much easier to digest than cow's milk, and many people think it tastes delicious.

**Directions:** Answer these questions about goats.

1. Use context clues to choose the correct definition of **goatherd**.
   - ☒ person who herds goats
   - ☐ goats in a herd
   - ☐ person who has heard of goats
2. Use context clues to choose the correct definition of **paddock**.
   - ☐ pad
   - ☐ fence
   - ☒ pen
3. Use context clues to choose the correct definition of **nibble**.
   - ☒ take small bites
   - ☐ take small drinks
   - ☐ take little sniffs
4. Use context clues to choose the correct definition of **delicious**.
   - ☐ delicate
   - ☒ tasty
   - ☐ terrible

## Page 147

### "The Man and the Snake"

**Directions:** Read the fable "The Man and the Snake." Then, number the events in order.

Once, a kind man saw a snake in the road. It was winter and the poor snake was nearly frozen. The man began to walk away, but he could not.

"The snake is one of Earth's creatures, too," he said. He picked up the snake and put it in a sack. "I will take it home to warm up by my fire. Then I will set it free."

The man stopped for lunch at a village inn. He put his coat and his sack on a bench by the fireplace. He planned to sit nearby, but the inn was crowded, so he had to sit across the room.

He soon forgot about the snake. As he was eating his soup, he heard screams. Warmed by the fire, the snake had crawled from the bag. It hissed at the people near the fire.

The man jumped up and ran to the fireplace. "Is this how you repay the kindness of others?" he shouted.

He grabbed a stick used for stirring the fire and chased the snake out of the inn.

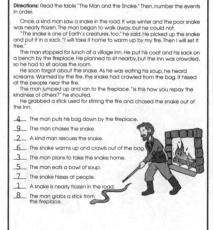

- 4 The man puts his bag down by the fireplace.
- 9 The man chases the snake.
- 2 A kind man rescues the snake.
- 6 The snake warms up and crawls out of the bag.
- 3 The man plans to take the snake home.
- 5 The man eats a bowl of soup.
- 7 The snake hisses at people.
- 1 A snake is nearly frozen in the road.
- 8 The man grabs a stick from the fireplace.

## Page 148

### "The Sly Fox"

**Directions:** Read the legend "The Sly Fox." Then answer the questions.

One evening, Fox met Wolf in the forest. Wolf was in a terrible mood. He felt hungry, too. So he said to Fox, "Don't move! I'm going to eat you this minute."

As he spoke, Wolf backed Fox up against a tree. Fox realized she couldn't run away.

"I will have to use my wits instead of my legs," she thought to herself.

Aloud to Wolf, Fox said calmly, "I would have made a good dinner for you last year. But I've had three little babies since then. I spend all my time looking for food to feed them."

Before she could go on, Wolf interrupted. "I don't care how many children you have! I'm going to eat you right now." Wolf began closing in on Fox.

"Stop!" shouted Fox. "Look how skinny I am. I ran off all my fat looking for food for my children. But I know where you can find something that's good and fat!" Wolf backed off to listen.

"There's a well near here. In the bottom of it is a big fat piece of cheese. I don't like cheese, so it's of no use to me. Come, I'll show you."

Wolf trotted off after Fox, making sure she could not run away.

"See," said Fox when they got to the well.

Inside was what looked like a round yellow piece of cheese. It was really the moon's reflection, but Wolf didn't know this. Wolf leaned over the well, wondering how to get the cheese. Fox jumped up quickly and pushed Wolf in.

"I am a sly, old thing," Fox chuckled as she trotted home to her children. And to this day, that's why foxes are sly.

1. What is the main idea of this legend? (Check one.)
   - ✓ Fox is cornered but uses her wits to outsmart Wolf and save her own life.
   - ___ Wolf is in a terrible mood and wants to eat Fox.
   - ___ Wolf thinks the moon was made of cheese.
2. Why did Fox say she will not make a good meal for Wolf? She was too thin because she spent all her time searching for food for her babies.
3. What happens to Wolf at the end? Fox pushes Wolf into the well.

## Page 149

### "The Sly Fox"

**Directions:** Review the legend "The Sly Fox." Then, answer the questions.

1. What are three events in the story that show Wolf's bad mood? Answers will vary.
2. What does Fox say she will have to use to get away from Wolf? her wits
3. Where does Fox tell Wolf he can find a nice fat meal? at the bottom of the well
4. How does Fox finally rid herself of Wolf? She pushes him into the well
5. What does Fox say as she trots home? "I am a sly old thing."
6. Have you ever been in a situation where you used words to solve a problem instead of fighting with someone? Write about it.
7. In addition to teaching why foxes are sly, what lesson does this story teach?

Answers will vary.

## Page 150

### "Grasshopper Green"

**Directions:** Read the poem "Grasshopper Green." Then answer the questions.

Grasshopper Green is a comical guy,
He lives on the best of fare.
Bright little trousers, jacket and cap,
These are his summer wear.

Out in the meadow he loves to go,
Playing away in the sun.
It's hopperty, skipperty, high and low,
Summer's the time for fun.

Grasshopper Green has a cute little house,
He stays near it every day.
It's under the hedge where he is safe,
Out of the gardener's way.

Gladly he's calling the children to play,
Out in the beautiful sun
It's hopperty, skipperty, high and low,
Summer's the time for fun.

1. What does **comical** mean in this poem? amusing or jolly
2. What are three things Grasshopper Green wears in the summer? trousers, jacket and cap
3. Where does he love to go and play? out in the meadow
4. Whom does Grasshopper Green call to play? the children
5. What is summer the time for? fun
6. Use a dictionary. What does **fare** mean in this poem? food
7. You won't find the words **hopperty** and **skipperty** in a dictionary. Based on the poem, write your own definitions of these words. Answers will vary.

## Page 151

### Oceans

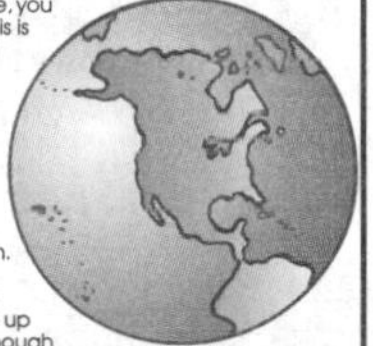

If you looked at Earth from up in space, you would see a planet that is mostly blue. This is because more than two-thirds of Earth is covered with water. You already know that this is what makes our planet different from the others, and what makes life on Earth possible. Most of this water is in the four great oceans: Pacific, Atlantic, Indian, and Arctic. The Pacific is by far the largest and the deepest. It is more than twice as big as the Atlantic, the second largest ocean.

The water in the ocean is salty. This is because rivers are always pouring water into the oceans. Some of this water picks up salt from the rocks it flows over. It is not enough salt to make the rivers taste salty. But the salt in the oceans has been building up over millions of years. The oceans get more and more salty every century.

The ocean provides us with huge amounts of food, especially fish. There are many other things we get from the ocean, including sponges and pearls. The oceans are also great "highways" of the world. Ships are always crossing the oceans, transporting many goods from country to country.

The science of studying the ocean is called oceanography. Today, oceanographers have special equipment to help them learn about the oceans and seas. Electronic instruments can be sent deep below the surface to make measurements. The newest equipment uses sonar or echo-sounding systems that bounce sound waves off the sea bed and use the echoes to make pictures of the ocean floor.

**Directions:** Answer these questions about the oceans.

1. How much of the Earth is covered by water? two-thirds
2. Which is the largest and deepest ocean? Pacific
3. What is the science of studying the ocean? oceanography
4. What new equipment do oceanographers use? sonar or echo sounding systems

## Page 152

### Your Five Senses

Your senses are very important to you. You depend on them every day. They tell you where you are and what is going on around you. Your senses are sight, hearing, touch, smell, and taste.

Try to imagine for a minute that you were suddenly unable to use your senses. Imagine, for instance, that you are in a cave and your only source of light is a candle. Without warning, a gust of wind blows out the flame.

Your senses are always at work. Your eyes let you read this book. Your nose brings the scent of dinner cooking. Your tongue helps you taste dinner later. Your hand feels the softness as you stroke a puppy. Your ears tell you that a storm is approaching.

Your senses also help keep you from harm. They warn you if you touch something that will burn you. They keep you from looking at a light that is too bright, and they tell you if a car is coming up behind you. Each of your senses collects information and sends it as a message to your brain. The brain is like the control center for your body. It sorts out the messages sent by your senses and acts on them.

**Directions:** Answer these questions about the five senses.

1. Circle the main idea:
   - (Your senses keep you from harm.)
   - Your senses are important to you in many ways.
2. Name the five senses.
   - a. sight
   - b. hearing
   - c. touch
   - d. smell
   - e. taste

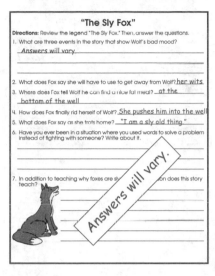

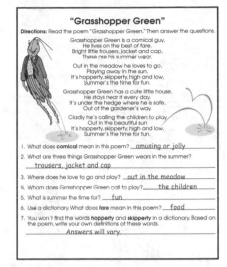

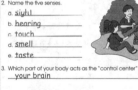

3. Which part of your body acts as the "control center"? your brain

## Page 153

### Hearing

Every sound you hear is made by the movement of air. These movements, called vibrations, spread out in waves. Your outer ear collects these "sound waves" and sends them down a tube to the inner ear. The vibrations hit the eardrum, a flap of skin stretched across the inner end of the tube. As the eardrum vibrates, a tiny bone called the hammer moves back and forth. This helps the vibrations move to three small bones and then to the cochlea, where they are changed to nerve impulses. The impulses travel to the brain where they are recognized as sounds.

Some people have trouble hearing or cannot hear at all. This is called being deaf. Some deaf people can understand what you are saying by watching how your lips move. They use their eyes as their ears. Sometimes a hearing aid can help improve hearing. It is like a tiny radio that fits into the ear. Sounds enter the hearing aid and are made much louder.

Deaf people also have difficulty learning to speak because they cannot hear how to say words. Many deaf people "talk" by making pictures with their hands. This kind of talking is called sign language. Every letter of the alphabet has a sign. These signs are shown above.

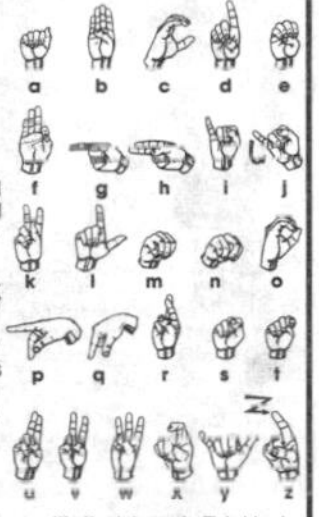


**Directions:** Answer these questions about the sense of hearing

1. Sound is made by movements of the air called vibrations.
2. The flap of skin stretched over the inner end of the tube inside your ear is called the eardrum.
3. People who cannot hear are said to be deaf.
4. The language of making pictures with your hands is called sign language.
5. Read this word in sign language. It says hear

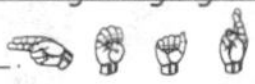

## Page 154

### Taste

The senses of taste and smell work very closely together. If you can't smell your food, it is difficult to recognize the taste. You may have noticed this when you've had a bad cold with a stuffed-up nose.

Tasting is the work of your tongue. All over your tongue are tiny taste sensors called taste buds. If you look at your tongue in a mirror, you can see small groups of taste buds. They are what give your tongue its rough appearance. Each taste bud has a small opening in it. Tiny pieces of food and drink enter this opening. These taste sensors gather information about the taste and send messages to your brain. Your brain decides what the taste is.

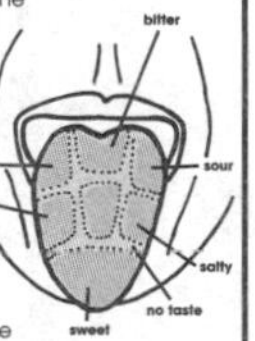


Taste buds located in different areas of your tongue recognize different tastes. There are only four tastes your tongue can recognize: sweet, sour, bitter, and salty. All other flavors are a mixture of taste and smell.

**Directions:** Answer these questions about the sense of taste.

1. It is difficult to taste your food if you can't smell.
2. The tiny taste sensors on your tongue are called taste buds.
3. The four tastes that your tongue can recognize are sweet, sour, bitter and salty.
4. All other flavors are a mixture of taste and smell.

## Page 155

### Deep-Sea Diving

One part of the world is still largely unexplored. It is the deep sea. Over the years, many people have explored the sea. But the first deep-sea divers wanted to find sunken treasure. They weren't really interested in studying the creatures or life there. Only recently have they begun to learn some of the mysteries of the sea.

It's not easy to explore the deep sea. A diver must have a way of breathing under water. He must be able to protect himself from the terrific pressure. The pressure of air is about 15 pounds on every square inch. But the pressure of water is about 1,300 pounds on every square inch!

The first diving suits were made of rubber. They had a helmet of brass with windows in it. The shoes were made of lead and weighed 20 pounds each! These suits let divers go down a few hundred feet, but they were no good for exploring very deep waters. With a metal diving suit, a diver could go down 700 feet. Metal suits were first used in the 1930s.

In 1937, a diver named William Beebe wanted to explore, deeper than anyone had ever gone before. He was not interested in finding treasure. He wanted to study deep-sea creatures and plants. He invented a hollow metal ball called the bathysphere. It weighed more than 5,000 pounds, but in it Beebe went down 3,028 feet. He saw many things that had never been seen by humans before.

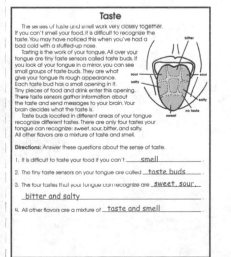

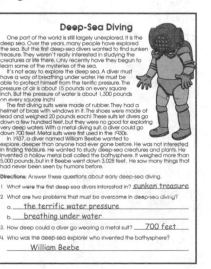

**Directions:** Answer these questions about early deep-sea diving.

1. What were the first deep-sea divers interested in? sunken treasure
2. What are two problems that must be overcome in deep-sea diving?
   - a. the terrific water pressure
   - b. breathing under water
3. How deep could a diver go wearing a metal suit? 700 feet
4. Who was the deep-sea explorer who invented the bathysphere? William Beebe

## Page 156

### Dolphins and Porpoises

Dolphins and porpoises are members of the whale family. In fact, they are the most common whales. If they have pointed or "beaked" faces, they are dolphins. If they have short faces, they are porpoises. Sometimes large groups of more than 1,000 dolphins can be seen.

Dolphins and porpoises swim in a special way called "porpoising." They swim through the surface waters, diving down and then leaping up—sometimes into the air. As their heads come out of the water, they breathe in air. Dolphins are acrobatic swimmers, often spinning in the air as they leap.

Humans have always had a special relationship with dolphins. Stories dating back to the ancient Greeks talk about dolphins as friendly, helpful creatures. There have been reports over the years of people in trouble on the seas who have been rescued and helped by dolphins.

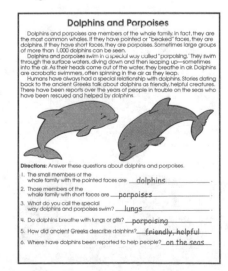

**Directions:** Answer these questions about dolphins and porpoises.

1. The small members of the whale family with the pointed faces are dolphins.
2. Those members of the whale family with short faces are porpoises.
3. What do you call the special way dolphins and porpoises swim? lungs
4. Do dolphins breathe with lungs or gills? porpoising
5. How did ancient Greeks describe dolphins? friendly, helpful
6. Where have dolphins been reported to help people? on the seas

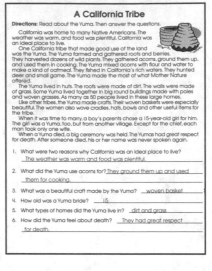

## Page 157

### Giraffes

**Directions:** Read about giraffes. Then answer the questions.

Giraffes are tall, beautiful, and graceful animals that live in Africa. When they are grown, male giraffes are about 18 feet tall. Adult females are about 14 feet tall. Giraffes are not fat animals, but because they are so big, they weigh a lot. The average male weighs 2,800 pounds. Females weigh about 400 pounds less. Giraffes reach their full height when they are four years old. They continue to gain weight until they are about eight years old.

If you have ever seen giraffes, you know their necks and legs are very long. They are not awkward, though! Giraffes can move very quickly. They like to jump over fences and streams. They do this gracefully. They do not trip over their long legs.

If they are frightened, they can run 35 miles an hour. When giraffes gallop, all four feet are sometimes off the ground! Usually, young and old giraffes pace along at about 10 miles an hour.

Giraffes are strong. They can use their back legs as weapons. A lion can run faster than a giraffe, but a giraffe can kill a lion with one quick kick from its back legs.

Giraffes do not look scary. Their long eyelashes make them look gentle. They usually have a curious look on their faces. Many people think they are cute. Do you?

1. What is the weight of a full-grown male giraffe?  _2,800 pounds_
2. What is the weight of an adult female?  _2,400 pounds_
3. When does a giraffe run 35 miles an hour?  _when it is fright_
4. What do giraffes use as weapons?  _their back legs_
5. For how long do giraffes continue to gain weight?  _until they are 8 years old_
6. When do giraffes reach their full height?  _when they are 4 years old_
7. Use a dictionary. What does **gallop** mean?  _to run quickly; to run at full speed_

## Page 158

### A California Tribe

**Directions:** Read about the Yuma. Then answer the questions.

California was home to many Native Americans. The weather was warm, and food was plentiful. California was an ideal place to live.

One California tribe that made good use of the land was the Yuma. The Yuma farmed and gathered roots and berries. They harvested dozens of wild plants. They gathered acorns, ground them up, and used them in cooking. The Yuma mixed acorns with flour and water to make a kind of oatmeal. They fished in California's rich waters. They hunted deer and small game. The Yuma made the most of what Mother Nature offered.

The Yuma lived in huts. The roofs were made of dirt. The walls were made of grass. Some Yuma lived together in big round buildings made with poles and woven grasses. As many as 50 people lived in these large homes.

Like other tribes, the Yuma made crafts. Their woven baskets were especially beautiful. The women also wove cradles, hats, bowls and other useful items for the tribe.

When it was time to marry, a boy's parents chose a 15-year-old girl for him. The girl was a Yuma, too, but from another tribe. Except for the chief, each man took only one wife.

When a Yuma died, a big ceremony was held. The Yumas had great respect for death. After someone died, his or her name was never spoken again.

1. What were two reasons why California was an ideal place to live?  _The weather was warm and food was plentiful._
2. What did the Yuma use acorns for?  _They ground them up and used them for cooking._
3. What was a beautiful craft made by the Yuma?  _woven basket_
4. How old was a Yuma bride?  _15_
5. What types of homes did the Yuma live in?  _dirt and grass_
6. How did the Yuma feel about death?  _They had great respect for death._

## Page 159

### The Yuma

**Directions:** Review what you read about the Yuma. Write the answers.

1. How did the Yuma make good use of the land?  _They farmed and gathered roots, acorns and berries. They fished and hunted._
2. How were the Yuma like the Pueblo people?  _Both hunted deer and small game, farmed, gathered berries and made crafts._
3. How were they different?  _The Yuma fished, made baskets and lived in huts. The Pueblos made pottery and jewelry and lived in adobe homes._
4. Why did the Yuma have homes different than those of the Pueblo tribes?  _Answers should indicate differences in natural materials available due to different climates._
5. When it was time for a young Yuma man to marry, his parents selected a fifteen-year-old bride for him from another tribe. Do you think this is a good idea? Why or why not?
6. Why do you suppose the Yuma ne___ ___ ___rson's name after he or she died?
7. Do you think this woul___ ___ ___ ___thing to do? Explain your answer.

_Answers will vary._

## Page 160

### "Over the Hills and Far Away"

**Directions:** Read "Over the Hills and Far Away." Then answer the questions.

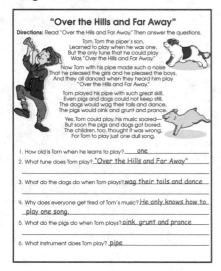

Tom, Tom the piper's son,
Learned to play when he was one,
But the only tune that he could play
Was "Over the Hills and Far Away."

Now Tom with his pipe made such a noise
That he pleased the girls and he pleased the boys,
And they all danced when they heard him play
"Over the Hills and Far Away."

Tom played his pipe with such great skill,
Even pigs and dogs could not keep still.
The dogs would wag their tails and dance,
The pigs would oink and grunt and prance.

Yes, Tom could play his music soared—
But soon the pigs and dogs got bored.
The children, too, thought it was wrong,
For Tom to play just one dull song.

1. How old is Tom when he learns to play?  _one_
2. What tune does Tom play?  _"Over the Hills and Far Away"_
3. What do the dogs do when Tom plays?  _wag their tails and dance_
4. Why does everyone get tired of Tom's music?  _He only knows how to play one song._
5. What do the pigs do when Tom plays?  _oink, grunt and prance_
6. What instrument does Tom play?  _pipe_

## Page 161

### Helen Keller

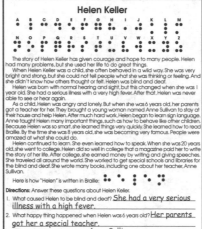

The story of Helen Keller has given courage and hope to many people. Helen had many problems, but she used her life to do great things.

When Helen Keller was a child, she often behaved in a wild way. She was very bright and strong, but she could not tell people what she was thinking or feeling. And she didn't know how others thought or felt. Helen was blind and deaf.

Helen was born with normal hearing and sight, but this changed when she was 1 year old. She had a serious illness with a very high fever. After that, Helen was never able to see or hear again.

As a child, Helen was angry and lonely. But when she was 6 years old, her parents got a teacher for her. They brought a young woman named Anne Sullivan to stay at their house and help Helen. After much hard work, Helen began to learn sign language. Anne taught Helen many important things, such as how to behave like other children. Because Helen was so smart, she learned things very quickly. She learned how to read Braille. By the time she was 8 years old, she was becoming very famous. People were amazed at what she could do.

Helen continued to learn. She even learned how to speak. When she was 20 years old, she went to college. Helen did so well in college that a magazine paid her to write the story of her life. After college, she earned money by writing and giving speeches. She traveled all around the world. She worked to get special schools and libraries for the blind and deaf. She wrote many books, including one about her teacher, Anne Sullivan.

Here is how "Helen" is written in Braille: 

**Directions:** Answer these questions about Helen Keller.

1. What caused Helen to be blind and deaf?  _She had a very serious illness with a high fever._
2. What happy thing happened when Helen was 6 years old?  _Her parents got her a special teacher._
3. What was her teacher's name?  _Anne Sullivan_

## Page 162

### Animal Legend Organizer

**Directions:** Follow the instructions to write a legend of your own.

1. Select one of the following titles for your legend. Circle the one you plan to use.
   How the Tiger Got Stripes — How the Elephant Got a Tusk
   How the Giraffe Got a Long Neck — How the Kangaroo Got Her Pouch
   How the Gazelle Got Twisty Horns — Why the Pig Has a Short Tail
   How the Elephant Got Big Ears — Why Birds Fly
   Why Rabbits Are Timid — How the Giraffe Got a Long Neck
   How the Mouse Got a Long Tail — Why Fish Swim
2. Briefly explain the type of conflict that will be in your legend.
3. Write words and phrases to show events you plan to include in your legend.
4. Summarize how you plan to settle the ___ ___ the problem.

**Directions:** Write your legend. ___ ___ ___ ___ate it if you like.

_Answers will vary._

## Page 163

### Kanati's Son

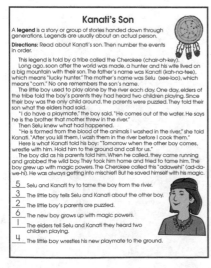

A **legend** is a story or group of stories handed down through generations. Legends are usually about an actual person.

**Directions:** Read about Kanati's son. Then number the events in order.

This legend is told by a tribe called the Cherokee (chair-oh-key).

Long ago, soon after the world was made, a hunter and his wife lived on a big mountain with their son. The father's name was Kanati (kah-na-tee), which means "lucky hunter." The mother's name was Selu (see-loo), which means "corn." No one remembers the son's name.

The little boy used to play alone by the river each day. One day, elders of the tribe told the boy's parents they had heard two children playing. Since their boy was the only child around, the parents were puzzled. They told their son what the elders had said.

"I do have a playmate," the boy said. "He comes out of the water. He says he is the brother that mother threw in the river."

Then Selu knew what had happened.

"He is formed from the blood of the animals I washed in the river," she told Kanati. "After you kill them, I wash them in the river before I cook them."

Here is what Kanati told his boy: "Tomorrow when the other boy comes, wrestle with him. Hold him to the ground and call for us."

The boy did as his parents told him. When he called, they came running and grabbed the wild boy. They took him home and tried to tame him. The boy grew up with magic powers. The Cherokee called him "adawehi" (ad-da-we-hi). He was always getting into mischief! But he saved himself with his magic.

_5_ Selu and Kanati try to tame the boy from the river.
_3_ The little boy tells Selu and Kanati about the other boy.
_2_ The little boy's parents are puzzled.
_6_ The new boy grows up with magic powers.
_1_ The elders tell Selu and Kanati they heard two children playing.
_4_ The little boy wrestles his new playmate to the ground.

## Page 164

### "Hickory, Dickory, Dock"

**Directions:** Read the poem "Hickory, Dickory, Dock." Then answer the questions.

Hickory, dickory, dock.
The mouse ran up the clock.
The clock struck one,
And down he run,
Hickory, dickory, dock.

Dickory, dickory, dare,
The pig flew in the air.
The man in brown
Soon brought him down,
Dickory, dickory, dare.

1. What is the main idea? (Check one.)
   ___ Mice and pigs can cause a lot of problems to clocks and men in brown suits.
   _✓_ There is no main idea. This poem is just for fun.
   ___ Beware of mice in your clocks and flying pigs.
2. Why do you think the mouse runs down the clock?  _Answers will vary._

**Directions:** Number these events in order.

_2_ The clock strikes one.
_3_ The mouse runs back down the clock.
_1_ The mouse runs up the clock.
_5_ The man in brown brings the pig down.
_4_ The pig flies in the air.

## Page 165

### "Mr. Nobody"

**Directions:** After reading the poem "Mr. Nobody," number in order the things people blame him for.

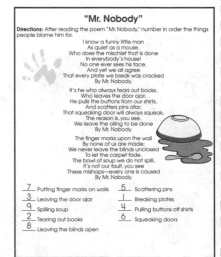

I know a funny little man
As quiet as a mouse,
Who does the mischief that is done
In everybody's house!
No one ever sees his face.
And yet we all agree
That every plate we break was cracked
By Mr. Nobody.

It's he who always tears out books,
Who leaves the door ajar,
He pulls the buttons from our shirts,
And scatters pins afar;
That squeaking door will always squeak,
The reason is, you see,
We leave the oiling to be done
By Mr. Nobody.

The finger marks upon the wall
By none of us are made;
We never leave the blinds unclosed
To let the carpet fade.
The bowl of soup we do not spill,
It's not our fault, you see
These mishaps—every one is caused
By Mr. Nobody.

_7_ Putting finger marks on walls  _5_ Scattering pins
_3_ Leaving the door ajar  _1_ Breaking plates
_9_ Spilling soup  _4_ Pulling buttons off shirts
_2_ Tearing out books  _6_ Squeaking doors
_8_ Leaving the blinds open

## Page 166

### Recipes

**Sequencing** is putting items or events in logical order.

**Directions:** Read the recipe. Then number the steps in order for making brownies.

Preheat the oven to 350 degrees. Grease an 8-inch square baking dish.

In a mixing bowl, place two squares (2 ounces) of unsweetened chocolate and 1/3 cup butter. Place the bowl in a pan of hot water and heat it to melt the chocolate and the butter.

When the chocolate is melted, remove the pan from the heat. Add 1 cup sugar and two eggs to the melted chocolate and beat it. Next, stir in 3/4 cup sifted flour, 1/2 teaspoon baking powder and 1/2 teaspoon salt. Finally, mix in 1/2 cup chopped nuts.

Spread the mixture in the greased baking dish. Bake for 30 to 35 minutes. The brownies are done when a toothpick stuck in the center comes out clean. Let the brownies cool. Cut them into squares.

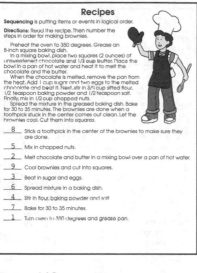

__8__ Stick a toothpick in the center of the brownies to make sure they are done.

__5__ Mix in chopped nuts.

__2__ Melt chocolate and butter in a mixing bowl over a pan of hot water.

__9__ Cool brownies and cut into squares.

__3__ Beat in sugar and eggs.

__6__ Spread mixture in a baking dish.

__4__ Stir in flour, baking powder and salt

__7__ Bake for 30 to 35 minutes.

__1__ Turn oven to 350 degrees and grease pan.

## Page 167

### Summarizing

A **summary** includes the main points from an article, book, or speech.

**Example:**
Tomb robbing was an important business in ancient Egypt. Often entire families participated in the plunder of tombs. These robbers may have been laborers, officials, tomb architects, or guards, but they all probably had one thing in common. They were involved in the building or designing of the tomb or they wouldn't have had the knowledge necessary to successfully rob the burial sites. Not only did tomb robbing ensure a rich life for the robbers but it also enabled them to be buried with many riches themselves.

**Summary:**
Tomb robbing occurred in ancient Egypt. The robbers stole riches to use in their present lives or in their burials. Tomb robbers usually had some part in the building or design of the tomb. This allowed them to find the burial rooms where the treasures were stored.

**Directions:** Read about life in ancient Egypt. Then write a three- to five-sentence summary.

Egyptologists have learned much from the pyramids and mummies of ancient Egypt from the items left by grave robbers.

Women of ancient Egypt wore makeup to enhance their features. Dark colored minerals called *kohl* were used as eyeliner and eye shadow. Men also wore eyeliner. Women used another mineral called *ocher* on their cheeks and lips to redden them. Henna, a plant which produces an orange dye, tinted the fingernails, the palms of their hands, and the soles of their feet.

Perfume was also important in ancient Egypt. Small cones made of wax were worn on top of the head. These cones contained perfume oils. The sun slowly melted the wax, and the perfume would scent the hair, head, and shoulders.

Sample answer:
We have learned much from the pyramids and mummies. Women wore makeup made out of the minerals kohl and ocher and a plant called henna. Men wore eyeliner, too. Perfume made out of wax was also important to the ancient Egyptians.

## Page 168

### Writing a Summary

**Directions:** Read the following selection. Then, write a summary of the selection.

**Man's First Flights**

In the first few years of the 20th century, the majority of people strongly believed that man could not and would not ever be able to fly. There were a few daring individuals who worked to prove the public wrong.

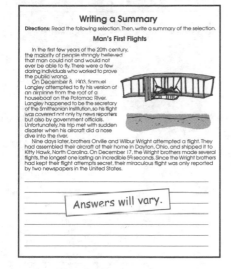

On December 8, 1903, Samuel Langley attempted to fly his version of an airplane from the roof of a houseboat on the Potomac River. Langley happened to be the secretary of the Smithsonian Institution, so his flight was covered not only by news reporters but also by government officials. Unfortunately, his trip met with sudden disaster when his aircraft did a nose dive into the river.

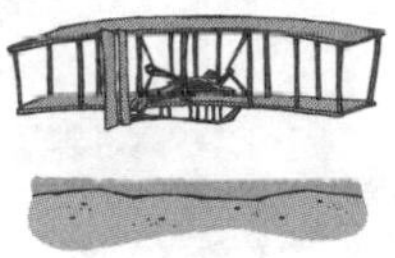

Nine days later, brothers Orville and Wilbur Wright attempted a flight. They had assembled their aircraft at their home in Dayton, Ohio, and shipped it to Kitty Hawk, North Carolina. On December 17, the Wright brothers made several flights, the longest one lasting an incredible 59 seconds. Since the Wright brothers had kept their flight attempts secret, their miraculous flight was only reported by two newspapers in the United States.

Answers will vary.

## Page 169

### Using an Outline to Write an Essay

Outlines help you organize information and notes into a manageable form. Outlines also help you prepare to write reports and essays by keeping your thoughts in a logical order or sequence. Once you have a good outline, converting it to paragraph form is easy.

To convert an outline to an essay, add your own words to expand the words and phrases in the outline into sentence form. Information from the first main topic becomes the first paragraph.

I. Painting the tree house
  A. Choose a color of paint
  B. Choose a kind of paint
    1. Cans of paint
    2. Spray paint

Information from the second and third main topics become the second and third paragraphs of the essay.

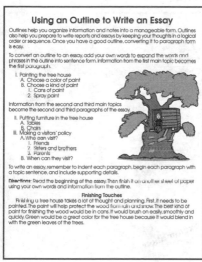

II. Putting furniture in the tree house
  A. Tables
  B. Chairs
III. Making a visitors' policy
  A. Who can visit?
    1. Friends
    2. Sisters and brothers
    3. Parents
  B. When can they visit?

To write an essay, remember to indent each paragraph, begin each paragraph with a topic sentence, and include supporting details.

**Directions:** Read the beginning of the essay. Then finish it on another sheet of paper using your own words and information from the outline.

**Finishing Touches**

Finishing a tree house takes a lot of thought and planning. First, it needs to be painted. The paint will help protect the wood from rain and snow. The best kind of paint for finishing the wood would be in cans. It would brush on easily, smoothly and quickly. Green would be a great color for the tree house because it would blend in with the green leaves of the trees.

## Page 170

### Making an Outline

An outline will help you organize your ideas before you begin writing your report.

Title
I. First Main Idea
  A. A supporting idea or fact
  B. Another supporting idea or fact
    1. An example or related fact
    2. An example or related fact
II. Second Main Idea
  A. A supporting idea or fact
  B. Another supporting idea or fact
III. Third Main Idea
  A. A supporting idea or fact
  B. Another supporting idea or fact

**Directions:** Use information from your notes to write an outline for your report. Follow the above format, but expand your outline to include as many main ideas, facts, and examples as necessary.

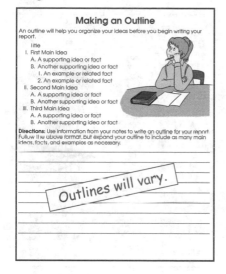

Outlines will vary.

## Page 171

### Building a Tree House

**Directions:** Study the sample outline for building a house. Then use words and phrases from the box to fill in the missing parts of the outline on how to build a tree house.

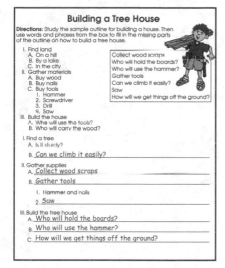

I. Find land
  A. On a hill
  B. By a lake
  C. In the city
II. Gather materials
  A. Buy wood
  B. Buy nails
  C. Buy tools
    1. Hammer
    2. Screwdriver
    3. Drill
    4. Saw
III. Build the house
  A. Who will use the tools?
  B. Who will carry the wood?

| |
|---|
| Collect wood scraps |
| Who will hold the boards? |
| Who will use the hammer? |
| Gather tools |
| Can we climb it easily? |
| Saw |
| How will we get things off the ground? |

I. Find a tree
  A. Is it sturdy?
  B. Can we climb it easily?
II. Gather supplies
  A. Collect wood scraps
  B. Gather tools
    1. Hammer and nails
    2. Saw
III. Build the tree house
  A. Who will hold the boards?
  B. Who will use the hammer?
  C. How will we get things off the ground?

## Page 172

### Writing the Paper

**Directions:** Read more about writing a report. Then write your report.

Before you begin, be certain you clearly understand what is expected. How long should your report be? Must it be typed? Can it be written in pen? Should it be double-spaced?

Begin the first draft of your report with a general introduction of your topic. In the introduction, briefly mention the main points you will write about. One paragraph is usually enough to introduce your paper.

Next, comes the body of your report. Start a new paragraph for each main point. Include information that supports that point. If you are writing a long report, you may need to write a new paragraph for each supporting idea and/or each example. Follow your outline to be certain you cover all points. Depending on the number of words required to cover your topic, the body of the report will be anywhere from three or four paragraphs to several pages long.

In one or two concluding paragraphs, briefly summarize the main points you wrote about in the body of the report and state any conclusions you have drawn as a result of your research.

Once you finish the first draft, you will need to edit and rewrite your report to make it read smoothly and correct errors. You may need to rewrite your report more than once to make it the best it can be.

If possible, put the report aside for a day or two before you rewrite it so you can look at it with fresh eyes and a clear mind. Professional writers often write several drafts, so don't be discouraged about rewrites! Rewriting and editing are the keys to good writing—keys that every writer, no matter how old or experienced, relies on.

**Directions:** Circle the words in the puzzle related to writing a report.

| | | | | | | | | | | | |
|---|---|---|---|---|---|---|---|---|---|---|---|
| K | K | N | K | T | O | P | I | C | D | T | B |
| L | D | O | B | T | T | O | D | P | T | D | O |
| I | N | T | R | O | D | U | C | T | I | O | N |
| E | N | E | R | G | D | E | E | O | O | O | N |
| D | W | S | R | G | E | Y | C | P | C | X | R |
| S | A | F | E | A | T | T | E | I | E | Y | O |
| R | W | A | Q | U | B | W | P | C | D | G | F |
| L | I | C | O | N | C | L | U | S | I | O | N |
| O | U | T | L | I | N | D | U | T | T | E | D |
| R | E | S | E | A | R | C | H | R | E | S | E |

topic
facts
outline
introduction
body
conclusion
notes
research
edit

## Page 173

### Author's Purpose

Authors write to fulfill one of three purposes: to **inform**, to **entertain**, or to **persuade**.

Authors who write to inform are providing facts for the reader in an informational context. **Examples:** Encyclopedia entries and newspaper articles

Authors who write to entertain are hoping to provide enjoyment for the reader. **Examples:** Funny stories and comics

Authors who write to persuade are trying to convince the reader to believe as they believe. **Examples:** Editorials and opinion essays

**Directions:** Read each paragraph. Write **inform, entertain**, or **persuade** on the line to show the author's purpose.

1. The whooping crane is a migratory bird. At one time, this endangered bird was almost extinct. These large white cranes are characterized by red faces and trumpeting calls. Through protection of both the birds and their habitats, the whooping crane is slowly increasing in number.
inform

2. It is extremely important that all citizens place bird feeders in their yards and keep them full for the winter. Birds that spend the winter in this area are in danger of starving due to lack of food. It is every citizen's responsibility to ensure the survival of the birds.
persuade

3. Imagine being able to hibernate like a bear each winter! Wouldn't it be great to eat to your heart's content all fall? Then, sometime in late November, inform your teacher that you will not be attending school for the next few months because you'll be resting and living off your fat? Now, that would be the life!
entertain

4. Bears, woodchucks and chipmunks are not the only animals that hibernate. The queen bumblebee also hibernates in winter. All the other bees die before winter arrives. The queen hibernates under leaves in a small hole. She is cold-blooded and therefore is able to survive slightly frozen.
inform

## Page 174

### Alliterative Poetry

**Alliteration** is the repetition of a consonant sound in a group of words.

**Example:** Barney Bear bounced a ball.

Alliterative story poems can be fun to read and write. Any of several rhyming patterns can be used. Possibilities include:
Every two lines rhyme.
Every other line rhymes.
The first line rhymes with the last line and the two middle lines rhyme with each other.
All four lines rhyme.

**Example:**
Thomas Tuttle tries to dine,
On turkey, tea and treats so fine.
Thomas eats tomatoes and tortellini,
He devours tuna and tettrazini.

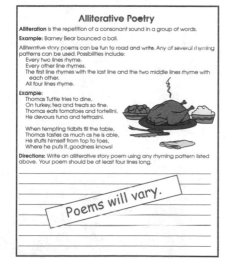

When tempting tidbits fill the table,
Thomas tastes as much as he is able,
He stuffs himself from top to toes,
Where he puts it, goodness knows!

**Directions:** Write an alliterative story poem using any rhyming pattern listed above. Your poem should be at least four lines long.

Poems will vary.

## Page 175

### Haiku

**Haiku** is a form of unrhymed Japanese poetry. A haiku poem has only three lines. Each line has a specific number of syllables.

Haiku poems usually describe a season or something in nature. Sometimes haiku are written about feelings.

**The Haiku pattern:**
Line 1 — 5 syllables
Line 2 — 7 syllables
Line 3 — 5 syllables

**Example haiku:**
Winter snow slides from
The eave. Drops—plop—on my head.
As I walk under.
— *D.S. Underwood*

When writing haiku you do not count words per line. Count only the number of syllables.

**Directions:** To prepare for writing your poem, think of words about a snowy day. Write them on the lines. After each word, write the number of syllables in the word.

frosty (2)    white (1)    snowflake

*Answers will vary.*

When writing any type of poetry, it is a good idea to start on scrap paper so you can write, erase, cross out, and rewrite.

**Directions:** Write a haiku poem about a snowy day on scrap paper. When you are satisfied with your poem, rewrite it below. At the end of each line, write the number of syllables in the line.

*Poems will vary.*
5
7
5

**Directions:** Select one of the topics in the box. Prewrite your poem on scrap paper. Write it on good paper when you are satisfied with it.

| rainy day | summer | spring | fall |
| a sparrow | joy | sadness | friendship |

## Page 176

### Tankas

Haiku poems are given to friends as gifts. A **tanka** is a poem written in response to haiku. If a person receives a haiku, he or she is supposed to send a tanka in reply! A tanka is much like a haiku but has two more lines.

**The tanka pattern:**
Line 1 — 5 syllables
Line 2 — 7 syllables
Line 3 — 5 syllables
Line 4 — 7 syllables
Line 5 — 7 syllables

**Example tanka:**
The snow on your head
It did plop—stop and slide down
Your neck to your socks.
The winter wind blew, gave you
A chill, now you sneeze—Ah choo!
— *D.S. Underwood*

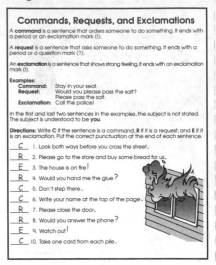

Remember to count syllables per line.

**Directions:** Write a tanka in response to one of the two haiku poems you wrote. Prewrite on scrap paper. When you are satisfied with your tanka, rewrite it below. At the end of each line, write the number of syllables in the line.

5
7
5
7
7

*Poems will vary.*

**Directions:** Trade your haiku _____ Write a tanka in response to your partner's haiku.

## Page 177

### Commands, Requests, and Exclamations

A **command** is a sentence that orders someone to do something. It ends with a period or an exclamation mark (!).

A **request** is a sentence that asks someone to do something. It ends with a period or a question mark (?).

An **exclamation** is a sentence that shows strong feeling. It ends with an exclamation mark (!).

**Examples:**
**Command:**    Stay in your seat.
**Request:**    Would you please pass the salt?
                Please pass the salt.
**Exclamation:**    Call the police!

In the first and last two sentences in the examples, the subject is not stated. The subject is understood to be **you.**

**Directions:** Write **C** if the sentence is a command, **R** if it is a request, and **E** if it is an exclamation. Put the correct punctuation at the end of each sentence.

C  1. Look both ways before you cross the street.
R  2. Please go to the store and buy some bread for us.
E  3. The house is on fire!
R  4. Would you hand me the glue?
C  5. Don't step there.
C  6. Write your name at the top of the page.
R  7. Please close the door.
R  8. Would you answer the phone?
E  9. Watch out!
C  10. Take one card from each pile.

## Page 178

### Run-On Sentences

A **run-on sentence** occurs when two or more sentences are joined together without the correct punctuation. A run-on sentence must be divided into two or more separate sentences.

**Example:**
**Run-on:**    On Tuesday my family went to the amusement park but unfortunately it rained and we got wet and it took hours for our clothes to dry.
**Correct:**    On Tuesday, my family went to the amusement park. Unfortunately, it rained and we got wet. It took hours for our clothes to dry.

**Directions:** Rewrite these run-on sentences correctly.

1. I have a dog named Boxer and a cat named Phoebe and they are both well-behaved and friendly.

   I have a dog named Boxer and a cat named Phoebe. They are both friendly and well-behaved.

2. Jacob's basketball coach makes the team run for 20 minutes each practice and then he makes them play a full game and afterwards he makes them do 50 push-ups and 100 sit-ups.

   Jacob's basketball coach makes the team run for 20 minutes each practice. Then he makes them play a full game. Afterwards he makes them do 50 push-ups and 100 sit-ups.

3. My family members each enjoy different hobbies Mom likes to paint Dad likes to read I like to play sports and my younger sister likes to build model airplanes although I think they are too hard.

   My family members each enjoy different hobbies. Mom likes to paint. Dad likes to read. I like to play sports. My younger sister likes to build model airplanes although i think they are too hard.

## Page 179

### Writing: Topic Sentences

The topic sentence in a paragraph usually comes first. Sometimes, however, the topic sentence can come at the end or even in the middle of a paragraph. When looking for the topic sentence, try to find the one that tells the main idea of a paragraph.

**Directions:** Read the following paragraphs and underline the topic sentence in each.

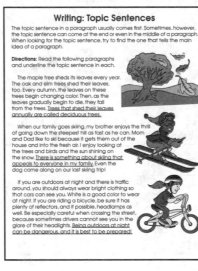

The maple tree sheds its leaves every year. The oak and elm trees shed their leaves, too. Every autumn, the leaves on these trees begin changing color. Then, as the leaves gradually begin to die, they fall from the trees. Trees that shed their leaves annually are called deciduous trees.

When our family goes skiing, my brother enjoys the thrill of going down the steepest hill as fast as he can. Mom and Dad like to ski because it gets them out of the house and into the fresh air. I enjoy looking at the trees and birds and the sun shining on the snow. There is something about skiing that appeals to everyone in my family. Even the dog came along on our last skiing trip!

If you are outdoors at night and there is traffic around, you should always wear bright clothing so that cars can see you. White is a good color to wear at night. If you are riding a bicycle, be sure it has plenty of reflectors, and if possible, headlamps as well. Be especially careful when crossing the street, because sometimes drivers cannot see you in the glare of their headlights. Being outdoors at night can be dangerous, and it is best to be prepared!

## Page 180

### Four Kinds of Sentences

**Directions:** For each pair of words, write two kinds of sentences (any combination of question, command, statement, or exclamation). Use one or both words in each sentence. Name each kind of sentence you wrote.

**Example:** pump    crop

Question: What kind of crops did you plant?
Command: Pump the water as fast as you can.

1. pinch    health

_____ : _____

2. fond    fact

*Answers will vary.*

3. insist    hatch

_____ : _____

exclamation    command    statement    question

Summer Link Super Edition Grade 5    190

# Developmental Skills for Fifth Grade Reading Success

Parents and educators alike know that the School Specialty name ensures outstanding educational experience and content. *Summer Link Reading* was designed to help your child retain those skills learned during the past school year. With *Summer Link Reading*, your child will be ready to review and master new material with confidence when he or she returns to school in the fall.

Use this checklist—compiled from state curriculum standards—to help your child prepare for proficiency testing. Place a check mark in the box if the appropriate skill has been mastered. If your child needs more work with a particular skill, place an "R" in the box and come back to it for review.

## Language Arts Skills

❑ Recognizes and correctly uses parts of speech: nouns, verbs, pronouns, adjectives, adverbs, articles, prepositions, and conjunctions.

❑ Understands and correctly uses mechanics conventions: capitalization, punctuation, correct verb tense, subject and verb agreement, complete sentences versus fragments, and compound and complex sentences.

❑ Uses a variety of vocabulary strategies: synonyms, antonyms, homophones, homographs, multiple meanings, affixes, and base words.

❑ Understands and correctly uses a variety of writing strategies: compare and contrast, cause and effect, fact and opinion, supporting facts and statistics, and proofreading and revising.

❑ Recognizes and writes various sentence types: statements, questions, exclamations. Uses multiple paragraphs in writing, such as: an introduction, body support, and conclusion.

❑ Can locate information in reference materials: dictionary, thesaurus, encyclopedia, atlas, almanac, and the Internet.

## Reading Skills

❑ Uses reading strategies to understand meaning: classification, themes, compare and contrast, cause and effect, context clues, and sequencing.

❑ Reads for different purposes: main idea, supporting details, following directions, predicting outcomes, and making inferences.

❑ Recognizes story elements: character, setting, point of view, mood, plot development and problem resolution.

❑ Distinguishes between fact and fiction and is familiar with different genres and forms of literature, such as: fantasy, fairy tale, folk tale, tall tale, historical fiction, realistic fiction, poetry, biography, and autobiography.

# Summer LINK
# TEST PRACTICE

# Summer Link Test Practice
# Table of Contents

## Just for Parents

About the Tests .................................................194
How to Help Your Child Prepare for Standardized Testing .....................198

## For All Students

Taking Standardized Tests ..........................................200
Terms to Know ................................................204

## Kinds of Questions

Multiple Choice Questions ..........................................206
Fill-in-the-Blank Questions ..........................................207
True/False Questions .............................................208
Matching Questions ..............................................209
Analogy Questions ...............................................210
Short Answer Questions ............................................211

## Subject Help

Reading .....................................................212
Language Arts .................................................213

## Practice Test and Final Test

Introduction ..................................................221
Practice Test Answer Sheet ..........................................222
Practice Test .................................................223
Final Test Answer Sheet ............................................259
Final Test ...................................................261
Answer Key ..................................................285
Test Practice Worksheet ............................................296

# About the Tests

## What Are Standardized Achievement Tests?

Achievement tests measure what children know in particular subject areas such as reading, language arts, and mathematics. They do not measure your child's intelligence or ability to learn.

When tests are standardized, or *normed*, children's test results are compared with those of a specific group who have taken the test, usually at the same age or grade.

Standardized achievement tests measure what children around the country are learning. The test makers survey popular textbook series, as well as state curriculum frameworks and other professional sources, to determine what content is covered widely.

Because of variations in state frameworks and textbook series, as well as grade ranges on some test levels, the tests may cover some material that children have not yet learned. This is especially true if the test is offered early in the school year. However, test scores are compared to those of other children who take the test at the same time of year, so your child will not be at a disadvantage if his or her class has not covered specific material yet.

## Different School Districts, Different Tests

There are many flexible options for districts when offering standardized tests. Many school districts choose not to give the full test battery, but select certain content and scoring options. For example, many schools may test only in the areas of reading and mathematics. Similarly, a state or district may use one test for certain grades and another test for other grades. These decisions are often based on the amount of time and money a district wishes to spend

on test administration. Some states choose to develop their own statewide assessment tests.

On pages 195–197 you will find information about these five widely used standardized achievement tests:

- California Achievement Tests (CAT)
- Terra Nova/CTBS
- Iowa Test of Basic Skills (ITBS)
- Stanford Achievement Test (SAT9)
- Metropolitan Achievement Test (MAT).

However, this book contains strategies and practice questions for use with a variety of tests. Even if your state does not give one of the five tests listed above, your child will benefit from doing the practice questions in this book. If you're unsure about which test your child takes, contact your local school district to find out which tests are given.

## Types of Test Questions

Traditionally, standardized achievements tests have used only multiple choice questions. Today, many tests may include constructed response (short answer) and extended response (essay) questions as well.

In addition, many tests include questions that tap students' higher-order thinking skills. Instead of simple recall questions, such as identifying a date in history, questions may require students to make comparisons and contrasts or analyze results among other skills.

## What the Tests Measure

These tests do not measure your child's level of intelligence, but they do show how well your child knows material that he or she has learned and that is also covered on the tests. It's important to remember

that some tests cover content that is not taught in your child's school or grade. In other instances, depending on when in the year the test is given, your child may not yet have covered the material.

If the test reports you receive show that your child needs improvement in one or more skill areas, you may want to seek help from your child's teacher and find out how you can work with your child to improve his or her skills.

# California Achievement Tests (CAT/5)

## What Is the California Achievement Test?

The California Achievement Test is a standardized achievement test battery that is widely used with elementary through high school students.

## Parts of the Test

The CAT includes tests in the following content areas:

**Reading**
- Word Analysis
- Vocabulary
- Comprehension

**Spelling**

**Language Arts**
- Language Mechanics
- Language Usage

**Mathematics**

**Science**

**Social Studies**

Your child may take some or all of these subtests if your district uses the *California Achievement Test*.

# Terra Nova/CTBS (Comprehensive Tests of Basic Skills)

## What Is the Terra Nova/CTBS?

The *Terra Nova/Comprehensive Tests of Basic Skills* is a standardized achievement test battery used in elementary through high school grades. While many of the test questions on the *Terra Nova* are in the traditional multiple-choice form, your child may take parts of the *Terra Nova* that include some open-ended questions (constructed-response items).

## Parts of the Test

Your child may take some or all of the following subtests if your district uses the *Terra Nova/CTBS*:

**Reading/Language Arts**
**Mathematics**
**Science**
**Social Studies**

Supplementary tests include:
- Word Analysis
- Vocabulary
- Language Mechanics
- Spelling
- Mathematics Computation

Critical thinking skills may also be tested.

# Iowa Tests of Basic Skills (ITBS)

## What Is the ITBS?

The *Iowa Test of Basic Skills* is a standardized achievement test battery used in elementary through high school grades.

## Parts of the Test

Your child may take some or all of these subtests if your district uses the *ITBS*, also known as the *Iowa*:

**Reading**
- Vocabulary
- Reading Comprehension

**Language Arts**
- Spelling
- Capitalization
- Punctuation
- Usage and Expression

**Math**
- Concepts/Estimate
- Problems/Data Interpretation

**Social Studies**

**Science**

**Sources of Information**

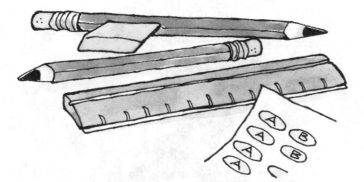

# Stanford Achievement Test (SAT9)

## What Is the Stanford Achievement Test?

The *Stanford Achievement Test, Ninth Edition (SAT9)* is a standardized achievement test battery used in elementary through high school grades.

Note that the *Stanford Achievement Test (SAT9)* is a different test from the *SAT* used by high school students for college admissions.

While many of the test questions on the *SAT9* are in traditional multiple choice form, your child may take parts of the *SAT9* that include some open-ended questions (constructed-response items).

## Parts of the Test

Your child may take some or all of these subtests if your district uses the Stanford Achievement Test.

**Reading**
- Vocabulary
- Reading Comprehension

**Mathematics**
- Problem Solving
- Procedures

**Language Arts**

**Spelling**

**Study Skills**

**Listening**

Critical thinking skills may also be tested.

# Metropolitan Achievement Test (MAT7 and MAT8)

## What Is the Metropolitan Achievement Test?

The *Metropolitan Achievement Test* is a standardized achievement test battery used in elementary through high school grades.

## Parts of the Test

Your child may take some or all of these subtests if your district uses the *Metropolitan Achievement Test*.

**Reading**
- Vocabulary
- Reading Comprehension

**Math**
- Concepts and Problem Solving
- Computation

**Language Arts**
- Pre-writing
- Composing
- Editing

**Science**

**Social Studies**

**Research Skills**

**Thinking Skills**

**Spelling**

# Statewide Assessments

Today the majority of states give statewide assessments. In some cases these tests are known as *high-stakes assessments*. This means that students must score at a certain level in order to be promoted. Some states use minimum competency or proficiency tests. Often these tests measure more basic skills than other types of statewide assessments.

Statewide assessments are generally linked to state curriculum frameworks. Frameworks provide a blueprint, or outline, to ensure that teachers are covering the same curriculum topics as other teachers in the same grade level in the state. In some states, standardized achievement tests (such as the five described in this book) are used in connection with statewide assessments.

## When Statewide Assessments Are Given

Statewide assessments may not be given at every grade level. Generally, they are offered at one or more grades in elementary school, middle school, and high school. Many states test at grades 4, 8, and 10.

## State-by-State Information

You can find information about statewide assessments and curriculum frameworks at your state Department of Education Web site. To find the address for your individual state go to www.ed.gov, click on Topics A–Z, and then click on State Departments of Education.
You will find a list of all the state departments of education, mailing addresses, and Web sites.

# How to Help Your Child Prepare for Standardized Testing

## Preparing All Year Round

Perhaps the most valuable way you can help your child prepare for standardized achievement tests is by providing enriching experiences. Keep in mind also, that test results for younger children are not as reliable as for older students. If a child is hungry, tired, or upset, this may result in a poor test score. Here are some tips on how you can help your child do his or her best on standardized tests.

**Read aloud with your child**. Reading aloud helps develop vocabulary and fosters a positive attitude toward reading. Reading together is one of the most effective ways you can help your child succeed in school.

**Share experiences.** Baking cookies together, planting a garden, or making a map of your neighborhood are examples of activities that help build skills that are measured on the tests such as sequencing and following directions.

**Become informed about your state's testing procedures.** Ask about or watch for announcements of meetings that explain about standardized tests and statewide assessments in your school district.

Talk to your child's teacher about your child's individual performance on these state tests during a parent-teacher conference.

**Help your child know what to expect.** Read and discuss with your child the test-taking tips in this book. Your child can prepare by working through a couple of strategies a day so that no practice session takes too long.

**Help your child with his or her regular school assignments.** Set up a quiet study area for homework. Supply this area with pencils, paper, markers, a calculator, a ruler, a dictionary, scissors, glue, and so on. Check your child's homework and offer to help if he or she gets stuck. But remember, it's your child's homework, not yours. If you help too much, your child will not benefit from the activity.

**Keep in regular contact with your child's teacher.** Attend parent-teacher conferences, school functions, PTA or PTO meetings, and school board meetings. This will help you get to know the educators in your district and the families of your child's classmates.

**Learn to use computers as an educational resource.** If you do not have a computer and Internet access at home, try your local library.

**Remember—simply getting your child comfortable with testing procedures and helping him or her know what to expect can improve test scores!**

# Getting Ready for the Big Day

There are lots of things you can do on or immediately before test day to improve your child's chances of testing success. What's more, these strategies will help your child prepare him or herself for school tests, too, and promote general study skills that can last a lifetime.

**Provide a good breakfast on test day.** Instead of sugar cereal, which provides immediate but not long-term energy, have your child eat a breakfast with protein or complex carbohydrates such as an egg, whole grain cereal or toast, or a banana-yogurt shake.

**Promote a good night's sleep.** A good night's sleep before the test is essential. Try not to overstress the importance of the test. This may cause your child to lose sleep because of anxiety. Doing some exercise after school and having a quiet evening routine will help your child sleep well the night before the test.

**Assure your child that he or she is not expected to know all of the answers on the test.** Explain that other children in higher grades may take the same test, and that the test may measure things your child has not yet learned in school. Help your child understand that you expect him or her to put forth a good effort—and that this is enough. Your child should not try to cram for these tests. Also avoid threats or bribes; these put undue pressure on children and may interfere with their best performance.

**Keep the mood light and offer encouragement.** To provide a break on test days, do something fun and special after school—take a walk around the neighborhood, play a game, read a favorite book, or prepare a special snack together. These activities keep your child's mood light—even if the testing sessions have been difficult—and show how much you appreciate your child's effort.

# Taking Standardized Tests

No matter what grade you're in, this is information you can use to prepare for standardized tests. Here is what you'll find:

- Test-taking tips and strategies to use on test day and year-round.
- Important terms to know for Language Arts, Reading, Math, Science, and Social Studies.
- A checklist of skills to complete to help you understand what you need to know in Language Arts, Reading Comprehension, Writing, and Math.
- General study/homework tips.

By opening this book, you've already taken your first step towards test success. The rest is easy—all you have to do is get started!

## What You Need to Know

There are many things you can do to increase your test success. Here's a list of tips to keep in mind when you take standardized tests—and when you study for them, too.

**Keep up with your school work.** One way you can succeed in school and on tests is by studying and doing your homework regularly. Studies show that you remember only about one-fifth of what you memorize the night before a test. That's one good reason not to try to learn it all at once! Keeping up with your work throughout the year will help you remember the material better. You also won't be as tired or nervous as if you try to learn everything at once.

**Feel your best.** One of the ways you can do your best on tests and in school is to make sure your body is ready. To do this, get a good night's sleep each night and eat a healthy breakfast (not sugary cereal that will leave you tired by the middle of the morning). An egg or a milkshake with yogurt and fresh fruit will give you lasting energy. Also, wear comfortable clothes, maybe your lucky shirt or your favorite color on test day. It can't hurt, and it may even keep you relax.

**Be prepared.** Do practice questions and learn about how standardized tests are organized. Books like this one will help you know what to expect when you take a standardized test.

**When you are taking the test, follow the directions.** It is important to listen carefully to the directions your teacher gives and to read the written instructions carefully. Words like *not*, *none*, *rarely*, *never*, and *always* are very important in test directions and questions. You may want to circle words like these.

**Look at each page carefully before you start answering.** In school you usually read a passage and then answer questions about it. But when you take a test, it's helpful to follow a different order.

If you are taking a Reading test, first read the directions. Then read the questions before you read the passage. This way you will know exactly what kind of information to look for as you read. Next, read the passage carefully. Finally, answer the questions.

On math and science tests, look at the labels on graphs and charts. Think about what each graph or chart shows. Questions often will ask you to draw conclusions about the information.

**Manage your time.** *Time management* means using your time wisely on a test so that you can finish as much of it as possible and do your best. Look over the test or the parts that you are allowed to do at one time. Sometimes you may want to do the easier parts first. This way, if you run out of time before you finish, you will have completed a good chunk of the work.

For tests that have a time limit, notice what time it is when the test begins and figure out when you need to stop. Check a few times as you work through the test to be sure you are making good progress and not spending too much time on any particular section.

**You don't have to keep up with everyone else.** You may notice other students in the class finishing before you do. Don't worry about this. Everyone works at a different pace. Just keep going, trying not to spend too long on any one question.

**Fill in answer sheets properly.** Even if you know every answer on a test, you won't do well unless you enter the answers correctly on the answer sheet.

Fill in the entire bubble, but don't spend too much time making it perfect. Make your mark dark, but not so dark that it goes through the paper! And be sure you only choose one answer for each question, even if you are not sure. If you choose two answers, both will be marked as wrong.

**It's usually not a good idea to change your answers.** Usually your first choice is the right one. Unless you realize that you misread the question, the directions, or some facts in a passage, it's usually safer to stay with your first answer. If you are pretty sure it's wrong, of course, go ahead and change it. Make sure you completely erase the first choice and neatly fill in your new choice.

**Use context clues to figure out tough questions.** If you come across a word or idea you don't understand, use context clues—the words in the sentences nearby—to help you figure out its meaning.

**Sometimes it's good to guess.** Should you guess when you don't know an answer on a test? That depends. If your teacher has made the test, usually you will score better if you answer as many questions as possible, even if you don't really know the answers.

On standardized tests, here's what to do to score your best. For each question, most of these tests let you choose from four or five answer choices. If you decide that a couple of answers are clearly wrong but you're still not sure about the answer, go ahead and make your best guess. If you can't narrow down the choices at all, then you may be better off skipping the question. Tests like these take away extra points for wrong answers, so it's better to leave them blank. Be sure you skip over the answer space for these questions on the answer sheet, though, so you don't fill in the wrong spaces.

**Sometimes you should skip a question and come back to it later.** On many tests, you will score better if you answer more questions. This means that you should not spend too much time on any single question. Sometimes it gets tricky, though, keeping track of questions you skipped on your answer sheet.

If you want to skip a question because you don't know the answer, put a very light pencil mark next to the question in the test booklet. Try to choose an answer, even if you're not sure of it. Fill in the answer lightly on the answer sheet.

**Check your work.** On a standardized test, you can't go ahead or skip back to another section of the test. But you may go back and review your answers on the section you just worked on if you have extra time.

First, scan your answer sheet. Make sure that you answered every question you could. Also, if you are using a bubble-type answer sheet, make sure that you filled in only one bubble for each question. Erase any extra marks on the page.

**Finally—avoid test anxiety!** If you get nervous about tests, don't worry. *Test anxiety* happens to lots of good students. Being a little nervous actually sharpens your mind. But if you get very nervous about tests, take a few minutes to relax the night before or the day of the test. One good way to relax is to get some exercise, even if you just have time to stretch, shake out your fingers, and wiggle your toes. If you can't move around, it helps just to take a few slow, deep breaths and picture yourself doing a great job!

# Terms to Know

Here's a list of terms that are good to know when taking standardized tests. Don't be worried if you see something new. You may not have learned it in school yet.

**acute angle:** an angle of less than 90°

**adjective:** a word that describes a noun (*yellow duckling, new bicycle*)

**adverb:** a word that describes a verb (*ran fast, laughing heartily*)

**analogy:** a comparison of the relationship between two or more otherwise unrelated things (*Carrot is to vegetable as banana is to fruit.*)

**angle:** the figure formed by two lines that start at the same point, usually shown in degrees **90°**

**antonyms:** words with opposite meanings (*big* and *small, young* and *old*)

**area:** the amount of space inside a flat shape, expressed in square units

**article:** a word such as *a, an*, or *the* that goes in front of a noun (*the chicken, an apple*)

**cause/effect:** the reason that something happens

**character:** a person in a story, book, movie, play, or TV show

**compare/contrast:** to tell what is alike and different about two or more things

**compass rose:** the symbol on a map that shows where North, South, East, and West are

**conclusion:** a logical decision you can make based on information from a reading selection or science experiment

**congruent:** equal in size or shape

**context clues:** language and details in a piece of writing that can help you figure out difficult words and ideas

**denominator:** in a fraction, the number under the line; shows how many equal parts a whole has been divided into ($\frac{1}{2}, \frac{6}{7}$)

**direct object:** in a sentence, the person or thing that receives the action of a verb (*Jane hit the ball hard.*)

**equation:** in math, a statement where one set of numbers or values is equal to another set (*6 + 6 = 12, 4 x 5 = 20*)

**factor:** a whole number that can be divided exactly into another whole number (*1, 2, 3, 4, and 6 are all factors of 12.*)

**genre:** a category of literature that contains writing with common features (*drama, fiction, nonfiction, poetry*)

**hypothesis:** in science, the possible answer to a question, most science experiments begin with a hypothesis

**indirect object:** in a sentence, the noun or pronoun that tells to or for whom the action of the verb is done (*Louise gave a flower to her sister.*)

**infer:** to make an educated guess about a piece of writing, based on information contained in the selection and what you already know

**main idea:** the most important idea or message in a writing selection

**map legend:** the part of a map showing symbols that represent natural or human-made objects

**noun:** a person, place, or thing (*president, underground, train*)

**numerator:** in a fraction, the number above the line; shows how many equal parts are to be taken from the denominator ($\frac{3}{4}, \frac{1}{5}$)

**operation:** in math, tells what must be done to numbers in an equation (such as add, subtract, multiply, or divide)

**parallel:** lines or rays that, if extended, could never intersect

**percent:** fraction of a whole that has been divided into 100 parts, usually expressed with % sign ($\frac{5}{100} = 5\%$)

**perimeter:** distance around an object or shape

3 ft.

3 ft. ▢ 3 ft.

3 ft.

Perimeter = 3 + 3 + 3 + 3 = 12 ft.

**perpendicular:** lines or rays that intersect to form a 90° (right) angle

90°

**predicate:** in a sentence, the word or words that tell what the subject does, did, or has (*The fuzzy kitten had black spots on its belly.*)

**predict:** in science or reading, to use given information to decide what will happen

**prefixes/suffixes:** letters added to the beginning or end of a word to change its meaning (*reorganize, hopeless*)

**preposition:** a word that shows the relationship between a noun or pronoun and other words in a phrase or sentence (*We sat by the fire. She walked through the door.*)

**probability:** the likelihood that something will happen, often shown with numbers

**pronoun:** a word that is used in place of a noun (*She gave the present to them.*)

**ratio:** a comparison of two quantities, often shown as a fraction (*The ratio of boys to girls in the class is 2 to 1, or 2/1.*)

**sequence:** the order in which events happen or in which items can be placed in a pattern

**subject:** in a sentence, the word or words that tell who or what the sentence is about (*Uncle Robert baked the cake. Everyone at the party ate it.*)

**summary:** a restatement of important ideas from a selection in the writer's own words

**symmetry:** in math and science, two or more sides or faces of an object that are mirror images of one another

line of symmetry

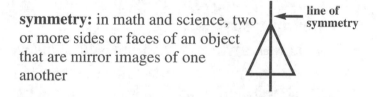

**synonyms:** words with the same, or almost the same, meaning (*delicious* and *tasty*, *funny* and *comical*)

**Venn diagram:** two or more overlapping circles used to compare and contrast two or more things

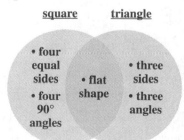

square    triangle

• four equal sides
• four 90° angles
• flat shape
• three sides
• three angles

**verb:** a word that describes an action or state of being (*He watched the fireworks.*)

**writing prompt:** on a test, a question or statement that you must respond to in writing

# Multiple Choice Questions

You have probably seen multiple choice questions before. They are the most common type of question used on standardized tests. To answer a multiple choice question, you must choose one answer from a number of choices.

---

**EXAMPLE**   **The word that means the opposite of <u>rapid</u> is _____ .**

    Ⓐ shallow        Ⓒ speedy

    Ⓑ sluggish       Ⓓ rabbit

---

Sometimes you will know the answer right away. Other times you won't. To answer multiple choice questions on a test, do the following:

- Read the directions carefully. If you're not sure what you're supposed to do, you might make a lot of mistakes.
- First answer any easy questions whose answers you are *sure* you know.
- When you come to a harder question, circle the question number. You can come back to this question after you have finished all the easier ones.
- When you're ready to answer a hard question, throw out answers that you know are wrong. You can do this by making an **X** after each choice you know is not correct. The last choice left is probably the correct one.

**Testing It Out**

Now look at the sample question more closely.

 **Think:** I know that rapid means "fast." So I must be looking for a word that means "slow." I have already eliminated *speedy* and *rabbit*. *Speedy* has the same meaning as *rapid*. *Rabbit* doesn't really have anything to do with *rapid*.

Now I have to choose between *shallow* and *sluggish*. *Shallow* means the opposite of *deep*, not the opposite of *fast*. I do not know the word *sluggish*, but I do know that slugs are slow-moving creatures. So I will choose **B**.

# Fill-in-the-Blank Questions

On some tests, you will be given multiple choice questions where you must fill in something that's missing from a phrase, sentence, equation, or passage. These are called "fill-in-the-blank" questions.

> **EXAMPLE**
>
> **Pablo was looking _____ to his family's camping trip.**
>
> Ⓐ foremost        Ⓒ former
>
> Ⓑ forehead       Ⓓ forward

To answer fill-in-the-blank questions, do the following:

- First read the item with a blank that needs to be filled.
- See if you can think of the answer even before you look at your choices.
- Even if the answer you first thought of is one of the choices, be sure to check the other choices. There may be an even better answer.
- For harder questions, try to fit every answer choice into the blank. Underline clue words that may help you find the correct answer. Write an **X** after answers that do not fit. Choose the answer that does fit. You can also use this strategy to double-check your answers.

**Testing It Out**

Now look at the sample question more closely.

 **Think:** "Pablo was looking _____ to his family's camping trip." If I were going on a camping trip, I would probably be excited about it—looking forward to it. Maybe one of the choices is *forward*. Yes, it is—the answer must be **D**.

To double-check, I'll try the other answer choices in the sentence. None of them makes sense: "looking foremost," "looking forehead," and "looking former" all sound wrong. Answer **D** still seems correct to me.

# True/False Questions

A true/false question asks you to read a statement and decide if it is right (true) or wrong (false). Sometimes you will be asked to write **T** for true or **F** for false. Most of the time you must fill in a bubble next to the correct answer.

---

**EXAMPLE**  **It is important to eat a good breakfast.**

Ⓐ true

Ⓑ false

---

To answer true/false questions on a test, think about the following:

- True/false sections contain more questions than other sections of a test. If there is a time limit on the test, you may need to go a little more quickly than usual. Do not spend too much time on any one question.
- First answer all of the easy questions. Circle the numbers next to harder ones and come back to them later.
- If you have time left after completing all the questions, quickly double-check your answers.
- True/false questions with words like *always*, *never*, *none*, *only*, and *every* are usually false. This is because they limit a statement so much.
- True-false questions with words like *most*, *many*, and *generally* are often true. This is because they make statements more believable.

**Testing It Out**

Now look at the sample question more closely.

**Think:** Is it important to eat a good breakfast? Yes, I've heard that before. I don't see any words like *always*, *never*, or *every* to limit the statement. My first instinct must be right. I'll choose **T** for true.

# Matching Questions

Matching questions ask you to find pairs of words or phrases that go together. The choices are often shown in columns.

**Match items that mean the same, or almost the same, thing.**

| | | | | | |
|---|---|---|---|---|---|
| **1** interest | A distress | **1** | Ⓐ Ⓑ Ⓒ Ⓓ |
| **2** discourage | B cheer up | **2** | Ⓐ Ⓑ Ⓒ Ⓓ |
| **3** encourage | C fascinate | **3** | Ⓐ Ⓑ Ⓒ Ⓓ |
| **4** worry | D disappoint | **4** | Ⓐ Ⓑ Ⓒ Ⓓ |

When answering matching questions on tests, follow these guidelines:

• Match the easiest choices first.
• If you come to a word you don't know, look for prefixes, suffixes, or root words to help figure out its meaning. Also, try using it in a sentence.
• Work down one column at a time. It is confusing to switch back and forth.

**Testing It Out**
Now look at the sample question more closely.

**Think:** I'll start with the first column. *Interest* is a word I've seen before. I think that *fascinate* means the same thing as, so I'll choose **C** to go with number 1.

I know that *disappointed* is the way people feel when they don't get something they want. *Let down* means the same thing. So I'll choose **D**.

I think that *support* might mean something similar to *help*. Let's see— "My mom gave me all the help she could." "My mom gave me all the support she could." Yes, both sentences make sense. I'll choose **B**.

The fourth word is *worry*. The only remaining choice is *distress*, but I don't know what it means. It might have something to do with being upset, but the only other possible word is *disappoint*, and I'm sure of my choice for that word. So I'll choose **A**.

# Analogy Questions

Analogies are a special kind of question. In an analogy question, you are asked to figure out the relationship between two things. Then you must complete another pair with the same relationship.

> **EXAMPLE**
>
> <u>Porcupine</u> is to <u>quills</u> as <u>bee</u> is to _____ .
>
> Ⓐ  sharp            Ⓒ  buzzing
>
> Ⓑ  insect           Ⓓ  stinger

Analogies usually have two pairs of items. In the question above, the two pairs are *porcupine/quills* and *bee/ _____* . To answer analogy questions on standardized tests, do the following:

• Try to form a sentence that explains how they are related.
• Next, use your sentence to figure out the missing word in the second pair of items.
• For more difficult analogies, try each answer choice in the sentence you formed. Choose the answer that fits best.

**Testing It Out**
Now look at the sample question more closely.

**Think:** How are *porcupine* and *quills* related? A porcupine has quills on its body; it uses its quills to protect itself. So if I use the word *bee* in this sentence, I'd say, "A bee has a _____ on its body; it uses its _____ to protect itself."

Choice **A** is *sharp*. If I use *sharp* to complete the sentence, I end up with, *A bee has sharp on its body; it uses its sharp to protect itself.* That makes no sense.

Choice **B** is *insect*. If I use *insect* to complete the sentence, I end up with *A bee has an insect on its body; it uses its insect to protect itself.* That makes no sense, either.

Choice **C** is *buzzing*. *A bee has a buzzing on its body; it uses its buzzing to protect itself.* Bees do buzz, but they don't have *buzzing* on their body.

Choice **D** is *stinger*. *A bee has a stinger on its body; it uses its stinger to protect itself.* Yes, both parts of that sentence are true. **D** is the correct choice.

# Short Answer Questions

Some test questions don't give you answers to choose from; instead, you must write short answers in your own words. These are called "short answer" or "open response" questions.

> **EXAMPLE**    **Ted saw that a rowboat had tipped over and two people were struggling in the water. He swam out to the boat. He calmed the two swimmers and showed them how to hold on to the overturned boat. Then he stayed with them until a rescue boat could get there.**
>
> 1. What word or words would you use to describe Ted? _____
>
> 2. How do you think the people in the water felt about Ted? _____

When you must write short answers to questions on a standardized test, do the following:

- Read each question carefully. Make sure to respond directly to the question that is being asked.
- Your response should be short but complete.
- Write in complete sentences unless the directions say you don't have to.
- Make sure to double-check your answers for spelling, punctuation, and grammar when you are done.

**Testing It Out**

Now reread the paragraph about Ted and the questions.

**Think**: From the story, I can tell that Ted is brave. He tried to save the swimmers even though it might have been dangerous. I know he is a good swimmer because he stayed in the water for a long time and showed the swimmers how to hold on to the boat. Even though the directions don't say, I know I should write in complete sentences. So I'll write:

1. *Ted is brave. He is also a good swimmer.*

The swimmers must have appreciated Ted's help. So I'll write:

2. *The swimmers were glad that Ted was there to help them.*

# Reading

Many standardized tests have sections called "Reading" or "Reading Comprehension." Reading Comprehension questions test your ability to read for detail, find meaning in a sentence or passage, and use context clues to figure out words or ideas you don't understand. The following is a list of topics covered on Reading Comprehension tests.

## Word Meaning

Word meaning questions test your vocabulary and your ability to figure out unfamiliar words. When answering questions about word meaning:

- See if you can find prefixes, suffixes, or root words for clues to their meaning.
- Look at the other words in the sentence or passage to help tell what the underlined word means.

> When the climbers reached the summit, they could see for miles.

The underlined word must mean "top" or "peak."

## Characterization

What characters say, do, and feel is an important part of many reading passages.

> When Jennie heard the news, she made a face and groaned.

Is Jennie happy about the news? No, her actions tell you she is unhappy.

## Cause and Effect

Look for **cause and effect** when you read. A **cause** is an event that makes another one happen. The **effect** is the event that is caused.

- Words like *before*, *after*, and *because* can provide clues to cause and effect.
- Sometimes you must use context clues and what you already know to figure out the cause or effect of something.

> Louis's grandmother was furious. "I told you not to swim in the pool without and adult nearby! I'm afraid you can't go to the movies tonight."

We can assume that Louis's grandmother is furious because he went in the pool without an adult nearby. We can also assume that she won't let him go to the movies for the same reason.

## Sequence

The **sequence of events** is the order in which events take place.

- Look for clue words such as first, next, last, finally, before, and after to help you tell the sequence of events in a story.
- Sometimes the events in a story won't be listed in sequence. Then you have to read carefully for other clues to the sequence.

> First, you mix the ingredients. Then, you roll the cookies into little balls. Next, you place the cookie sheet into the oven. Finally, they are done and ready to eat!

# Language Arts

## Language Mechanics and Expression

Standardized tests usually include questions about spelling, grammar, punctuation, and capitalization. These questions are often grouped together in sections called "Language Mechanics and Expression" or "Language Arts."

The following is a list of different topics included under Language Mechanics and Expression. Look at the tips and examples that go with each topic. If you have trouble with one of the topics listed, talk to a teacher or parent about getting extra help.

### Grammar

Grammar is the set of rules that helps you write good, clear sentences. Whether you are answering a multiple choice question, writing a short answer, or responding to a writing prompt, you should:

- Be sure the subject and verb of each sentence agree with one another.

Daryl | usually | wins | the class
*singular subject*          *singular verb*

spelling bee.

Daryl and Linda | usually | win | the class
*plural subject*          *plural verb*

spelling bee.

- Remember how to use different parts of speech such as nouns, verbs, adjectives, adverbs, pronouns, and conjunctions.

Sam | studies | constantly. | He | is | an |
*noun*   *verb*   *adverb*   *pronoun* *verb* *article*

amazing | student | and | always | gets | A's.
*adjective*   *noun* *conjunction* *adverb*   *verb* *noun*

### Capitalization

You may be asked to identify words that should be capitalized and words that shouldn't. Remember:

- Always capitalize the first word in a sentence.
- Always capitalize the names of people, places, and other proper nouns.

My friend Chow celebrates Chinese New Year.

On the other hand, Alana and Lakeisha celebrate Kwanzaa.

- Capitalize proper adjectives.

We went out for Vietnamese food on my mother's birthday.

# Language Arts

**Directions:** Choose the punctuation that is missing from numbers 1–3.

**1**   **Do you think the film is scary__**

.        ,        ?        !
**A**     **B**     **C**     **D**

**2**   **It__s more funny than scary.**

?        ,        .        ,
**F**     **G**     **H**     **J**

**3**   **Lookout, here comes an avalanche__**

!        .        ?        ,
**A**     **B**     **C**     **D**

**Directions:** For question 4, choose the correct capitalized sentence.

**4**   **i took jake's dog ben for a walk.**

**F**   I took Jake's dog ben for a walk.

**G**   I took jake's dog Ben for a walk.

**H**   I took Jake's Dog ben for a walk.

**J**   I took Jake's dog Ben for a walk.

**Directions:** For questions 5–7, choose the verb that best completes each sentence.

**5**   **Mr. Jacobs _____ the school band.**

**A**   leading

**B**   lead

**C**   leads

**D**   are leading

**6**   **The horn players _____ in the city finals.**

**F**   competes

**G**   is competing

**H**   compete

**J**   competing

**7**   **My mother _____ for three hours.**

**A**   drive

**B**   driven

**C**   has drove

**D**   drove

# Writing

Many tests will ask you to respond to a writing prompt. A writing prompt is a question or statement that you are asked to respond to.

> Why is George Washington often called "The Father of Our Country"? Explain your answer.

The following is a list of guidelines to use when responding to a writing prompt.

## Read the Prompt
- Read the instructions carefully. Sometimes you will be given a choice of questions or topics to write about. You don't want to respond to more questions than you need to.
- Remember, there is no one right response to a writing prompt; there are only stronger and weaker arguments.

## Prewrite
- Before you write your answer, jot down some details to include.
- You may find it helpful to use a chart, web, illustration, or outline to help you organize the information you want to include in your response.
- Even if you aren't asked to, it is always a good idea to include facts and examples that support your answer. If the prompt asks you to respond to a reading passage, you can include specific examples from the passage to strengthen your argument.

## Draft
- Begin your answer with a **topic sentence** that answers the main question and gives the main idea.
- Write **supporting sentences** that give details and tell more about your main idea. All of these sentences should relate to the topic sentence.
- If you are allowed, skip lines as you write. That way you'll have space to correct your mistakes once you're done writing.

## Proofread
- Make sure to proofread your draft for missing words, grammar, punctuation, capitalization, indentation, and spelling. Correct your mistakes.

## Testing It Out
Now read the following topic sentence that is the beginning of a response to the sample prompt. It has been formatted correctly, beginning with an indentation. All spelling and grammar mistakes have been corrected.

> I think that George Washington is called "The Father of Our Country" because he played such an important role in the American Revolution and he was our first President. He was the general of the colonial army when it fought against the British, and if it hadn't been for his good leadership the colonies might not have won the war.

# Math: Trick Questions

Sometimes you're given trick questions on tests. You may be able to solve a trick question but the answer is not one of the choices given. In this case, you fill in "None of these."

**EXAMPLE**

**There were 488 balloons decorating the gymnasium for a party. There were 97 students at the party. If each student brought home an equal number of balloons after the party, how many balloons were left over?**

Ⓐ    2 balloons        Ⓒ    12 balloons

Ⓑ    46 balloons       Ⓓ    None of these

• First, determine what you need to do to solve the problem. Since you have to know the number of balloons left over, you need to find a remainder from a division problem.

• The correct answer is not one of your answer choices. Check your work and then fill in D, the "None of these" choice.

$$\begin{array}{r} 5R3 \\ 97\overline{)488} \\ -485 \\ \hline 3 \end{array}$$

When you have to solve questions for which the answer may not be given:

❑ Read the problem carefully.

❑ Determine what information you need to solve the problem.

❑ Solve the problem.

❑ Check for the correct answer.

❑ Review your work for accuracy and then mark "None of these."

# Math: Paper and Pencil

It often helps to work through problems using paper and pencil. It allows you to see and check the work you have done. Some test questions do not give multiple choice answers. You will need to use paper and pencil when you have to find answers to these questions.

---

**EXAMPLE**
**There are 32 cartons of yo-yos. Each carton has 145 yo-yos. They are ready to be shipped to several stores in a truck. How many yo-yos in total are being shipped on the truck?**

---

- Since you do not have any answers to choose from, you have to figure out the answer to the question using paper and pencil.

- Use paper and pencil to multiply 145 x 32. This is the total number of yo-yos on the truck.

- Then, use paper and pencil again to check the answer you found the first time. When checking multiplication, you change the order of the factors.

- You know the answer is 4,640 yo-yos.

$$\begin{array}{r} 145 \\ \times\ \ 32 \\ \hline 290 \\ 435\ \ \\ \hline \end{array}$$
4,640 yo-yos

$$\begin{array}{r} 32 \\ \times\ \ 145 \\ \hline 160 \\ 128\ \\ 32\ \ \\ \hline \end{array}$$
4,640 yo-yos

When you use pencil and paper, do the following:

- ☐ Read the problem carefully.
- ☐ Write neatly so that you do not make errors.
- ☐ Solve the problem.
- ☐ Check your work.

# Math: Estimation

On multiple choice tests you can estimate the answer as a way to eliminate some of the choices.

---

**EXAMPLE**

**A sailboat takes 124 passengers on a cruise on a lake. If the sailboat makes 53 tours a month, how many people ride on the boat?**

Ⓐ   5,789

Ⓒ   6,845 people

Ⓑ   5,499

Ⓓ   6,572 people

---

• First, estimate the answer by rounding. You should round to the most precise place needed for the problem. In this case, round to the nearest ten.

124 rounds to 120

53 rounds to 50

120 x 50 = 6,000

• You can cross off choices A and B since they have a 5 rather than a 6 in the thousands place.

• Find the exact answer by multiplying:

$$\begin{array}{r} 124 \\ \times\ \ 53 \\ \hline 372 \\ 620\ \ \\ \hline 6,572 \end{array}$$

• There would be 6,572 riders. The correct answer is **D**.

When you estimate, do the following:

❑   Read the problem carefully.

❑   Round the numbers you need.

❑   Estimate the answer.

❑   Cross off any answers that are not close to your estimate.

❑   Find the exact answer.

# Math: Concepts

Standardized tests also test your understanding of important math concepts you will have learned about in school.

The following is a list of concepts that you may be tested on when you take a standardized test with math problems.

### Number Concepts
You may have to show that you understand the following number concepts:

- recognizing the standard and metric units of measure used for weighing and finding length and distance.
- equivalent measures (how many fcct in a yard, etc.).
- recognizing place value (the ones, tens, hundreds, and thousands places; the tenths and hundredths places).
- telling time to the minute.
- using a calendar.
- reading a thermometer.
- rounding up and down to the nearest five, ten, or hundred.
- fraction/decimal equivalents.
- reading/writing numbers in expanded notation.

### Geometry
It's also common to see questions about geometry on standardized tests. You may be asked to:
- identify solid shapes such as prisms, spheres, cubes, cylinders, and cones.
- calculate the perimeter and area of flat shapes.

- find the line of symmetry in a flat shape.
- tell about thc number of angles and sides of flat shapes.
- recognize parallel and perpendicular lines.
- recognize congruent shapes.

### Other Things to Keep in Mind
The best way to prepare for concept questions is **to study math words and definitions in advance**. However, if you come to a difficult problem, think of what you know about the topic and **eliminate answer choices that don't make sense**. For example, if you are asked to identify a shape that you don't recognize, you may recognize some of othcr shapes mentioned and know that they couldn't be correct. Use the process of elimination whenever you come to a tough question.

# Math: Applications

You will often be asked to apply what you know about math to a new type of problem or set of information. Even if you aren't exactly sure how to solve a problem of this type, you can usually draw on what you already know to make the most logical choice.

When preparing for standardized tests, you may want to practice some of the following:

- how to use a number line with whole numbers and decimals.
- putting numbers in order from least to greatest and using greater than/less than symbols.
- recognizing basic number patterns and object patterns and extending them.
- writing an equation to solve a problem.
- reading bar graphs, tally charts, or pictographs.
- reading pie charts.
- reading simple line graphs.
- reading and making Venn diagrams.

**Other Things to Keep in Mind**
When answering application questions, be sure to **read each problem carefully**. You may want to **use scrap paper to help you work out some problems**.

Again, if you come to a problem you aren't sure how to solve or a word/idea you don't recognize, try to **eliminate answer choices** by using what you do know. Then go back and check your answer choice in the context of the problem.

# Practice Test and Final Test Information

The remainder of this book is made up of two tests. On page 223, you will find a Practice Test. On page 261, you will find a Final Test. These tests will give you a chance to put the tips you have learned to work. There is also a name and answer sheet preceding each test and an answer key at the end of the book.

**Here are some things to remember as you take these tests:**

- Be sure you understand all the directions before you begin each test.

- Ask an adult questions about the directions if you do not understand them.

- Work as quickly as you can during each test. There are no time limits on the Practice Test, but you should try to make good use of your time. There are suggested time limits on the Final Test to give you practice managing your time.

- You will notice little GO and STOP signs at the bottom of the test pages. When you see a GO sign, continue on to the next page if you feel ready. The STOP sign means you are at the end of a section. When you see a STOP sign, take a break.

- When you change an answer, be sure to erase your first mark completely.

- You can guess at an answer or skip difficult items and go back to them later.

- Use the tips you have learned whenever you can.

- It is OK to be a little nervous. You may even do better.

- After you have completed your tests, check your answers with the answer key.

- When you complete all the lessons in this book, you will be on your way to test success!

Name _____

# Practice Test Answer Sheet

Fill in **only one** letter for each item. If you change an answer, make sure to erase your first mark completely.

## Unit 1: Reading, pages 223-237

| | | | | |
|---|---|---|---|---|
| **A** A B C D | **7** A B C D | **15** A B C D | **22** A B C D | **29** F G H J |
| **B** F G H J | **8** F G H J | **16** F G H J | **23** F G H J | **30** A B C D |
| **1** A B C D | **9** A B C D | **17** A B C D | **24** A B C D | **31** F G H J |
| **2** F G H J | **10** F G H J | **18** F G H J | **25** F G H J | **32** A B C D |
| **3** A B C D | **11** A B C D | **19** A B C D | **26** A B C D | **33** F G H J |
| **4** F G H J | **12** F G H J | **20** F G H J | **27** F G H J | **34** A B C D |
| **5** A B C D | **13** A B C D | **21** A B C D | **D** A B C D | |
| **6** F G H J | **14** F G H J | **C** A B C D | **28** A B C D | |

## Unit 2: Language Arts, pages 238-248

| | | | | |
|---|---|---|---|---|
| **A** A B C D | **9** A B C D | **18** F G H J K | **25** A B C D | **34** F G H J |
| **1** A B C D | **10** F G H J | **19** A B C D E | **26** F G H J | **35** A B C D |
| **2** F G H J | **C** A B C D | **20** F G H J | **G** A B C D E | **36** F G H J |
| **B** A B C D | **11** A B C D | **D** A B C D | **27** A B C D | **37** A B C D |
| **3** A B C D | **12** F G H J | **21** A B C D | **28** F G H J | **38** F G H J |
| **4** F G H J | **13** A B C D | **22** F G H J | **29** A B C D | **39** A B C D |
| **5** A B C D | **14** F G H J K | **E** A B C D E | **30** F G H J | **40** F G H J K |
| **6** F G H J | **15** A B C D E | **23** A B C D E | **31** A B C D | **41** A B C D E |
| **7** A B C D | **16** F G H J K | **24** F G H J K | **32** F G H J | **42** F G H J K |
| **8** F G H J | **17** A B C D E | **F** A B C D | **33** A B C D | **43** A B C D E |

## Unit 3: Mathematics, pages 249-258

| | | | | |
|---|---|---|---|---|
| **A** A B C D E | **6** F G H J K | **14** F G H J | **21** A B C D E | **28** A B C D |
| **B** F G H J K | **7** A B C D E | **15** A B C D | **22** F G H J K | **29** F G H J |
| **1** A B C D E | **8** F G H J K | **16** F G H J K | **23** A B C D E | **30** A B C D |
| **2** F G H J K | **9** A B C D E | **17** A B C D E | **D** A B C D | **31** F G H J |
| **3** A B C D E | **10** F G H J | **18** F G H J K | **24** A B C D | |
| **4** F G H J K | **11** A B C D | **E** F G H J K | **25** F G H J | |
| **C** A B C D | **12** F G H J | **19** A B C D E | **26** A B C D | |
| **5** A B C D | **13** A B C D | **20** F G H J K | **27** F G H J | |

# Reading

| Lesson 1 | **Reading Nonfiction** |

Did you ever hear about the "7–11 rule"? It's about something you use every day. Steps are supposed to have a tread—the part you step on—that is about 11 inches wide. The riser—the distance from one step to another—is supposed to be 7 inches high. Steps that use these dimensions are easiest to climb.

**This passage is mostly about**

    **A** the invention of steps.

    **B** exercising on steps.

    **C** things you use every day.

    **D** steps made the right way.

**Find the word that best completes the sentence.**

The ball _____ down the steps.

    **F** rolled        **H** rolling

    **G** roll         **J** having rolled

Be careful! There are two sets of letters for the answer choices. Skip difficult items and come back to them later. If you aren't sure which answer is correct, take your best guess.

## *Listening and Looking*

It's amazing what you can learn by listening and looking. In this lesson, you will read about two interesting school projects that you might want to try.

GO

**Directions:** Tomas keeps a journal for his All-Year Project in English. On the entry for this day, he wrote about an assignment one of his teachers had given him. Read the journal entry, then do numbers 1–6.

October 19

"Boy, does this sound like a goofy assignment," I said to Kendra, rolling my eyes. We were walking home after school talking about what Mr. Stewart had given us for homework this week. We were supposed to listen—just listen—for a total of two hours this week. We could do it any time we wanted, in short periods or long, and write down some of the things we heard. We also had to describe where we listened and the time of day.

As we walked by a small corner park, Kendra stopped for a moment and suggested, "Hey, I have an idea. Let's start right here. It's just about two-thirty, my parents won't be home for two more hours, and neither will your mother. We should just sit down in the park and get part of the assignment done. It will be a breeze."

For once, she had something. I told her it was a great idea, then spotted a bench beside the fountain. "Let's get started," I said.

We sat down and pulled out notebooks and pencils. After just a few seconds, Kendra began writing something down. I started right after her, and for the next half hour, we did nothing but sit, listen, and take notes.

**GO**

At about three o'clock, Kendra said, "That's enough for me now. Do you want to compare notes? I want to be sure I did this right."

"Sure," I answered. "I can't believe all the things I heard. Maybe this isn't such a goofy assignment after all."

**1**  **About how long did Tomas and Kendra listen in the park?**

  **A**  two hours

  **B**  half an hour

  **C**  a few seconds

  **D**  a few minutes

**2**  **Kendra said the homework assignment would <u>be a breeze</u>.**
That means the assignment would be

| hard. | long. | easy. | outside. |
|:---:|:---:|:---:|:---:|
| **F** | **G** | **H** | **J** |

**3**  **The first sound Kendra probably wrote about is**

  **A**  the fountain.     **C**  crickets.

  **B**  a fire engine.     **D**  her watch.

GO

**4** **Why did Mr. Stewart probably give the students this assignment?**

    **F** It would be an easy way for them to get a good grade.

    **G** It would give them a chance to work together.

    **H** It would give them more free time for other assignments.

    **J** It would help them understand the world around them better.

**5** **Tomas and Kendra live in a city. Which of these sounds are they most likely to hear on the way home?**

    **A** birds chirping

    **B** the wind in the trees

    **C** traffic sounds

    **D** planes landing

**6** **What lesson did Tomas probably learn?**

    **F** Some assignments are better than they first seem.

    **G** Kendra is a better student than he first thought.

    **H** Mr. Stewart usually gives easy assignments.

    **J** There is no reason to go right home after school.

GO

Name _____

**Directions:** For numbers 7 and 8, find the word that best completes the sentence.

**7** **The water _____ in the fountain.**

  **A** splash        **C** splashing

  **B** having splashed   **D** splashed

**8** **Kendra _____ a report next weekend.**

  **F** will write

  **G** wrote

  **H** having written

  **J** writing

**9** **Find the simple predicate, or action word, of the sentence below.**

Two people listen better than one person.
  **A**   **B**   **C**      **D**

GO

Summer Link Super Edition Grade 5

**Directions:** This set of directions suggests an easy project for a class of students or even a whole school. Read the directions to find out how you can get an "up close and personal" view of birds. Then do numbers 10–21.

# Birds: Up Close and Personal

Many schools and communities now have small nature areas. These nature areas have a bird feeder of some kind. If the nature area in your community has a feeder, try this observation activity. If not, try setting one up in your school! The activity works best when a number of students are involved, and it can continue from year to year.

1. Find a spot that is close enough to the feeder to see the birds but not so close that you scare them away. Binoculars will help you get a better look at the birds.

2. Throughout the day, keep a record of the birds that are at the feeder. Note the type of bird and how many there are of each kind. If possible, observe the feeder at the same time each day.

3. Create a "lifetime list" of birds that appear at the feeder. This could be a wall chart with the name of each bird that appears at the feeder. In addition, keep a detailed notebook showing the results of each observation.

This activity can lead to many other projects. For example, you can create a computer database showing the kind and number of birds that come to the feeder throughout the year. It's also possible to do an in-depth study of bird families, or identify times of the day that are best for

**10** **This passage is mostly about**

   **F** feeding birds.

   **G** observing birds.

   **H** building a bird feeder.

   **J** bird migrations.

**11** **In this picture, students are probably**

   **A** putting seed in a feeder.

   **B** taking notes about birds.

   **C** observing birds.

   **D** making a lifetime list.

**12** **Binoculars are important because they let you**

   **F** choose the right seed.

   **G** organize your notes.

   **H** take good notes.

   **J** observe birds closely.

**13** **It is important to look at the birds at the same time each day so you can**

   **A** make comparisons from day to day.

   **B** get to all your classes on time.

   **C** meet the same friends each day.

   **D** talk about birds with your teacher.

**14** **In the text, a "lifetime list" of birds is a**

    **F**  book.        **H**  wall chart.

    **G**  computer program.    **J**  journal.

**15** **Find the sentence that best completes this description of a bird.**

This bird was about the size of a robin. _____ . I saw it near a pond.

    **A**  My friends and I go there often.

    **B**  Birds seem to be more active in the morning.

    **C**  It was mostly black with red marks on its wings.

    **D**  Robins fly south in the winter.

**16** **The last sentence in the introduction is about**

    **F**  collecting information.

    **G**  drawing conclusions.

    **H**  comparing different birds.

    **J**  sharing information.

**17** **Find the sentence that is complete and correctly written.**

    **A**  To take good notes.

    **B**  Some birds feed early.

    **C**  Using a computer.

    **D**  A detailed wall chart.

GO

**18**   **Find the word that fits in both sentences.**

What _____ will you be on vacation?
I enjoy eating _____ .

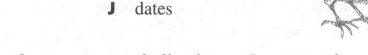

**F**   days

**G**   fruit

**H**   weeks

**J**   dates

**19**   **Find the sentence that has correct capitalization and punctuation.**

**A**   my sister takes good notes.

**B**   This is a good bird book

**C**   What kind of bird was that?

**D**   Did you put seed in the feeder.

**20**   **Choose the sentence that best combines these two sentences into one.**

A bird landed on a tree.
The tree was an apple tree.

**F**   The bird landed on an apple tree.

**G**   The bird landed and it landed on an apple tree.

**H**   On an apple tree the bird landed.

**J**   An apple tree, on which the bird landed.

**21**   **Choose the sentences that best support this topic sentence.**

Birds eat many different things.

**A**   Their colors vary from drab to colorful. Some drab birds have small patches
of color.

**B**   Small birds generally eat seeds and insects. Larger birds eat small animals and
even fish.

**C**   They also fly in different ways. Gulls soar, but hummingbirds flap their
wings often.

**D**   Even in cities, birds can survive. Some hawks now make their homes
in skyscrapers.

GO

## Lesson 2 Reading Fiction

# Family Traditions

Many families have traditions that are their very own. Think about your family. You probably have some traditions that are so natural you don't think about them anymore.

Buster was the neighborhood cat. His favorite spot was on Mrs. Wilson's car. He sat on the hood while everyone walked by and petted him.

**This story suggests that Buster is**

**A** cautious.          **C** friendly.

**B** large.             **D** curious.

Skim the story then read the questions. Look back at the story to find the answers. Some questions won't be answered directly in the story. Answer the easiest questions first.

**Directions:** Here is a story about an unusual family tradition. Read the story and then do numbers 22 and 23.

# The **Un**-Birthday

In my family we don't celebrate birthdays. At least we don't celebrate them like most families. My friends say I have an "un-birthday."

The tradition started with my grandmother. She and grandfather grew up in Poland. They escaped before World War II and made their way to America. When they got here, they were so grateful that they decided to share what they had with others. On their birthdays, they gave each other just one small gift. Then they each bought a gift for someone who needed it more than they did.

GO

As the years passed and the family grew, the tradition continued. On my last birthday, I got a backpack for school. We had a little party with cake and all of that, and then we headed off to the Lionel School. This is a school for kids who are disabled. Some of the children are in electric wheelchairs, and only a few can walk. I picked this school out because one of my friends has a sister there.

When we walked in with our arms full of gifts, the kids were really excited. Even though we gave them just little things—sticker books, puzzles, that sort of thing—all the presents were wrapped and had bows.

I gave Maggie, my friend's sister, a floppy stuffed animal. Her mom said Maggie's old stuffed animal had just worn out. I helped Maggie open it and made sure it didn't fall out of her wheelchair. Maggie can't talk, but she hugged her stuffed animal and looked at me so I knew she was grateful.

I don't get as much stuff as my friends, but I don't feel bad, even though I want a new skateboard. I have enough stuff, probably too much. Seeing Maggie and the other kids receive their gifts was a lot better than getting a bunch of presents myself.

**22**  **This passage is mostly about**

    **A**  a child's disappointing birthday.

    **B**  a school for disabled children.

    **C**  a family that lives in Poland.

    **D**  an unusual birthday tradition.

**23**  **What does the family do to show they want the children at the Lionel School to feel important?**

    **F**  drive to the school      **H**  have just a small party

    **G**  wrap the presents carefully      **J**  give them small gifts

GO

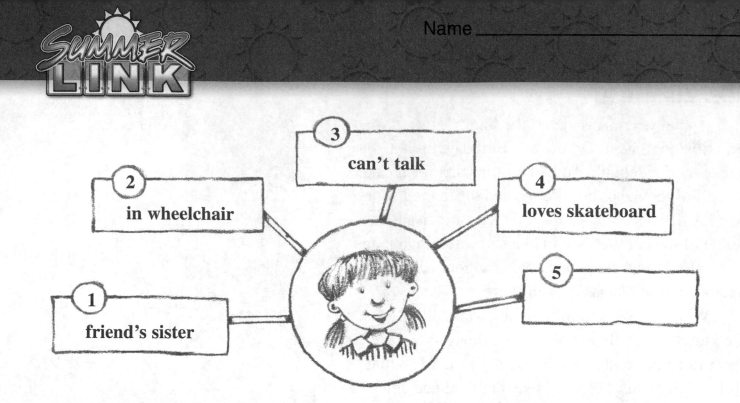

**Directions:** Use this web about the passage to do numbers 24 and 25.

**24** **Which phrase would best fit in Box 5?**

   **A** shows gratitude

   **B** learns to read

   **C** drops stuffed animal

   **D** grew up in Poland

**25** **Which box contains information that does not belong in the web?**

   **F** Box 1

   **G** Box 2

   **H** Box 4

   **J** Box 5

**Directions:** For numbers 26 and 27, choose the sentence that is written correctly.

**26** **A** the party will happen last week.

   **B** the presents was all wrapped.

   **C** Maggie will soon learn to read.

   **D** The kids at the school excited.

**27** **F** he doesn't celebrate birthdays.

   **G** She don't have a party.

   **H** Got one gift.

   **J** She hugged her stuffed animal.

STOP

## Lesson 3  Review

SAMPLE
D

[1]Natural fires are good for forests. [2]Burning dead wood and heavy brush. [3]This helps new trees and grass grow better.

**Choose the best way to write Sentence 2.**

A   Having burned dead wood and heavy brush.

B   They burn dead wood and heavy brush.

C   Dead wood and heavy brush they burn.

D   Dead wood will burn heavy brush.

**Directions:** Greg is writing a story for the Young Author's column of the school paper. The first draft of the story needs some editing. Here is the first part of the story.

[1]Our town's name is Lost City.  [2]It has an unusual history. [3]First of all, it was founded in 1886 by accident. [4]A group of pioneers thought they were headed toward San Francisco. [5]Instead, they ended up hundreds of miles farther up the coast.

**28**  **Which of these best combines Sentences 1 and 2 into one sentence?**

A   Lost City has an unusual history and it is our town.

B   An unusual history, our town is Lost City.

C   Our town, Lost City, has an unusual history.

D   With an unusual history, our town is Lost City.

**29**  **Which is the best way to write Sentence 4?**

F   A group of pioneers toward San Francisco were headed.

G   Toward San Francisco a group of pioneers thought they were headed.

H   San Francisco, they thought the pioneers were headed.

J   Best as it is

GO

Now read the next part of the story.

> [1]The founders of Lost City from Baltimore came. [2]They knew about fishing, trapping crabs, and gathering oysters and clams. [3]It was only natural that they would use their skills in the Pacific Ocean. [4]Soon, Lost City was known for its fine seafood. [5]Wagons packed with ice and snow brought fish, oysters, and crabs to inland towns. [6]Seafood restaurants were on almost every corner.

**30**  **Select the best way to write Sentence 1.**

   **A**  The founders of Lost City came from Baltimore.

   **B**  From Baltimore the founders of Lost City came.

   **C**  Coming from Baltimore were the founders of Lost City.

   **D**  Best as it is

**31**  **Choose the best way to write Sentence 4.**

   **F**  Lost City was known soon for its fine seafood.

   **G**  For its fine seafood, Lost City was known soon.

   **H**  Lost City, for its fine seafood, was soon known.

   **J**  Best as it is

GO

Name _____

This is the last part of the story.

> [1]The sleepy little fishing town doubled in size almost overnight. [2]Harriet Johnson decided to build a resort on the cliffs near the beach. [3]With her fortune, she hired hundreds of workers to complete the job. [4]Many of them decided to stay when the job was finished. [5]The workers lived in tents on the beach. [6]These workers the logging industry that exists even today helped build.

**32  Choose the sentence that does not belong in the paragraph.**

**A**  Sentence 2          **C**  Sentence 4

**B**  Sentence 3          **D**  Sentence 5

**33  Select the best way to write Sentence 6.**

**F**  The workers in the logging industry that exists today helped build.

**G**  These workers, they helped build the logging industry. It exists even today.

**H**  These workers helped build the logging industry that exists even today.

**J**  Best as it is

**Greg's friend, Betty, wrote a paragraph about the school play.**

**34  Find the sentence that best completes Betty's story.**

The junior high play will take place on Friday and Saturday nights. _____ . The play will be held in the school auditorium.

**A**  Tryouts were last month.          **C**  My sister likes plays.

**B**  Tickets cost $2.50 per person.     **D**  Did you like it?

STOP

237          Summer Link Super Edition Grade 5

# Language Arts

 **Lesson 1** **Vocabulary**

**Directions:** For Sample A and numbers 1 and 2, choose the word that correctly completes both sentences.

**Directions:** For Sample B and numbers 3 and 4, choose the word that means the **opposite** of the underlined word.

**SAMPLE A**
The player began to _____ .
Put the new _____ on the car.

**A** run

**B** fender

**C** weaken

**D** tire

**SAMPLE B**
<u>recall</u> information

**A** forget

**B** remember

**C** write

**D** find

---

**1** The sun _____ at 5:45.
A _____ grew beside the steps.

**A** appeared

**B** rose

**C** flower

**D** set

**2** My _____ is in the closet.
Add a new _____ of paint.

**F** hat

**G** color

**H** shirt

**J** coat

**3** <u>valuable</u> painting

**A** strange

**B** expensive

**C** worthless

**D** humorous

**4** left <u>promptly</u>

**F** late

**G** recently

**H** quietly

**J** slowly

---

Try each answer choice in BOTH blanks. Use the meaning of a sentence to find the answer.

**Directions:** For number 5, read the sentence with the missing word and the question about that word. Choose the word that best answers the question.

**5** Let's _____ the ripe apples. Which word means to gather the ripe apples?

    **A** eat

    **B** collect

    **C** check

    **D** sell

**Directions:** For numbers 6 and 7, choose the word that means the same, or about the same, as the underlined word.

**6** fast <u>vehicle</u>

    **F** runner     **H** car

    **G** animal     **J** computer

**7** baggy <u>trousers</u>

    **A** shirt     **C** clothes

    **B** pants     **D** coat

**Directions:** For numbers 8–10, read the paragraph. For each numbered blank, there is a list of words with the same number. Choose the word from each list that best completes the meaning of the paragraph.

      Glass is an amazing substance. Made by heating sand with a few other simple chemicals, glass is both useful and beautiful. In the __(8)__ you drink your juice in a glass. At your school, you may __(9)__ the building through a glass door. The lights inside the school are made of glass, as is the screen of the computer you will use. If you go to gym class, the basketball backboard might even be made of glass. Your fami' may have pieces of glass as decorations around the house, and if you go to a museum, you might see __(10)__ glass from hundreds of years ago.

**8**  **F** evening     **H** morning

    **G** time     **J** mood

**9**  **A** open     **C** like

    **B** see     **D** enter

**10**  **F** new     **H** full

    **G** antique     **J** broken

STOP

## Lesson 2  Language Mechanics

 **SAMPLE C**  **Directions:** Choose the answer that is written correctly and shows the correct capitalization and punctuation.

    **A**  Rudy gave janet a gift.

    **B**  We can leave now but, the party isn't until seven.

    **C**  Do you think she will be surprised?

    **D**  This cake looks wonderful?

 **TIPS**  Be sure you know if you are to look for correct or incorrect capitalization and punctuation.

**Directions:** For numbers 11 and 12, decide which punctuation mark, if any, is needed in the sentence.

**11**  **The puppy couldn't find the food dish**

      ,        .        ?      None

     **A**      **B**      **C**      **D**

**12**  **"This is fun, answered Lettie.**

      ,        ?        "      None

     **F**      **G**      **H**      **J**

**Directions:** For numbers 13 and 14, choose the answer that is written correctly and shows the correct capitalization and  punctuation.

**13**  **A**  The tennis courts are full

       **B**  Venus put our names on the list.

       **C**  Did you remember your racket.

       **D**  This can of tennis balls is new?

**14**  **F**  Tell Mrs Jensen I called.

       **G**  Miss. Richards will be late.

       **H**  Our coach is Mr. Wanamaker

       **J**  Dr. Cullinane was here earlier.

 **GO**

Name _____

**Directions:** For numbers 15–20, look at the underlined part of the sentence. Choose the answer that shows the best capitalization and punctuation for that part.

**15** **Winters are warm in Tucson Arizona.**

  **A** Tucson, arizona

  **B** Tucson Arizona,

  **C** Tucson, Arizona.

  **D** Correct as it is

**16** **The play will be held on Wednesday, Thursday, and Friday, nights.**

  **F** Thursday, and Friday

  **G** Thursday, and, Friday

  **H** Thursday and Friday,

  **J** Correct as it is

**(17)** January 5 2001,

**(18)** dear Burt

    My mom said you are coming to see us next month.

**(19)** If the weather is right, we can go skiing, sledding, or ice skating. You can borrow my brother's skis and skates.

    See you soon.

          **(20)** Your Cousin,

              Sarah

**17** **A** January 5, 2001

  **B** January 5 2001

  **C** January 5, 2001,

  **D** Correct as it is

**18** **F** Dear Burt

  **G** dear burt

  **H** Dear Burt,

  **J** Correct as it is

**19** **A** skiing sledding or

  **B** skiing, sledding, or,

  **C** skiing sledding or,

  **D** Correct as it is

**20** **F** Your Cousin

  **G** Your cousin,

  **H** your Cousin,

  **J** Correct as it is

STOP

## Lesson 3   Spelling

**Directions:** For Sample D and numbers 21 and 22, choose the word that is spelled correctly and best completes the sentence.

SAMPLE **D**   Harry wrote a _____ to the paper.

    **A**  leter    **C**  ledder

    **B**  lettir    **D**  letter

**Directions:** For Sample E and numbers 23 and 24, read each phrase. Find the underlined word that is <u>not</u> spelled correctly. If all words are spelled correctly, mark "All correct."

SAMPLE **E**

  **A**  college <u>dormitory</u>

  **B**  <u>assemble</u> a toy

  **C**  <u>loyal</u> dog

  **D**  <u>pause</u> briefly

  **E**  All correct

**21**  Tomorrow will be _____ .

  **A**  rainee

  **B**  rainie

  **C**  ranie

  **D**  rainy

**23**  **A**  <u>lene</u> meat

    **B**  <u>demonstrate</u> a toy

    **C**  <u>reflect</u> light

    **D**  <u>terrible</u> food

    **E**  All correct

**22**  Did you finish the _____ yet?

  **F**  lesson

  **G**  leson

  **H**  lessin

  **J**  lessan

**24**  **F**  make me <u>yawn</u>

    **G**  <u>wooden</u> bench

    **H**  <u>accidentally</u> drop it

    **J**  <u>ajust</u> the radio

    **K**  All correct

Don't spend too much time looking at the words. Pretty soon, they all begin to look like they are spelled wrong.

STOP

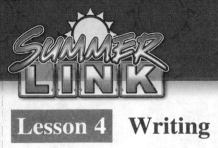

## Lesson 4    Writing

**Directions:** Read the paragraph about a book one student really liked. Then write one or two sentences to answer each question below.

> I really liked the book *The Wizard of Oz* and think others will like it, too. It was very exciting, especially the part where Dorothy went to the Wicked Witch's castle and made the Witch melt. I also liked the way the characters worked together to solve their problems. Finally when Dorothy says, "There's no place like home," I thought about my home and the many wonderful things I have.

**Think of a book you really liked. What is its title?**

_____

_____

_____

**Why do you think others should read it?**

_____

_____

_____

**What are some specific parts of the book that you think others would enjoy?**

_____

_____

_____

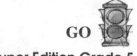

GO

**Directions:** Read the short story about one child's problem. Then think about a fiction story that you would like to write. Write one or two sentences to answer each question below.

Shandra kicked a rock. She shook her head. She had missed the bus again, and she knew she'd be late for school.

That night, Shandra set two alarms. She put them on the other side of her room. She asked her friend to call her to make sure she was up.

The next morning Shandra was smiling. For once, she would be on-time with everyone else.

**Think about the main character. Who is it? What is he or she like? Why are you writing about this character?**

_____

_____

_____

**What is the setting of the story?**

_____

_____

**What kind of problem will the main character have? How will the character solve the problem?**

_____

_____

_____

_____

STOP

## Lesson 5  Review

**Directions:** For Sample F and numbers 25 and 26, read the sentences with the missing word and the question about that word. Choose the word that best answers the question.

**SAMPLE F**

**The owner had to _____ the puppy for chewing the shoes.** Which word means to speak harshly to the puppy?

**A** scold     **C** alert

**B** pursue     **D** inspire

---

**25 We hiked to a _____ campsite.** Which word means the campsite was far away?

**A** remote     **C** crowded

**B** pleasant     **D** level

**26 The bird _____ from branch to branch.** Which word means to fly quickly from branch to branch?

**F** coasted

**G** hopped

**H** darted

**J** paced

---

**SAMPLE G**

**Directions:** Find the underlined word that is <u>not</u> spelled correctly.

**A** avoid <u>capture</u>

**B** hate to <u>complane</u>

**C** <u>empty</u> room

**D** <u>fourteen</u> points

**E** All correct

**Directions:** For number 27, choose the word that means the **opposite** of the underlined word.

**27 <u>rough</u> board**

**A** large

**B** heavy

**C** smooth

**D** long

**Directions:** For number 28, choose the word that means the same, or about the same, as the underlined word.

**28 attend a <u>conference</u>**

**F** party

**G** game

**H** meeting

GO

Name _____

**Directions:** For number 29, decide which punctuation mark, if any, is needed in the sentence.

**29** **The clouds were dark and the wind was getting stronger.**

|   !   |   .   |   ?   | None |
|:-----:|:-----:|:-----:|:----:|
| **A** | **B** | **C** | **D** |

**Directions:** For numbers 30 and 31, choose the answer that is written correctly and shows the correct capitalization and punctuation.

**30**
**F** Suzie whispered, "This is a great movie."

**G** "Don't forget your money said Mother."

**H** Are there seats up front?" asked Bruce?

**J** "Let's get popcorn" suggested Wanda.

**31**
**A** Dad bought seeds plants, and fertilizer.

**B** The shovel rake and hoe are in the garage.

**C** We usually camp with Jan, Bob and, Annie.

**D** The garden had corn, beans, and peas.

**Directions:** For numbers 32–35, look at the underlined part of the paragraph. Choose the answer that shows the best capitalization and punctuation for that part.

(32)　　　Ricky said, "Watch what I can do." He rode his
(33)　bike to the middle of the driveway. And balanced himself
(34)　on the back wheel. Il'l bet there isn't another kid in
(35)　mayfield who can do that.

**32**
**F** said, Watch

**G** said, "watch

**H** said "Watch

**J** Correct as it is

**33**
**A** driveway and

**B** driveway and,

**C** driveway And

**D** Correct as it is

**34**
**F** Ill bet

**G** Ill' bet

**H** I'll bet

**J** Correct as it is

**35**
**A** mayfield. Who

**B** Mayfield who

**C** mayfield, who

**D** Correct as it is

GO

**Directions:** For numbers 36–39, choose the word that is spelled correctly and best completes the sentence.

**36** The _____ is narrow here.

   **F** channel

   **G** channle

   **H** chanel

   **J** chanell

**37** Do you like _____ movies?

   **A** horrorr

   **B** horor

   **C** horror

   **D** horrer

**38** Three _____ people lived in the city.

   **F** milion

   **G** millun

   **H** millione

   **J** million

**39** The train _____ arrived.

   **A** finaly

   **B** finnaly

   **C** finely

   **D** finally

**Directions:** For numbers 40–43, read each phrase. Find the underlined word that is <u>not</u> spelled correctly. If all the underlined words are spelled correctly, mark "All correct."

**40** **F** smart <u>dicision</u>

   **G** <u>favorite</u> teacher

   **H** <u>gather</u> wood

   **J** famous <u>legend</u>

   **K** All correct

**41** **A** <u>hardest</u> job

   **B** <u>invite</u> them

   **C** this <u>month</u>

   **D** too much <u>luggage</u>

   **E** All correct

**42** **F** daring <u>rescue</u>

   **G** <u>solid</u> rock

   **H** <u>oister</u> shell

   **J** blue <u>plastic</u>

   **K** All correct

**43** **A** A <u>certain</u> number

   **B** good <u>citizen</u>

   **C** <u>ceiling</u> fan

   **D** <u>Wenesday</u> night

   **E** All correct

**GO**

**Directions:** Read the flyer that two girls designed to advertise their landscaping business. Then think about what you could do around your neighborhood to make money. Write one or two sentences to answer each question below.

## Hire us to take care of your yard this summer.

We will mow, edge, water, and care for your flowers. Our prices are reasonable. We work hard. We can give you letters from other neighbors who have used our yard services. Call for more information!

### Tina and Yani
### 123-4567

**Pick one thing you could do around your neighborhood to make money. Describe what you would do.**

_____

_____

_____

**Why should your neighbors hire you to do this for them?**

_____

_____

_____

**How would you convince your neighbors to hire you?**

_____

_____

_____

**STOP**

# Mathematics

## Lesson 1   Computation

**SAMPLE A**

31
+ 25

**A**   6

**B**   56

**C**   54

**D**   46

**E**   None of these

**SAMPLE B**

$3\overline{)90}$

**F**   20

**G**   40

**H**   87

**J**   93

**K**   None of these

Look carefully at the operation sign.
Work neatly on scratch paper.

---

**1**

78
+ 46

**A**   32

**B**   114

**C**   122

**D**   124

**E**   None of these

**3**

**A**   328

**B**   1296

**C**   320

**D**   1396

**E**   None of these

**2**

0.4
− 0.4

**F**   0

**G**   0.8

**H**   0.04

**J**   1

**K**   None of these

**4**

$182 \div 5 =$

**F**   36

**G**   36 R2

**H**   32

**J**   30 R2

**K**   None of these

STOP

## Lesson 2  Mathematics Skills

**SAMPLE C**

Which of these number sentences would help you find the total number of flags?

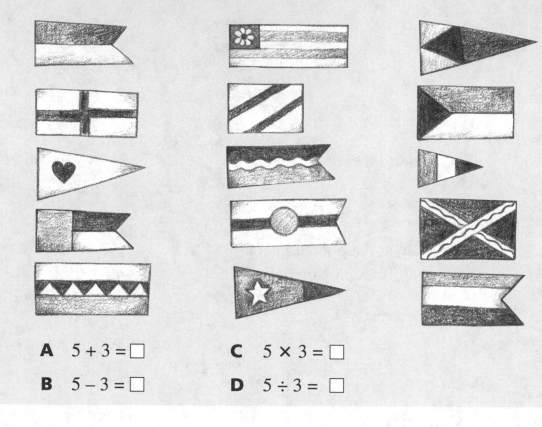

**A** $5 + 3 = \square$

**B** $5 - 3 = \square$

**C** $5 \times 3 = \square$

**D** $5 \div 3 = \square$

**TIPS**

Read the problem carefully. Look for key words, numbers, and figures.

Think about what you are supposed to do before you start working.

Stay with your first answer. Change it only if you are sure it is wrong and another answer is better.

GO

# The Community Pool

**Directions:** The town of Middlebury opened a community pool with a snack bar last year. Do numbers 5–9 about the pool.

SNACK BAR

**5** The only charge to use the pool is the $3 parking charge. Which of these number sentences should be used to find how much money the parking lot made on a day when 82 cars were parked there?

**A** $82 + 3 =$

**B** $82 - 3 =$

**C** $82 \times 3 =$

**D** $82 \div 3 =$

**6** To be allowed into the deep end of the pool, children must swim 12 laps across the shallow end without stopping. If Jessica has completed 8 laps, how many more laps must she swim to pass the test?

**F** 3

**G** 4

**H** 8

**J** 12

**K** None of these

GO

**7** Last week, the snack bar sold 1024 hot dogs. This week, it sold 1155 hot dogs. What was the total number of hot dogs served for the two weeks?

**A** 131

**B** 1179

**C** 2079

**D** 2179

**E** None of these

**8** The 4th grade had their class party at the pool. There are 120 4th graders, but 5 were absent that day. How many students attended the class party?

**F** 115

**G** 125

**H** 24

**J** 105

**K** None of these

**9** Ms. Fava divided her class of 24 students into groups of 2 students so that each child would have a buddy. How many groups of 2 students were there?

**A** 2

**B** 48

**C** 12

**D** 22

**E** None of these

GO

**Directions:** For numbers 10–12, you do not need to find exact answers. Use estimation to choose the best answer.

**10**  **Which of these is the best estimate of 767 ÷ 7 =      ?**

   **F**  10

   **G**  11

   **H**  100

   **J**  110

**11**  **Use estimation to find which problem will have the greatest answer.**

   **A**      357
           −   63

   **C**      888
           − 666

   **B**      615
           − 485

   **D**      915
           − 769

**12**  **Leah is making an orange punch recipe in a very large punch bowl. Orange juice comes in different-sized containers. Which sized container should she buy in order to purchase the fewest number of containers?**

   **F**  A one-cup container

   **G**  A one-gallon container

   **H**  A one-pint container

   **J**  A one-quart container

GO

**13** Juan kept a log of the number of minutes he spent practicing the trumpet for the past three weeks. Which is the best estimate of the number of minutes he practiced during that time period?

**A** 200

**B** 300

**C** 400

**D** 500

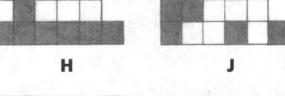

Practice Log

Week 1    128 min.
Week 2     87 min.
Week 3    185 min.

Total _____ min.

**14** Which of these shows the top view of the figure above?

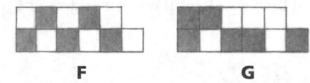

**F**          **G**          **H**          **J**

**15** Use the ruler at the right to help you solve this problem. Which of these paper clips is approximately 2 inches long?

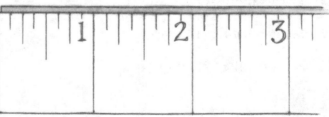

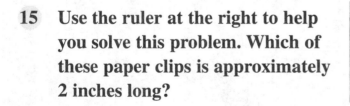

**A**          **B**          **C**          **D**

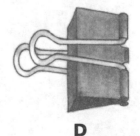

STOP

## Lesson 3   Review

**16**

6.89
+ 3.00
_____

F   3.89
G   3.98
H   0.88
J   9.89
K   None of these

**17**

925
−   6
_____

A   919
B   931
C   4650
D   4660
E   None of these

**18**

5 × 40 =

F   45
G   240
H   450
J   540
K   None of these

**19**

15) 90

A   5 R4
B   6
C   8
D   8 R4
E   None of these

**20**

794
− 318
_____

F   384
G   484
H   476
J   1112
K   None of these

**21**

$\frac{4}{7}$
+ $\frac{3}{7}$
_____

A   $\frac{1}{7}$
B   $\frac{5}{7}$
C   $\frac{6}{7}$
D   1
E   None of these

**22**

132
×   4
_____

F   528
G   136
H   478
J   476
K   None of these

**23**

125
− 19
_____

A   144
B   124
C   106
D   116
E   None of these

 SAMPLE D   150 ☐ 6 =

Look at the problem above. Which of these symbols goes in the box to get the smallest answer?

A  +          C  ×

B  −          D  ÷

24  Kim made one straight cut across the trapezoid. Which pair of figures could be the two cut pieces of the trapezoid?

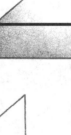

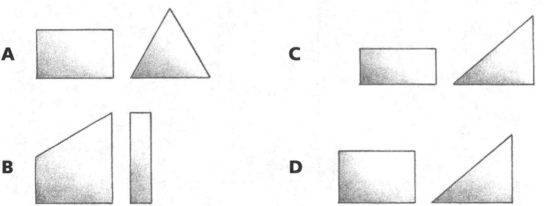

A

C

B

D

25  Look at the thermometers. How did the temperature change between Saturday and Sunday? On Sunday it was

F  5 degrees cooler than on Saturday.

G  10 degrees cooler than on Saturday.

H  5 degrees warmer than on Saturday.

J  10 degrees warmer than on Saturday.

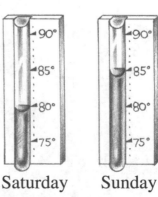

Saturday    Sunday

GO

# School Olympics

**Directions:** The fourth grade has School Olympics after the last day of school. Do numbers 26–31.

Make sure you are on number 26 on your answer sheet.

**26**  **The School Olympics start the Tuesday after school ends. If school ends on Friday, May 30, on what date do the School Olympics begin?**

**A**  May 31

**B**  June 1

**C**  June 2

**D**  June 3

*MAY calendar*

| SUN | MON | TUE | WED | THUR | FRI | SAT |
|---|---|---|---|---|---|---|
|  |  |  |  | 1 | 2 | 3 |
| 4 | 5 | 6 | 7 | 8 | 9 | 10 |
| 11 | 12 | 13 | 14 | 15 | 16 | 17 |
| 18 | 19 | 20 | 21 | 22 | 23 | 24 |
| 25 | 26 | 27 | 28 | 29 | 30 | 31 |

**27**  **Yusef is in line to take his turn at the long jump. There are 13 people in line and he is in the middle. What is his place in line?**

**F**  fifth

**G**  tenth

**H**  seventh

**J**  sixth

**28**  **There are an even number of events in which students can participate. Which of these could be the number of events?**

| 23 | 19 | 24 | 31 |
|---|---|---|---|
| **A** | **B** | **C** | **D** |

**Directions:** The graph shows how many students participated in certain events. Study the graph. Then do numbers 29–31.

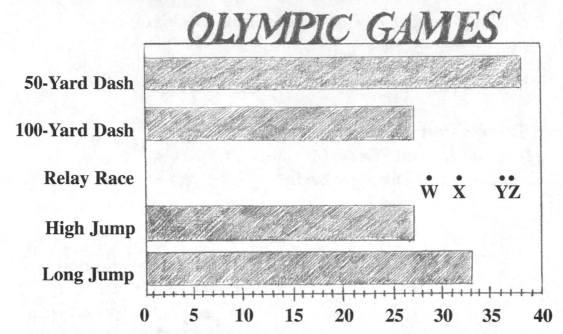

# OLYMPIC GAMES

50-Yard Dash

100-Yard Dash

Relay Race          W   X   YZ

High Jump

Long Jump

0   5   10   15   20   25   30   35   40

**29** **In which two events did the same number of students participate?**

F   50-yard dash and high jump

G   50-yard dash and long jump

H   100-yard dash and high jump

J   long jump and high jump

**30** **After this graph was made, 4 students switched from the 50-yard dash to the high jump. How many students then competed in the high jump?**

A   29

B   30

C   31

D   33

**31** **The graph is not complete. There are 28 students who competed in the relay race. Which point should the bar be drawn to?**

F   Point W

G   Point X

H   Point Y

J   Point Z

STOP

# Final Test Answer Sheet

Fill in **only one** letter for each item. If you change an answer, make sure to erase your first mark completely.

## Unit 1: Reading, pages 261–266

| | | | | |
|---|---|---|---|---|
| **A** A B C D | **8** F G H J | **16** F G H J | **24** A B C D | **32** A B C D |
| **1** A B C D | **9** A B C D | **17** A B | **25** F G H J | **33** A B C D |
| **2** F G H J | **10** F G H J | **18** A B | **26** A B | **34** A B C D |
| **3** A B C D | **11** A B C D | **19** A B | **27** A B | **35** A B C D |
| **4** F G H J | **12** F G H J | **20** A B | **28** A B C D | **36** F G H J |
| **5** A B C D | **13** A B C D | **21** A B | **29** F G H J | **37** F G H J |
| **6** F G H J | **14** F G H J | **22** A B C D | **30** A B C D | **38** F G H J |
| **7** A B C D | **15** A B C D | **23** F G H J | **31** F G H J | **39** F G H J |

## Unit 2: Language Arts, pages 267–275

| | | | | |
|---|---|---|---|---|
| **A** A B C D | **11** A B C D | **22** F G H J | **33** A B C D | **44** F G H J |
| **1** A B C D | **12** F G H J | **23** A B C D | **34** F G H J | **45** A B C D |
| **2** F G H J | **13** A B C D | **24** F G H J | **35** A B C D | **46** F G H J |
| **3** A B C D | **14** F G H J K | **25** A B C D | **36** F G H J | **47** A B C D |
| **4** F G H J | **15** A B C D E | **26** F G H J | **37** A B C D | **48** F G H J |
| **5** A B C D | **16** F G H J K | **27** A B C D | **38** F G H J | **49** A B C D |
| **6** F G H J | **17** A B C D E | **28** F G H J | **39** A B C D | **50** F G H J |
| **7** A B C D | **18** F G H J | **29** A B C D | **40** F G H J | **51** A B C D |
| **8** F G H J | **19** A B C D E | **30** F G H J | **41** A B C D | |
| **9** A B C D | **20** F G H J | **31** A B C D | **42** F G H J | |
| **10** F G H J | **21** A B C D | **32** F G H J | **43** A B C D | |

GO

# Final Test Answer Sheet

Fill in **only one** letter for each item. If you change an answer, make sure to erase your first mark completely.

## Unit 3: Mathematics, pages 276–284

| | | | | | |
|---|---|---|---|---|---|
| **1** A B C D E | **10** F G H J | **21** A B C D | **32** F G H J | **43** A B C D |
| **2** F G H J K | **11** A B C D | **22** F G H J | **33** A B C D | **44** F G H J |
| **3** A B C D E | **12** F G H J | **23** A B C D | **34** F G H J | **45** A B C D |
| **4** F G H J K | **13** A B C D | **24** F G H J | **35** A B C D | **46** F G H J |
| **5** A B C D E | **14** F G H J | **25** A B C D | **36** F G H J | **47** A B C D |
| **6** F G H J K | **15** A B C D | **26** F G H J | **37** A B C D | **48** F G H J |
| **7** A B C D E | **16** F G H J | **27** A B C D | **38** F G H J | |
| **8** F G H J K | **17** A B C D | **28** F G H J | **39** A B C D | |
| **A** A B C D | **18** F G H J | **29** A B C D | **40** F G H J | |
| **9** A B C D | **19** A B C D | **30** F G H J | **41** A B C D | |
| | **20** F G H J | **31** A B C D | **42** F G H J | |

# Reading

Some people complain when their dog's hair gets all over the house. Others welcome the problem by spinning the hair into yarn and knitting with it. In some cities, you can even find craftspeople who will knit you a sweater from your dog's hair.

**This passage is mostly about**

**A** how to clean up dog hair.

**C** an unusual way to use dog hair.

**B** how people love their pets.

**D** why people knit sweaters.

**Directions:** People are sometimes surprised when they discover talents they never knew they had. Leslie is both a painter and an athlete. Read the story about how she got started painting, then do numbers 1–5.

# Accidental Artist

It all started by accident. I was in a summer day camp when I was about ten. I loved sports and was disappointed when it rained. One rainy day my counselor took us to the art room. I grabbed a pencil and some paper and drew a soccer ball. It was kind of fun, so I added some grass around the ball and a pair of shoes. When it was finished, everybody—including me—was amazed at how good it was.

From then on, I still played lots of sports, but I always found time to draw and paint.

When I got older and was on the high school soccer and basketball teams, I took my sketch pad with me. In the bus on the way home, I drew things that happened during the games.

When I went to college, everyone was surprised when I chose art as my major. I even got a scholarship, which really helped my parents out. I played soccer, of course, but art was the chief reason I went to college. I knew that when I finished school, I wanted to be an artist.

**1** **This story is mostly about**

   **A** soccer, basketball, and art.

   **B** a girl growing up.

   **C** summer camp and college.

   **D** how a girl became an artist.

**2** **At first, Leslie was most interested in**

   **F** camp.    **H** drawing.

   **G** sports.    **J** studying.

**3** **How did Leslie feel after she completed her first drawing?**

   **A** amazed

   **B** amused

   **C** disappointed

   **D** relaxed

**4** **Leslie's scholarship "really helped her parents out." What does this mean?**

   **F** They wanted to be artists.

   **G** They wanted Leslie to be a soccer player.

   **H** It saved them money.

   **J** It surprised them.

**5** **The story says that Leslie was disappointed at camp when it rained. A word that means the opposite of *disappointed* is**

   **A** saddened.

   **B** pleased.

   **C** relieved.

   **D** entertained.

**Directions:** Leslie's brother, Lee, wrote this about her. For numbers 6 and 7, find the words that best complete the paragraph.

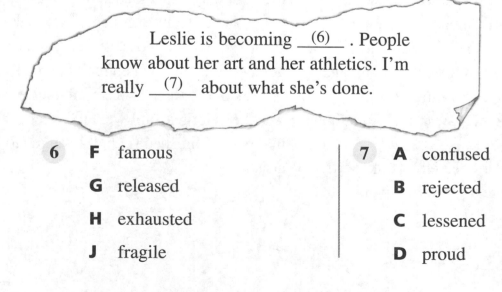

Leslie is becoming ___(6)___ . People know about her art and her athletics. I'm really ___(7)___ about what she's done.

**6**   **F** famous

     **G** released

     **H** exhausted

     **J** fragile

**7**   **A** confused

     **B** rejected

     **C** lessened

     **D** proud

GO

**Directions:** Read the passage. Then answer questions 8–21.

# Snakes

How much do you know about snakes? Read these snake facts and find out.

- A snake skeleton has **numerous** ribs. A large snake may have as many as 400 pairs!
- Most snakes have **poor** eyesight. They **track** other animals by sensing their body heat.
- Snakes can't blink! They sleep with their eyes open.
- Although all snakes have teeth, very few of them—only the **venomous** ones—have fangs.
- Many snakes arc very **docile** and unlikely to bite people.
- Pet snakes recognize their owners by smell. They flick their tongues in the air to **detect** smells.
- Snakes have special ways of hearing. Sound vibrations from the earth pass through their bellies to **receptors** in their spines. **Airborne** sounds pass through snakes' lungs to receptors in their skin.

**8** **What is this passage mainly about?**

   **F** keeping snakes as pets

   **G** snakes' body parts

   **H** venomous snakes

   **J** snakes' eyesight

**9** **In this passage, *poor* means the opposite of**

   **A** rich.

   **B** good.

   **C** happy.

   **D** broke.

**10** ***Numerous* means about the same as**

   **F** number.

   **G** many.

   **H** few.

   **J** special.

**11** **What does *track* mean as it is used in this passage?**

   **A** the rails on which a train moves

   **B** a sport that includes running, jumping, and throwing

   **C** to follow the footprints of

   **D** to find and follow

**GO**

**12** **Which word is a synonym for** *venomous*?

   **F** vicious      **H** sharp

   **G** poisonous     **J** huge

**13** **Which word means the opposite of** *docile*?

   **A** vicious      **C** shy

   **B** gentle       **D** active

**14** **Which word means the same as** *detect*?

   **F** enjoy       **H** arrest

   **G** find        **J** hide

**15** **A** *receptor* _____ **something.**

   **A** throws      **C** takes in

   **B** gives       **D** sees

**16** **Airborne sounds are**

   **F** carried through the air.

   **G** carried through the earth.

   **H** always made by wind.

   **J** louder than other sounds.

**Directions:** For numbers 17–21, decide whether each statement is true or false.

**17** **A large snake may have 800 pairs of ribs.**

   **A** true       **B** false

**18** **Most snakes have very good eyesight.**

   **A** true       **B** false

**19** **Everyone is a little afraid of snakes.**

   **A** true       **B** false

**20** **Only a few kinds of snakes are venomous.**

   **A** true       **B** false

**21** **Snakes detect sound in their spines and skin.**

   **A** true       **B** false

GO

**Directions:** Read the following passage. Then answer questions 22–27.

# Helping the Mountain Gorilla

Mountain gorillas live in the rainforests in Rwanda, Uganda, and the Democratic Republic of the Congo. These large, beautiful animals are becoming very rare. They have lost much of their **habitat** as people move in and take over gorillas' lands. Although there are strict laws protecting gorillas, **poachers** continue to hunt them.

Scientists observe gorillas to learn about their habits and needs. Then scientists write about their findings in magazines. Concerned readers sometimes contribute money to help safeguard the mountain gorillas.

Many other people are working hard to protect the mountain gorillas. Park rangers patrol the rainforest and arrest poachers. Tourists bring much-needed money into the area, encouraging local residents to protect the gorillas, too.

**22**  **What is this passage mainly about?**

  **A**  mountain gorillas' family relationships

  **B**  scientists who study mountain gorillas

  **C**  ways that gorillas are threatened and helped

  **D**  poachers and wars that threaten gorillas' survival

**23**  **Which words help you figure out the meaning of *habitat*?**

  **F**  "large, beautiful animals"

  **G**  "gorillas' lands"

  **H**  "the human population"

  **J**  "recent civil wars"

**24**  **In this passage, *poacher* means**

  **A**  park ranger.

  **B**  mountain gorilla.

  **C**  unlawful hunter.

  **D**  scientist.

**25**  **The writer of the passage thinks that tourism**

  **F**  is very harmful to mountain gorillas.

  **G**  is one cause of civil wars in Africa.

  **H**  can be helpful to mountain gorillas.

  **J**  is one cause of overpopulation in Africa.

**GO**

**Directions:** For numbers 26 and 27, decide whether each statement is true or false.

**26** **Mountain gorillas live in African deserts.**

    **A** true     **B** false

**27** **People who live near the mountain gorillas have little need for money.**

    **A** true     **B** false

**Directions:** For numbers 28–31, choose the correct answer to each question.

**28** **Apple is to orange as lettuce is to** _____ .

    **A** grapefruit     **C** apple

    **B** vegetable     **D** spinach

**29** **Happy is to sad as beautiful is to** _____ .

    **F** ugly     **H** pretty

    **G** unhappy     **J** angry

**30** **Car is to driver as train is to** _____ .

    **A** passenger     **C** conductor

    **B** headmaster     **D** inspector

**31** **Jupiter is to planet as United States is to** _____ .

    **F** Washington, D. C.

    **G** state

    **H** nation

    **J** North America

**Directions:** Match words with the same meanings.

| | | | |
|---|---|---|---|
| **32** | ruin | **A** | annoy |
| **33** | aid | **B** | attempt |
| **34** | try | **C** | help |
| **35** | irritate | **D** | destroy |

**Directions:** Match words with opposite meanings.

| | | | |
|---|---|---|---|
| **36** | funny | **F** | boring |
| **37** | exciting | **G** | nice |
| **38** | mature | **H** | serious |
| **39** | mean | **J** | childish |

STOP

# Language Arts

**Directions:** For Sample A and numbers 1 and 2, read the sentences. Choose the word that correctly completes both sentences.

**SAMPLE A**
Do you feel _____ ?
We get our water from a _____ .

    **A** well    **B** good    **C** pipe    **D** sick

**1** It's not safe to _____ a boat.
This _____ is too heavy to move.

  **A** sink    **C** push
  **B** stone    **D** rock

**2** The photography _____ meets today.
The cave man carried a _____ .

  **F** group    **H** spear
  **G** club    **J** class

**Directions:** For numbers 3 and 4, read the paragraph. For each numbered blank, choose the word that best completes the paragraph.

## *Roller Blading*

    In-line skating, also known as rollerblading, might be the fastest growing __(3)__ in America. Each day, millions of people step into their skates and take off for miles of exercise and enjoyment. Typical __(4)__ follow roads, sidewalks, or bikepaths, but "extreme skaters" build half-pipes of plywood or seek expert terrain like steps or steep hills. This sport is relatively new, but it is already enjoyed by people young and old.

**3**  **A** thing
    **B** people
    **C** town
    **D** sport

**4**  **F** skaters
    **G** vehicles
    **H** hikers
    **J** results

GO

**Directions:** For number 5, decide which punctuation mark, if any, is needed in the sentence.

**5** **"Your brother just called," said Kyle.**

    .             ,              !          None

    **A**         **B**         **C**        **D**

**Directions:** For numbers 6 and 7, choose the answer that is written correctly and shows the correct capitalization and punctuation.

**6** **F** Mrs. shields writes about sports for our local newspaper.

    **G** Did Dr. Robinson call yet?

    **H** Please give this to miss Young.

    **J** This is Mr McCoy's bicycle.

**7** **A** I cant see the game from here.

    **B** Kim wasn't able to play this week.

    **C** Dont' worry if you forgot.

    **D** The coach would'nt let us in.

**Directions:** For numbers 8 and 9, look at the underlined part of each sentence. Choose the answer that shows the best capitalization and punctuation for that part.

(8)    We moved into our new house on <u>June 5, 2001</u>.

(9)    The <u>garage bathroom, and</u> kitchen still weren't finished.

**8** **F** June 5 2001

    **G** June, 5 2001

    **H** june 5 2001

    **J** Correct as it is

**9** **A** garage, bathroom, and

    **B** garage bathroom, and,

    **C** garage, bathroom. And

    **D** Correct as it is

GO

**Directions:** For numbers 10–13, choose the word that is spelled correctly and best completes the sentence.

**10**   This _____ leads to the gym.

   **F**   stareway

   **G**   stareweigh

   **H**   stairweigh

   **J**   stairway

**11**   Hand me the _____ , please.

   **A**   chalk

   **B**   chaulk

   **C**   chawlk

   **D**   challk

**12**   We went on a _____ walk.

   **F**   nachur

   **G**   nature

   **H**   nayture

   **J**   nachure

**13**   Please _____ your work.

   **A**   revew

   **B**   reeview

   **C**   review

   **D**   revyoo

**Directions:** For numbers 14–17, read each phrase. Find the underlined word that is <u>not</u> spelled correctly. If all the underlined words are spelled correctly, mark "All correct."

**14**   **F**   <u>shallow</u> water

   **G**   confusing <u>siginal</u>

   **H**   find <u>something</u>

   **J**   <u>sparkle</u> brightly

   **K**   All correct

**15**   **A**   no <u>trouble</u>

   **B**   <u>unusual</u> bird

   **C**   play the <u>violin</u>

   **D**   cat's <u>whisker</u>

   **E**   All correct

**16**   **F**   white <u>geese</u>

   **G**   <u>lively</u> conversation

   **H**   <u>relaxing</u> music

   **J**   local <u>libary</u>

   **K**   All correct

**17**   **A**   good <u>condition</u>

   **B**   book <u>shelvs</u>

   **C**   <u>through</u> the door

   **D**   <u>eagerly</u> waiting

   **E**   All correct

GO

**Directions:** For numbers 18-25, find the answer that shows the correct capitalization and punctuation.

**18** **521 north Main st**

  **F** 521 North Main st

  **G** 521 North Main St

  **H** 521 North Main St.

  **J** Correct as is

**19** **West Hills, PA 11123**

  **A** West hills, Pa 11123

  **B** West Hills PA 11123

  **C** West Hills, pa 11123

  **D** Correct as is

**20** **aug 12 2001**

  **F** AUG 12, 2001

  **G** Aug. 12, 2001

  **H** Aug. 12 2001

  **J** Correct as is

**21** **Mrs Ann c James**

  **A** Mrs. Ann c. James

  **B** Mrs. Ann C James

  **C** Mrs. Ann C. James

  **D** Correct as is

**22** **432 East oak Ave**

  **F** 432 East Oak Ave

  **G** 432 East Oak Ave.

  **H** 432 east Oak Ave.

  **J** Correct as is

**23** **Newton valley  oh 42111**

  **A** Newton Valley, OH  42111

  **B** Newton Valley  OH  42111

  **C** Newton Valley, oh 42111

  **D** Correct as is

**24** **dear mrs. James**

  **F** Dear mrs. James,

  **G** Dear Mrs. James—

  **H** Dear Mrs. James,

  **J** Correct as is

**25** **thank you for the cool camera**

  **A** Thank you, for the cool camera

  **B** thank you for the cool camera.

  **C** Thank you for the cool camera.

  **D** Correct as is

**GO**

**Directions:** For numbers 26-33, find the sentence that is correctly written.

**26**  **F**  Those muffins was delicious!

    **G**  Those blueberries is so sweet and juicy.

    **H**  We done picked them yesterday afternoon.

    **J**  Please have another muffin.

**27**  **A**  We are awful glad you made it.

    **B**  We've been waiting anxiously.

    **C**  The roads are real bad.

    **D**  It's been snowing something heavy for hours.

**28**  **F**  Ray and I raked the leaves into a huge pile.

    **G**  My friend Ann helped him and I.

    **H**  Her and I jumped onto the leaf pile

    **J**  Ray took a great picture of me and her.

**29**  **A**  Of all the days for the bus to be late.

    **B**  We had to wait in the pouring rain.

    **C**  Even though I had an umbrella.

    **D**  Absolutely soaked by the time it came.

**30**  **F**  Last night at 7 o'clock in the school auditorium.

    **G**  The third annual school talent show.

    **H**  Our class put on the funniest skit of the show.

    **J**  Heard my parents laughing and applauding.

**31**  **A**  I was late because the bus broke down.

    **B**  I was late even though the bus broked down.

    **C**  I was late the bus broke down.

    **D**  I was late because the bus is broke.

**32**  **F**  Dan ate a sandwich and a apple.

    **G**  Jake has a cup of soup and a salad.

    **H**  May I please have a extra cookie?

    **J**  I'd like an ham and cheese omelet?

**33**  **A**  Come and see this spider.

    **B**  Watched curiously as it spun.

    **C**  Here an unsuspecting fly.

    **D**  How patiently the spider?

GO

**Directions:** For numbers 34–43, find the word that completes the sentence and is spelled correctly.

**34** That is the _____ story I've ever read.

  **F** funniest     **H** funnyst

  **G** funnyest     **J** funnest

**35** I grew three _____ this year.

  **A** inchs     **C** inchys

  **B** inchies     **D** inches

**36** We planted _____ along the fence.

  **F** daisyes     **H** daisys

  **G** daisies     **J** daises

**37** My brother _____ the coolest gift.

  **A** recieved     **C** received

  **B** receeved     **D** receaved

**38** I _____ at the store after school.

  **F** stopt     **H** stoppt

  **G** stoped     **J** stopped

**39** He is my best _____ .

  **A** frind     **C** friend

  **B** frend     **D** freind

**40** Miss Lambert was _____ about the litter on her lawn.

  **F** fuious     **H** furius

  **G** furious     **J** fiurius

**41** I can't _____ it!

  **A** belive     **C** beleive

  **B** believe     **D** beleve

**42** Her cousin is the most _____ person I've ever met.

  **F** polight

  **G** pollite

  **H** pollight

  **J** polite

**43** The garage needed a _____ cleaning.

  **A** thoroh

  **B** thurow

  **C** thourough

  **D** thorough

GO

Name _____

**Directions:** Find the punctuation mark that is missing from each sentence.

**44** Jody please don't forget to feed the cat.

,     !     ,     Correct as is

**F**    **G**    **H**    **J**

**45** Max said hed help me rake the leaves.

"    '    ,    Correct as is

**A**    **B**    **C**    **D**

**46** "Why aren't you coming with us" asked Julie.

.    ,    ?    Correct as is

**F**    **G**    **H**    **J**

**47** No, we're not going to the mall today.

'    ,    "    Correct as is

**A**    **B**    **C**    **D**

**48** I ate the whole box I had such a stomach ache!

,    !    ;    Correct as is

**F**    **G**    **H**    **J**

**Directions:** For numbers 49–51, find the answer with the correct capitalization of the underlined words.

**49** The last thing I meant to do was <u>annoy the Andersons on arbor day.</u>

**A** annoy the andersons on arbor day

**B** Annoy The Andersons on arbor day

**C** annoy the Andersons on Arbor Day

**D** Correct as is

**50** The neighbors got back from a long trip to the <u>south of china.</u>

**F** south of China

**G** South of china

**H** South Of China

**J** Correct as is

**51** Somehow, the shoe landed on <u>Felipe sanchez's lawn.</u>

**A** felipe sanchez's lawn

**B** Felipe Sanchez's lawn

**C** Felipe Sanchez's Lawn

**D** Correct as is

STOP

273     

**Directions:** Read the paragraph that tells about one student's great experience. Then think about all the good experiences you have ever had. Write one or two sentences to answer each question below.

> My violin competition was one of the best experiences I've ever had. I met people from all over the city. I learned to feel comfortable in front of an audience. I felt good about playing for so many people. When everyone clapped, I felt very proud.

**Think about all your good experiences. Which one was the best?**

_____

_____

_____

**Why was this experience so good?**

_____

_____

_____

**How did the experience make you feel?**

_____

_____

_____

GO

**Directions:** Read the paragraph below about how to plant a seed. Then think of something you know how to do. Write a paragraph that explains how to do it. Use words such as *first*, *next*, *then*, *finally*, *last*.

> I found out how to plant a seed and make it grow. First, I found a spot where the plant would get the right amount of sunshine. Next, I dug a hole, put the seed into the soil, and then covered the seed with soil. Then I watered the seed. After a couple weeks it began to grow into a beautiful plant.

_____

_____

_____

_____

_____

_____

_____

_____

_____

_____

_____

_____

_____

STOP

# Mathematics

**1**

$$282$$
$$422$$
$$+\ 116$$

- **A** 810
- **B** 710
- **C** 830
- **D** 819
- **E** None of these

**2**

$$0.6 - 0.6 =$$

- **F** 0
- **G** 0.8
- **H** 0.04
- **J** 1
- **K** None of these

**3**

$$2 \times 5 \times 9 =$$

- **A** 16
- **B** 47
- **C** 19
- **D** 91
- **E** None of these

**4**

$$4\tfrac{6}{11}$$
$$+3\tfrac{2}{11}$$

- **F** 8
- **G** $1\tfrac{4}{11}$
- **H** $7\tfrac{8}{11}$
- **J** $1\tfrac{8}{11}$
- **K** None of these

**5**

$$37$$
$$\times\ \ 8$$

- **A** 296
- **B** 255
- **C** 45
- **D** 166
- **E** None of these

**6**

$$88 \div 8 =$$

- **F** 8
- **G** 0
- **H** 1
- **J** 11
- **K** None of these

**7**

$$2.5$$
$$-\ 1.5$$

- **A** 1.5
- **B** 3.0
- **C** 3.5
- **D** 5
- **E** None of these

**8**

$$2\tfrac{1}{5} + 1\tfrac{3}{5} =$$

- **F** 4
- **G** $1\tfrac{2}{5}$
- **H** $3\tfrac{4}{5}$
- **J** $3\tfrac{2}{5}$
- **K** None of these

GO

Name _____

**SAMPLE A** Hillary spent between $11 and $12. Which two items did she buy?

A leash and food    C collar and food

B collar and leash    D collar and bowl

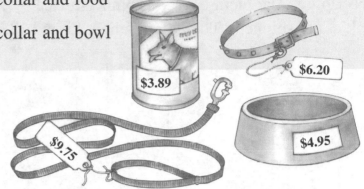

# COLLECTING BASEBALL CARDS

**Directions:** The binders below show four students' baseball card collections. Look at the picture. Then do numbers 9 and 10.

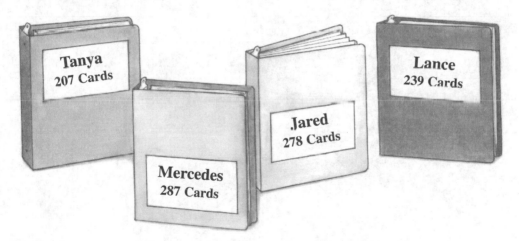

**9** The plastic inserts in the binders hold 9 cards each. Which student has a notebook in which every inserted page is full?

A Tanya

B Mercedes

C Jared

D Lance

**10** Which of these shows the baseball card collections arranged from fewest cards to most?

F Tanya, Lance, Mercedes, Jared

G Tanya, Lance, Jared, Mercedes

H Lance, Tanya, Mercedes, Jared

J Mercedes, Jared, Lance, Tanya

 GO

277    Summer Link Super Edition Grade 5

Name _____

# Rainy Day Game

**Directions:** The picture shows spinners made by four children who used them in a game. Look at the spinners. Then do numbers 11 and 12.

**11** Whose spinner will land on a square more than half the time?

   **A** Marci's

   **B** Eric's

   **C** Jeffrey's

   **D** Lauren's

**12** Whose spinner has the best chance of landing on a triangle?

   **F** Marci's

   **G** Eric's

   **H** Jeffrey's

   **J** Lauren's

GO

**13** Jodi bought cans of tennis balls that cost $2.50 per can. What else do you need to know to find out how much money Jodi spent in all?

  **A** whether she played singles or doubles

  **B** how many cans of tennis balls she bought

  **C** whether she won her tennis match

  **D** how many cans of tennis balls the store had in stock

**14** The computer screen shows some of the top scores earned on a computer game. Ricky earned the top score at level 10. Which was most likely his score?

  **F** 17,000

  **G** 18,000

  **H** 20,000

  **J** 21,000

| TOP SCORES | | |
|---|---|---|
| Alice | 19,000 | 12 |
| Ricky | _____ | 10 |
| Walter | 17,000 | 8 |
| Adele | 9,000 | 5 |
| Elena | 8,000 | 4 |

**15** To win at this board game, you need to cover 16 spaces with chips you earn. How many more chips does Marla need to earn so that she can cover $\frac{3}{4}$ of her spaces?

  **A** 1

  **B** 2

  **C** 3

  **D** 4

GO

Name_____

**16** Lillian rode her bicycle to the supermarket for her mother. Here is the change she was given when she bought one of the items on the table with a five-dollar bill. Which item did she buy?

$3.65                $4.55            $3.50              $4.79

Detergent          (cheese)        IceCream          Coffee

F                    G                H                  J

**17** Yoshi used this clue to find the secret number to open the briefcase. What is the secret number?

A  12

B  10

C  8

D  6

If you double the secret number and then add 4, the answer is 20.

**18** Which of these figures is 4/7 shaded?

F                    G                H                  J

GO

**Directions:** Choose the answer that correctly solves each problem.

**19**

A B | C | D |
●●   |  ● |  ● |
1    2    3    4

**What point represents $\frac{3}{4}$?**

**A** A    **B** B    **C** C    **D** D

**20** **What is the next number in this pattern?**

1  2  4  8  16  32  64....

**F** 80    **G** 81    **H** 84    **J** 128

**21** **Which figure is symmetric?**

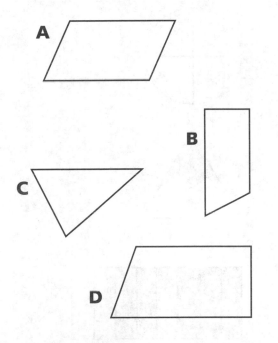

A

B

C

D

**22** **How many sides does a rectangle have?**

**F** 0    **G** 2    **H** 3    **J** 4

**23** **Which unit would be best for measuring the length of a new pencil?**

**A** feet

**B** meters

**C** inches

**D** liters

CENTER CINEMAS
MOVIE TICKET SALES

MONDAY ▢▢▢▢▢▢▢▢▢
TUESDAY ▢▢▢▢▢▢▢▢▢▢
WEDNESDAY ▢▢▢▢▢▢▢▢▢▢▢▢◁
THURSDAY ▢▢▢▢▢ ▢▢▢▢▢▢▢ ▢▢
FRIDAY ▢▢▢▢▢▢ ▢▢▢▢▢▢▢▢▢◁

KEY: 10 TICKETS = ▢

**24** **How many more tickets were sold on Friday than on Tuesday?**

**F** 45    **G** 55    **H** 75    **J** 295

**25** **Which number has an 8 in the thousands place?**

**A** 81,428

**B** 78,643

**C** 42,638

**D** 29,821

GO

**26** What is the perimeter of the rectangle?

**F** 22 meters

**G** 18 meters

**H** 11 meters

**J** 3 meters

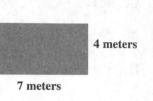

4 meters

7 meters

**27** How many sides does a circle have?

**A** 12  **B** 2  **C** 1  **D** 0

**28** What is the temperature on the thermometer?

**F** 87 °F

**G** 82 °F

**H** 80 °F

**J** 78 °F

**29** What is the least favorite pet in Ms. Sheely's class?

**A** dog

**B** cat

**C** gerbil

**D** fish

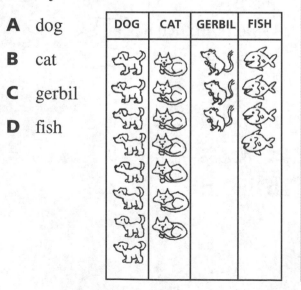

**30** What fraction does the shaded portion of the picture represent?

**F** $\frac{1}{4}$

**G** $\frac{1}{3}$

**H** $\frac{1}{2}$

**J** $1\frac{1}{4}$

**31** Which letter has a line of symmetry?

**A** J  **B** S  **C** M  **D** Q

**32** What picture shows a fraction equivalent to $\frac{3}{10}$?

**F**

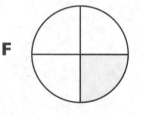

**G**

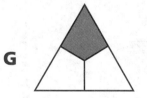

**H**

**J**

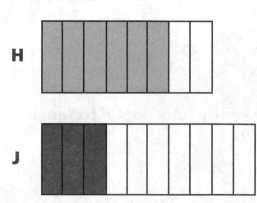

GO

Name _____

**Directions:** Choose the answer that correctly solves each problem.

**33**

879 + 43 =

  **A** 1,309
  **B** 922
  **C** 836
  **D** 122

**34**

46 × 82 =

  **F** 3,772
  **G** 3,672
  **H** 3,662
  **J** 128

**35**

281 − 93 =

  **A** 188
  **B** 212
  **C** 288
  **D** 374

**36**

8,941 + 1,278 =

  **F** 9,119
  **G** 9,219
  **H** 10,119
  **J** 10,219

**37**

369 × 4 =

  **A** 1,476
  **B** 1,264
  **C** 123
  **D** 92

**38**

445 ÷ 6 =

  **F** 78 R1
  **G** 63 R4
  **H** 74 R3
  **J** None of these

**39**

84.62 ☐ 84.26

  **A** >
  **B** =
  **C** <
  **D** None of these

**40**

$\frac{1}{4} + \frac{3}{4} =$

  **F** $\frac{2}{4}$
  **G** $\frac{1}{2}$
  **H** 1
  **J** 4

**41**

431 + 622 + 58 =

  **A** 1110
  **B** 1010
  **C** 111
  **D** None of these

**42**

12 × 12 =

  **F** 240
  **G** 144
  **H** 140
  **J** 24

**GO**

**Directions:** Choose the answer that correctly solves each problem.

**43** Colleen found 16 shells on Saturday and 17 shells on Sunday. Al found 12 shells on Saturday and 22 shells on Sunday. Who found the greater number of shells altogether?

**A** Al

**B** Colleen

**C** They each found the same number of shells.

**D** Not enough information

**44** Angela saved her allowance to buy a new pair of sneakers. She had $70.00. After buying the sneakers, how much money did she have left?

**F** $9.25

**G** $8.75

**H** $7.65

**J** Not enough information

**45** David has 72 baseball cards that he is sorting into three equal piles. How many cards are in each pile?

**A** 216 cards

**B** 24 cards

**C** 20 R4 cards

**D** 18 cards

**46** Toby left his house for school at 7:35 a.m. He arrived to school at 7:50 a.m. How many minutes did it take Toby to get to school?

**F** 15 minutes

**G** 20 minutes

**H** 25 minutes

**J** 10 minutes

**47** Rosendo and his sister combine their money to buy a new game. Rosendo has $7.48 and his sister has $8.31. How much money do they have in all?

**A** $0.83

**B** $15.79

**C** $16.89

**D** Not enough information

**48** What equation would you use to solve the following problem?

Tyrone and Lawrence have a total of 26 CDs. They each have the same number of CDs. How many CDs does Tyrone have?

**F** $26 \times 2 =$

**G** $26 + 2 =$

**H** $26 - 2 =$

**J** $26 \div 2 =$

STOP

# Grade 4 Answer Key

**Page 214**
1. C
2. J
3. A
4. J
5. C
6. H
7. D

**Page 223**
A. D
B. F

**Page 225**
1. B
2. H
3. A

**Page 226**
4. J
5. C
6. F

**Page 227**
7. D
8. F
9. C

**Page 229**
10. G
11. A
12. J
13. A

**Page 230**
14. J
15. C
16. F
17. B

**Page 231**
18. J
19. C
20. F
21. B

**Page 232**
C. C

**Page 233**
22. D
23. J

**Page 234**
24. A
25. H
26. C
27. J

# Grade 4 Answer Key

*Page 235*
  **D.** B
  **28.** C
  **29.** J

*Page 236*
  **30.** A
  **31.** J

*Page 237*
  **32.** D
  **33.** H
  **34.** B

*Page 238*
  **A.** D
  **1.** B
  **2.** J
  **B.** A
  **3.** C
  **4.** F

*Page 239*
  **5.** B
  **6.** H
  **7.** B
  **8.** H
  **9.** D
  **10.** G

*Page 240*
  **C.** C
  **11.** B
  **12.** H
  **13.** B
  **14.** J

*Page 241*
  **15.** C
  **16.** F
  **17.** A
  **18.** H
  **19.** D
  **20.** G

*Page 242*
  **D.** D
  **21.** D
  **22.** F
  **E.** E
  **23.** A
  **24.** J

*Page 245*
  **F.** A
  **25.** A
  **26.** H
  **G.** B
  **27.** C
  **28.** H

# Grade 4 Answer Key

*Page 246*
**29.** D
**30.** F
**31.** D
**32.** J
**33.** A
**34.** H
**35.** B

*Page 247*
**36.** F
**37.** C
**38.** J
**39.** D
**40.** F
**41.** E
**42.** H
**43.** D

*Page 249*
**A.** B
**B.** K
**1.** D
**2.** F
**3.** B
**4.** G

*Page 250*
**C.** C

*Page 251*
**5.** C
**6.** G

*Page 252*
**7.** D
**8.** F
**9.** C

*Page 253*
**10.** J
**11.** A
**12.** G

*Page 254*
**13.** C
**14.** G
**15.** C

*Page 255*
**16.** J
**17.** A
**18.** K
**19.** B
**20.** H
**21.** D
**22.** F
**23.** C

# Grade 4 Answer Key

*Page 256*
**D.** D
**24.** C
**25.** H

*Page 257*
**26.** D
**27.** H
**28.** C

*Page 258*
**29.** H
**30.** C
**31.** F

*Page 261*
**A.** C

*Page 262*
**1.** D
**2.** G
**3.** A
**4.** H
**5.** B
**6.** F
**7.** D

*Page 263*
**8.** G
**9.** B
**10.** G
**11.** D

*Page 264*
**12.** G
**13.** A
**14.** G
**15.** C
**16.** F
**17.** B
**18.** B
**19.** B
**20.** A
**21.** A

*Page 265*
**22.** C
**23.** G
**24.** C
**25.** H

# Grade 4 Answer Key

*Page 266*
26. B
27. B
28. D
29. F
30. C
31. H
32. D
33. C
34. B
35. A
36. H
37. F
38. J
39. G

*Page 267*
A. A
1. D
2. G
3. D
4. F

*Page 268*
5. D
6. G
7. B
8. J
9. A

*Page 269*
10. J
11. A
12. G
13. C
14. G
15. E
16. J
17. B

*Page 270*
18. H
19. D
20. G
21. C
22. G
23. A
24. H
25. C

*Page 271*
26. J
27. B
28. F
29. B
30. H
31. A
32. G
33. A

# Grade 4 Answer Key

*Page 272*

**34.** F
**35.** D
**36.** G
**37.** C
**38.** J
**39.** C
**40.** G
**41.** B
**42.** J
**43.** D

*Page 273*

**44.** H
**45.** B
**46.** H
**47.** D
**48.** H
**49.** C
**50.** F
**51.** B

*Page 276*

**1.** E
**2.** F
**3.** E
**4.** H
**5.** A
**6.** J
**7.** E
**8.** H

*Page 277*

**A.** D
**9.** A
**10.** G

*Page 278*

**11.** B
**12.** J

*Page 279*

**13.** B
**14.** G
**15.** C

*Page 280*

**16.** F
**17.** C
**18.** J

*Page 281*

**19.** A
**20.** J
**21.** A
**22.** J
**23.** C
**24.** G
**25.** B

# Grade 4 Answer Key

*Page 282*
26. F
27. D
28. G
29. C
30. F
31. C
32. J

*Page 283*
33. B
34. F
35. A
36. J
37. A
38. J
39. A
40. H
41. D
42. G

*Page 284*
43. A
44. H
45. B
46. F
47. B
48. J

# Grade 4 Answer Key

**Writing**

*Page 243*

Answers will vary, but should identify a book the student has read. Sample answer: *The Lion, the Witch, and the Wardrobe.*

Answers will vary, but should include supporting statements with reference to specific aspects of the book, including characters, setting, and plot. See sample paragraph in writing prompt for examples.

Answers will vary, but should include reference to one specific aspect of the book, rather than reference to the entire book. Sample answer: I think others will especially like the part of the book where the main character spoke out about his feelings.

*Page 244*

Answers will vary, but should identify a fictional character who could support a story. Students' reasoning should clearly show why the character was chosen. Sample answer: I would write about José, a boy who wants to build a submarine that to explore the deepest depths of the ocean. He will be the main character because he has not been able to follow through with things he has wanted to do in the past. In this story, he will follow through.

Answers will vary, but should include one or more settings. Sample answer: The story will take place now in a small city in California and in the ocean.

Answers will vary, but should include a clear problem and solution. More sophisticated answers might include a character's inner personal conflict, as well as the conflict happening externally within the story. Sample answer: José will need to invent the submarine to help find clues to solve a mystery. He will push past his own lack of ability to finish things he starts as he solves the problem.

# Grade 4 Answer Key

*Page 248*

Answers will vary, but should include chores that could realistically be done by children in a neighborhood. Sample answers: mow lawns, feed pets, clean garages.

Answers will vary, but should give specific reasons that tell why the child would do a good job. Sample answer: My neighbors should hire me to clean garages because I am a hard worker. I like to make things nice and tidy.

Answers will vary, but should show persuasive techniques. Sample answer: I would tell my neighbors to talk to others to find out how hard I work. I would tell them that I would return their money if they were not happy with my work.

# Grade 4 Answer Key

*Page 274*

Answers will vary, but should include a specific positive experience, rather than a general statement. Sample answer: One of the best experiences I can remember is our vacation to the mountains.

Answers will vary, but should show clear reasons that explain why the experience was a positive one. Sample answer: This was a great experience because I learned how to cook over a campfire and set up a tent.

Answers will vary, but should include specific feelings that make sense in the context of the experience. Sample answer: I felt happy and proud when I learned that I could set up a tent and cook over a campfire with my family.

*Page 275*

Paragraphs will vary, but should focus on topic and knowledge of an informative how-to paragraph, including time-order words. The steps should be written in a logical order. Topics might include: *how to bathe a pet, how to build a model, how to fix a meal.* See sample paragraph in writing prompt.

# Test Practice Worksheet

# Test Practice Worksheet

# Test Practice Worksheet

# Test Practice Worksheet

# Test Practice Worksheet

# Test Practice Worksheet

# Test Practice Worksheet

# Test Practice Worksheet

# Test Practice Worksheet

# Test Practice Worksheet

# Test Practice Worksheet

# Test Practice Worksheet

# Test Practice Worksheet

# Test Practice Worksheet

# Test Practice Worksheet

# Test Practice Worksheet

# Test Practice Worksheet

# Test Practice Worksheet

# Test Practice Worksheet

# Test Practice Worksheet

# Test Practice Worksheet

# Test Practice Worksheet

# Test Practice Worksheet

# Test Practice Worksheet

# Test Practice Worksheet